THE
COMPLETE
FIRST
TIME
GARDENER

THE COMPLETE FIRST TIME GARDENER

Geoff Hamilton & Gay Search

BBC BOOKS

Published by BBC Books,
an imprint of BBC Worldwide Publishing.
BBC Worldwide Limited, Woodlands,
80 Wood Lane, London W12 0TT

First published as *The First Time Garden* by Geoff Hamilton
in 1988 and *First Time Planting* by Gay Search and
Geoff Hamilton in 1989.

This revised omnibus edition first published 1996
Reprinted 1996
© Geoff Hamilton and Gay Search 1996
The moral right of the authors has been asserted

ISBN 0 563 37135 8

Set in Monophoto Sabon by Ace Filmsetting Ltd, Frome
Printed in Great Britain by Cambus Litho Ltd, East Kilbride
Bound in Great Britain by Hunter & Foulis Ltd, Edinburgh
Colour separations by Technik Litho, Berkhampsted
Cover printed by Richard Clays Ltd, St Ives plc

CONTENTS

INTRODUCTION

The most exciting thing you'll ever do in your gardening life is to create your first new garden.

Oh, certainly your initial reaction when you first look out of the window at a sea of mud liberally sprinkled with bricks, roofing tiles, bits of rusty wire, concrete bags and probably even a kitchen sink or two, will be a groan of dismay. How on earth are you ever going to turn that disaster area into a thing of beauty?

Well, that's just why we wrote this book. With a little bit of help, you certainly *can* do it, and once you get started, you'll enjoy every minute.

Look upon your new, expensive rubbish tip as a clean canvas and yourself as a latter-day Leonardo. You have the most marvellous opportunity to create a *masterpiece* exactly as you want it.

It all sounds rather far-fetched perhaps, at the moment, but believe me, it's not such a daft analogy as it sounds. *Everyone* can make a beautiful garden because you'll be working in close

However much of a mess the site may look at the outset, it really is possible to create a garden within six months.

7

cooperation with an old master – Nature. She's made millions of gardens in her time and she'll be just as keen to make yours a success as all the others.

What's more, in just one season you'll be able to transform the bare, cluttered soil into a little bit of paradise.

You may feel that the cost is going to be beyond you. After all, some of the prices at the garden centre are – well, optimistic to say the least! And we're always hearing about how expensive gardening has become. Well, that's just so much stuff and nonsense.

Half of what you'll be pressured to buy is quite unnecessary and much can be made at home or bought slowly. There's certainly no need to break the bank or even go without the curtains or the carpets. The thing to remember is *always* to buy good quality. Buying the cheapest plants, tools or sundries is often the most expensive way in the end.

Some of the tools and equipment needed in the construction of the garden are, admittedly, expensive. What's more, you'll probably only use them when you actually build the garden. After that, they'll sit in the shed until you move to the next garden. But all this equipment can be hired at a fraction of the cost of buying it. Everything from a cold chisel to a cement mixer is available at your local tool-hire shop, so one of the first jobs should be to get hold of their price list and find out what's available. It could save you pounds.

You may be put off by the thought of all the work a good garden entails. Well, I can tell you this. A well-thought-out and properly planted garden will take half the work demanded by a weed-infested mess. Cutting a good lawn once a week, for example, takes a fifth of the time needed to cut a poor one once a month! Weeding a well-planted garden is something you'll actually look forward to doing once or twice a year. Well-grown plants in well-planned borders just won't put up with an invasion by the riff-raff!

But worst of all, you may feel that you just don't *like* gardening. Most of us have memories of all that interminable, boring weeding we had to do for Dad when we were kids, and anyway, gardening is supposed to be an old man's sport!

All I can say is – look, just give it a go. It's pretty dumb to condemn anything out of hand without giving it a good chance. That way you'll never know what you're missing. Sure, we all hated the enforced weeding sessions and I have to agree that trolling round with the mower is not the most exciting thing in the world. But take my word for it, creating a thing of beauty from scratch certainly *is* exciting and it's very rewarding indeed.

The great thing about the art of gardening design and construction is that it's not the exclusive domain of the highly talented. You may not be able to blow a trumpet, paint in oils or write a best-seller. But you *can* make a beautiful garden, because that's something we can *all* do.

When we set out to make the TV series, *The First Time Garden*, a few years ago, we decided right from the start that *realism* was essential. It was very tempting to locate it in my own garden at Barnsdale where all the facilities are to hand and where the soil has been worked to a high state of fertility. There are no kitchen sinks buried there and no manhole covers stuck up in the air! But no, that just wouldn't do. If you were going to have problems, we wanted them too!

So, we prevailed upon Barratt Homes to get the permission of one of their first-time buyers to let us use the garden on a new development in Birmingham. We were lucky. Not only were the new owners just about the most cooperative people we could have wished for (they rewarded the constant disruption and the sea of mud with cheery smiles and endless cups of tea!), but they were blessed with *all* the problems any new home-owner is ever likely to encounter. I won't depress you with a catalogue now, but the sad story will unfold as you read on!

I've tried to keep everything as simple as possible and to make the instructions clear and graphic. I hope that real first-timers will soon begin to realize that there's not as much magic and mystery about the noble art of making a garden as they first thought. And I fervently pray that 'old hands' will bear with me for giving away some of their secrets!

PLANNING

Planning a garden is not a thing to do in a hurry. When we took our first look at the little plot we'd acquired for the *First Time Garden* series, we realized that the problems we'd taken on would take a fair bit of head-scratching to sort out. Mind you, we saw it at its worst.

I arrived with fellow presenter Gay Search one cold, wet December day to a scene of utter chaos! The road was a sea of mud, the house itself was still just a half-completed shell and the 'garden' was somewhere under an enormous pile of rubble. We wondered, when we got out of the car, about the cause of the dull thudding noise we could all hear. On enquiry, it turned out to be the sound of explosives blasting away the solid block of 4.5-metre (15-foot) thick concrete that had once supported a factory on the site. We discovered later that it was from underneath that concrete that our new garden had been delivered. Not a promising start.

The view was not exactly inspiring either – not unless you have a liking for dilapidated nineteenth-century chemical factories! It was certainly no 'rural idyll'.

We were about to seek the sanctuary of the car and go for a quick morale booster in the nearest local when we were dealt the final blow. With a screeching whistle, a roar and a rush, an Intercity Express flashed past the garden – no more than 6 metres (20 feet) from our patio doors!

'Well,' said my producer, 'you wanted a challenge!'

Now, looked at like that, I began to realize how barmy I'd been to suggest a difficult site in the first place! But what we did have here was one garden that encapsulated all the problems any unsuspecting first-timer was likely to encounter. Restricted space, terrible soil, enough builders' rubble to build the Great Wall of China, a regular, nerve-jangling noise every half-hour or so and a view of billows of acrid smoke rising from a heap of grime. We could certainly not be accused of making it easy for ourselves!

It took a long time to decide what to do. Alison Hainey, our designer, and I plodded round the plot like a couple of inmates of Wormwood Scrubbs on exercise, just getting the 'feel' of the site. Then long discussions followed.

I suppose it could be argued that the planning stage of any garden is just about the most important. After all, that garden will be with you for a long time, so it's worth getting it at least near enough right first time.

Basics

The first thing to do is to decide what the garden is *for*. If you have small children, for example, you may decide that it has to be devoted exclusively to them as a play area. In that case, the design will be very different to that of a garden meant to be used as an extension of the house. Very often a young couple will look upon it as an outside room to be used mainly for relaxation. Or you may be keen on collecting plants or growing vegetables or, more likely, you'll want a combination of all these things.

It's also wise to project forward a few years and think about what the future use may be. Bear in mind that eventually a young couple, who now want the garden only for leisure, may decide to start a family. And, projecting even further, that children will grow up and won't need the play area any more. Sometimes a lot of time and expense can be saved by looking that far ahead. The stone circle feature in our design is a good example.

This is intended as a sunbathing area. It catches all the afternoon sun, so it's the warmest spot in the place. But it's

It seems hard to believe that this was our first sight of the plot. Not exactly designed to encourage!

11

also easily seen from the kitchen and living-room windows, so it would make an ideal play area for a family with very small children. Mum or Dad could keep a close eye on them from the house. So it might be an idea, in the early stages, to put a wooden edging round the circle and to fill it with sand for the kids to play. When they grow out of that, it could then be paved with stone blocks, straight on top of the sand.

Keep that final use to the forefront of your mind and then start making lists.

List number one should contain all the things that you simply can't do without. You're quite likely, for example, to need a washing line. If you have small children it's almost a certainty. Don't worry about where it will go just yet, just put on the list. You may decide that you need somewhere to hide the dustbins, or a coal-bunker or even a tall, lockable gate to imprison little Johnny while you get on with the chores. Rack your brains and get them all down.

Then try to decide those features you *want* in the garden and make list number two. You're quite likely to decide that, since you want to use the garden as another 'room' for relaxing and entertaining, you need a paved area and a barbecue. Gardens aren't all hard work you know! A lawn may be considered essential if you have young children or, if you have a passion for flowers in the house, you may want a greenhouse.

Of course, this list is bound to be much too long ever to get everything in. So that's where list number three comes in. This is the 'compromise list' which is the result of honing everything down a scale or two. You may, for example, decide that a paved area *and* a lawn are too much of a luxury. You may have to compromise on the greenhouse and settle for a smaller lean-to against one of the house walls, or you may kiss the vegetable plot goodbye and decide to grow a few salads in amongst the flower borders instead.

Eventually, you'll finish up with something like the real thing (though I'll guarantee you'll still have too much to fit in!) and the planning can start.

Surveying the plot
The first job is to draw a 'masterplan' of the plot, including just the bare bones – the boundaries, the position of the house and any permanent features that already exist, like established trees, for example. And to do that, you'll need an elementary knowledge of basic surveying. Sounds daunting, but it's as easy as anything really.

Of course, if your garden is exactly square or rectangular, there's no problem. Just measure the lengths of each side and the boundaries can be drawn straight onto the plan. Unfortunately, very few are. Our plot looked for all the world as if it was square, until we measured it, when it turned out to be anything but. So to place the boundaries accurately, we had to resort to a technique called 'triangulation'. The only equipment you need is a surveyor's tape, which can be hired quite cheaply.

Start by measuring up the house. It can be assumed that the walls are straight and that all the angles are accurate right-angles, so there is no difficulty in transferring these measurements to paper.

Obviously you'll have to scale the measurements down and we found a scale of 1 to 50 most convenient. In other words, 1 centimetre on paper represents 50 centimetres on the ground. If you're working in metric measurements, this is a most convenient scale, but if, like me, you're an old-fashioned reactionary and have never got the hang of these 'foreign' ways, you may prefer to work in something like 1 inch to 5 feet. It doesn't matter at all which way you do it, so long as it's reasonably easy to work out and it fits your bit of paper! But, having been forced to work in metric because that's what Alison always uses (well, she's younger than me!), I must grudgingly admit that once you get the hang of it, it's by far the easiest!

Draw the outline of the house on the paper and then use it to get all your other measurements.

You need two fixed points to measure from and the two corners of the house are certainly the most convenient. All you do is measure to a corner of the plot from one fixed point on the house and then to the same corner from another. Do the same thing with the other corners of the plot and you're ready to transfer the measurements to paper.

Scale down these measurements and, with a pair of compasses, draw an arc whose radius is equal to the first measurement and with the centre on one of the fixed points on the house. Draw another arc whose radius is equal to the second measurement from the other fixed point on the house, and where the arcs cross is the corner of the garden.

Repeat the process for the other corners of the garden and you can draw in the boundaries. Other existing features, like trees or outhouses etc., can be drawn in in the same way.

When you've committed all this to paper, it's best to get a

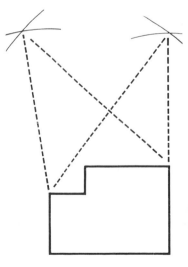

Triangulation is a simple system of measuring and marking fixed points, using the corners of the house as a 'benchmark'.

In a small garden, it's best to keep the design simple to avoid the 'cluttered' look.

piece of tracing paper and pin it over the top of your master-plan. You'll be doing a lot of scribbling, rubbing out and moving things about and this way, you can make as many mistakes as you like without losing the original plan. It's also a good idea, if you haven't got a drawing board, to tape the plan onto a bit of plywood or hardboard (masking tape is ideal), because you'll be referring to it regularly for at least a year and probably more.

Then you're ready to start drawing. Remember, when you do, that what you're seeing is a bird's eye view and what you'll want in the garden is a different perspective. Still, this shouldn't be allowed to worry you too much. I've found that, generally, a good, well-balanced design on paper looks good on the ground too. And, of course, you can always change the layout slightly when it comes to transferring it to the ground if it doesn't look quite right.

General principles

I don't believe there are, or should be, any hard-and-fast rules about garden design. After all, your garden is very much a personal thing and it should be made to suit you. If your neighbour doesn't like the design, well he doesn't have to look!

Quite frankly, the last thing I want to be seen as is an arbiter of 'taste', because I think that a great deal of the so-called 'fashion' in gardens and gardening is so much pretentious nonsense. So, please regard the following as a set of guidelines only. My observations may help you avoid making a few mistakes and so perhaps save you a little time and money, and

I hope they'll start you thinking. But at the end of the day, you must do what *you* want to do!

My own first rule is to keep things simple. There's a great temptation to try to cram too much into the garden and, if it's tiny, that's a great mistake. It results only in an uncoordinated clutter with no strong focal points. It's much better to err on the side of simplicity with either straight lines or bold, sweeping curves and large expanses of materials.

It's important to think about maintenance too. If you're a busy person, a simple design will be much easier to maintain. Make sure, for example that there are no awkward corners to mow when you design the lawn. Long, sweeping curves are not only easier but will also add to the illusion of space. Make most of the planting permanent, using trees, shrubs and herbaceous perennials which will come up every year, rather than leaving a lot of space for annuals which must be replanted each year.

Again with simplicity in mind, you should try to avoid too many different types of material in the garden. If, for example, you need a paved area and a wall, use walling blocks made of the same material as the paving or get hold of some of the same bricks used to build the house. The garden is essentially a peaceful place and my own feeling is that a jumble of different materials tends to jangle the nerves a bit!

So having determined to keep the design simple and to bear in mind the problems of maintenance, you're sitting there in front of a bare outline, wielding a sharpened pencil. What then? Where do you start?

Well, the first job is to decide on the main axis of the new garden. If you look at the plan of our plot, you'll see what I mean. Because it was so small, the garden actually appeared to be wider than it was long – a quite uncomfortable dimension. So to increase the apparent length, the axis was designed to run from corner to corner. The main viewing point would be in the corner just outside the patio doors, so the scheme is designed to draw the eye from that point to the opposite corner across the main feature – the stone circle and planted urn. Almost as soon as we decided to do that, the garden began to look twice the size!

The tricks you can play on your *perception* of space and dimension are quite surprising. If, for example, you put a striking ornament – a planted urn, a bright foliage shrub or even a statue – in one corner of the garden, the eye is automatically drawn to it. In the process, it seems to ignore what's outside the narrow tunnel of vision, making the feature look further away. If you arrange the borders so that the path to the feature – perhaps grass – narrows towards it, you create false lines of perspective and place the feature even further in the distance. Of course there are limits, but you certainly increase the *apparent* size of the garden by careful manipulation.

It's obviously vital to take into account the position of the sun. Most of us will want to position our sitting-out area in the sunniest spot, though it might also be useful to have a cool, shady place out of the glare too. That could be especially important for retired people. When it comes to planting, obviously you'll need to put sun-lovers in an open spot and shade-lovers in the cool.

The view will be an important aspect of any garden and will inevitably prompt design decisions. If you live in beautiful countryside, you'll not want to hide stunning views; it is much better to try to incorporate the surroundings in the design. I well remember being faced with this situation in a garden I built a while ago. To make it more difficult, the plot was high up in an exposed spot, so I needed to screen it from the wind without detracting from the view.

I solved it by planting on the boundaries but leaving 'windows'. Some trees, like laburnum and the popular double-flowering cherry, have a useful habit of growth in that their branches ascend fairly steeply, rather like a triangle standing on its point. By planting two close to each other, their branches met at the top, but left a viewing hole at about eye level.

Our plot held no such delights. The view of the chemical works simply *had* to be screened, so we decided to increase the height of the fence to 3 metres (9 feet) to blot the offending factory from our eyes and, we hoped, from our minds too! Of course, a 3-metre (9-foot) solid fence begins to look like Colditz, so to avoid the claustrophobic effect we used a trellis extension. This would give a more open aspect and climbing plants would soon hide the view. And, if you really looked for it, way out on the horizon were distant views of the countryside, so it would be nice to allow a peek through the foliage here and there to see that, without the ugly foreground.

Apart from the unattractive view, we also had the problem of noise from the railway line just a stone's throw away. Well, the high fence would help, but we also allowed for wide borders at that end. Massed planting really does do a very good job of damping down noise. So, we decided that the planting in front of the fence would be a mixture of trees and evergreens to give cover throughout the year.

Massed planting would have another beneficial effect. It's a strange paradox but luxuriant planting – almost overplanting if you like – also makes the small garden bigger. It would be logical to think that the narrower the borders and the larger the space in the middle the bigger the garden would look. But the effect of mass planting is to hide those claustrophobic fences and make it seem that your 'jungle' goes on for ever.

I visited a garden not long ago that measured just 4 metres (14 feet) wide and about 9 metres (30 feet) long. If you were going to swing a cat it would have to be a small one! The owner was a keen plantsman and the result was a density of planting like I'd never seen before. And that garden looked ten times the size and was an absolute delight. It can be done.

So, make the borders a little wider than you thought you might and, instead of making them straight, vary the width by curving the edges. Not only does this give a more attractive, informal shape to them, but it also allows some wider spaces for larger plants. Thus you'll be able to vary the heights and spreads of the plants you use, resulting in a more varied and much more attractive effect.

Paths and steps are also subject to this 'optical illusion'. Wide paths make the garden look even wider while, if they are too narrow, they look cramped and mean. Mind you, once again you have to strike the happy medium. Wide paths and steps may look more noble and generous but, of course, they do take up a lot of room. And in a tiny garden, most 'proper' gardeners are going to begrudge space that could be used for plants. So you might kill two birds with one stone and use a planted stepping-stone path.

Sloping sites

These days, building land is much too valuable to waste, so you could well find your house built on a steep slope. The first reaction is to curse your luck. Yes, there certainly is going to be more work involved but, at the end of the day, you'll be much, much happier that you've inherited that slope. There's no doubt that a garden with contours is much more interesting than a perfectly flat one.

The way to cope with the slope is to terrace it into a series of plateaux, divided either by walls or banks of grass or plants. Of course, stone or brick walls will be quite expensive, but

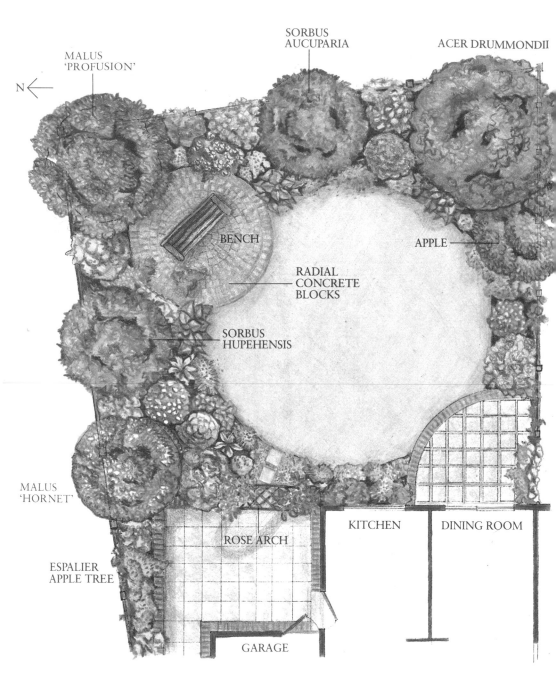

MALUS 'PROFUSION'

SORBUS AUCUPARIA

ACER DRUMMONDII

N

BENCH

APPLE

RADIAL CONCRETE BLOCKS

SORBUS HUPEHENSIS

MALUS 'HORNET'

KITCHEN

DINING ROOM

ESPALIER APPLE TREE

ROSE ARCH

GARAGE

The design for our garden in Birmingham was deliberately simple. Note that the axis runs from corner to corner to increase the apparent length.

consider using railway sleepers or some of the new log-roll products that are available now. If you're in a naturally rocky area, the local rockery stone may be cheap, or you can get away with simple grass or planted banks.

When it comes to designing the terraces, try to avoid simply cutting the garden up into equal strips across from side to side. This will have the effect of foreshortening it and looks ugly. Work out a twisting path with steps at intervals and level areas of grass, paving and planting on either side.

Buildings

Most new houses these days have a garage, so a garden shed may not be absolutely necessary. If you can store your tools, machines and sundries in the garage, so much the better. But if you are misguided enough to decide that the car is more important than the mower and the spade, there are several

Top: Curving the edge of the border makes lawn mowing easier, allows a greater variation of planting heights and gives a more informal appearance.

Bottom: Sloping sites may look daunting at first but by terracing you can create a very interesting effect.

quite attractive small buildings available that will fit in even the tiniest garden. If you have no room to hide a shed out of the way, make a feature of it by fixing wires to the outside and planting it with climbing plants.

If you can run to a greenhouse, then take the plunge and do it. Not only will it extend the gardening season right through the winter, but it will also be invaluable in raising plants. By growing all your own bedding plants and vegetable seedlings, your pot plants and cut flowers for the house plus food crops from spring to autumn, it'll very soon pay for itself.

Naturally, greenhouses should be sited in the sunniest spot and fairly near to the house if possible. That will greatly reduce the cost of putting in facilities like electricity, gas or water, and it will make those night-time trips in January to check the temperatures just a little more comfortable.

In my view, wooden greenhouses have the edge as far as looks are concerned but they do have certain disadvantages too. The big snag is that they're more expensive than aluminium and, unless you go for the astronomically priced cedar, you'll need to do a spot of painting every so often.

It's often said that aluminium is better than wood because it allows more light in. For the commercial grower who starts his tomatoes off in October and grows them right through the winter, it may be important. But for the amateur who starts sowing in February or March, when there's plenty of light for the plants to develop strongly, it's just not a factor to worry about.

If you have no room in the garden for a greenhouse, you may consider a conservatory. They're very popular these days as a means of cheaply extending the house, and they provide not only somewhere to raise plants but a place to lounge in the sun even when it's quite cold outside.

If you have room for another structure, like a pergola, a summerhouse or a rose arbour, you'll be able to provide almost instant height. Climbers will rapidly cover one of these and the garden will begin to take on an air of maturity in months rather than years.

Just one point to consider about these structures, especially if you are going to make them yourself. It's well worth asking the timber merchant for timber that has been pressure-treated with a preservative. It'll cost a little more but it more or less guarantees the wood against rotting for life.

Existing features

Sometimes, I think it's necessary to reassure new gardeners and put their minds at rest.

There is a tremendous amount of pressure these days to conserve our natural resources and no one would deny that that's a good and necessary thing. None the less, there are sometimes cases where existing plantings, and trees in particular, simply *have* to go.

If you are blessed with an enormous great sycamore in the garden that shades it out completely and allows nothing underneath but a scrappy bit of grass, then have no hesitation in getting rid of it! Well, in fact you should have just enough hesitation to check that it's not protected by a preservation order – your local council surveyor will be able to tell you that. Even if it is, you may well be able to appeal against the order and reverse it.

It's quite important to bear in mind that large, hungry trees can have a disastrous effect on the house itself. If you have a large tree like a sycamore, a poplar or a willow within about 12 metres (40 feet) of the house, it could well do damage, especially if your soil is heavy. Clay soils in particular expand and contract considerably, depending on the amount of water in them. A large tree can remove an enormous amount of water in a dry spell, and this could lead to the soil under the foundations of the house contracting. Then it's possible for the footings to crack, causing serious structural damage.

It's obvious, then, that if you have a tree close to your new house, it's wise to get rid of it. You should also, of course, avoid planting one! And I would go further. If you inherit trees or shrubs that are obviously much too large for the site, there is nothing wrong with pulling them out to allow you to grow more suitable subjects.

But if you remove a tree or shrub, remember that you're morally obliged to plant another somewhere! And when you do, you'll have the opportunity of planting subjects that are more in scale with their surroundings. There is more on choice of plants later in this book.

A much knottier problem arises when the large trees shading your garden belong to your next-door neighbour. What can you do then?

Well the answer in a nutshell is, not a lot. If his trees are taking light from your house you may be able to force him to do something, but otherwise you'll just have to tailor your planting scheme to the conditions that prevail.

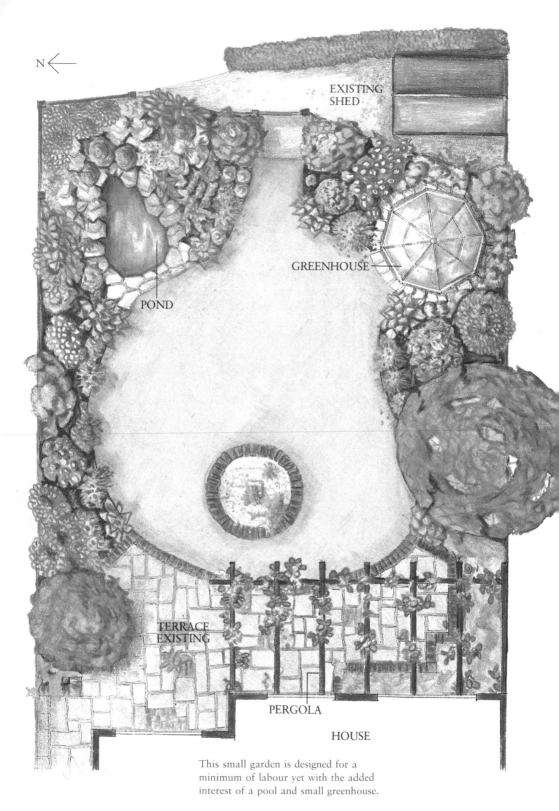

N

EXISTING
SHED

GREENHOUSE

POND

TERRACE
EXISTING

PERGOLA

HOUSE

This small garden is designed for a
minimum of labour yet with the added
interest of a pool and small greenhouse.

Of course, you are entitled to cut off branches and to sever the roots of his tree if they encroach into your garden. But there's little joy there, since a lop-sided tree presenting to your side of the garden nothing but a set of cut-off stumps is hardly an improvement. It may be worthwhile approaching your neighbour with your problem, but you can do little more. Still, you shouldn't despair, because there are plenty of marvellous plants that will thrive in shady conditions and make a great garden.

Transferring the plan

When you've finally finished the drawing and got all the discussions, arguments, disagreements and decisions out of the way, you need to preserve it with the greatest care. This is a document that's as valuable as the house deeds and has certainly taken a lot more blood, sweat and heartache to achieve. Not only will you refer to it continually during the building process but, as the first garden you've designed, it is certain to have a lot of value both in sentimental and educational terms. You'll soon discover mistakes you've made and, when you do, you'll have the plan to remind you never to commit the same error again.

If you've drawn it in pencil, it's well worth inking it in with a black pen. While you're at it, make sure you mark the centres of any circles or arcs you may have drawn. You'll be able to see them by the hole in the paper made by the compasses. When it comes to marking out the plan on the ground, those marks will be invaluable.

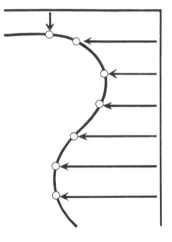

To mark curved borders, measure at intervals from the fence and use canes as markers.

If possible, leave the plan on the board or re-tape it to a piece of strong cardboard and then cover the whole thing with a sheet of clear polythene stuck on with waterproof tape. That way you'll be able to take it into the garden for reference, even if your fingers are covered in mud!

Marking straight lines on the ground is, of course, fairly straightforward. Just measure from the fences and put in a garden line at the appropriate points.

Marking a circle is no more difficult provided you've remembered to mark the centre point on your plan. Simply measure from two fixed points to find the centre, and put in a strong cane. Then measure the radius of the circle and cut a length of string to the required length leaving enough to make a loop to slip over the cane in the centre and to tie on to a marking stick at the other end. The marking stick can then be used either to scratch a line in the soil or to put in a series

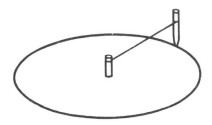

of markers round the perimeter of the circle. Remember, too, to leave that centre cane in position until the very last minute, just in case you need to clarify the mark for some reason.

Marking out curves is a little more arduous. Here you should measure at fixed intervals along a straight line – perhaps the fence or the edge of a path – putting in marker canes at the appropriate distances. The drawing clearly shows the method.

Naturally, you won't need to mark out the whole garden all at once right at the start. That way you'd have so many canes in the garden it would be like a slalom obstacle course! Much better set out each feature as you come to it.

When you've done your marking out and before you actually commit yourself, take a long, hard look at the line from all angles. Bear in mind that you are viewing it from a different angle now, so it might well need adjusting a little. Since garden design is essentially a visual art, the golden rule of landscaping is that 'if it *looks* right, it *is* right'.

The plan for our garden

Our Birmingham garden was faced with just the kind of problems encountered in most modern estate houses. It was small – 12 × 11 metres (35 × 38 feet) – square and surrounded by high fences. In other words, it was just like living in a matchbox! The bare site looked *awful*, but a glance at the plan shows how attractive it will look in a few years' time.

The first decision was to swing the axis of the garden so that, instead of looking from front to back, the eye was taken from corner to corner. That increases the apparent length at a stroke. The main viewing point would be from the small quadrant of paving outside the dining-room doors, so the circular feature was planned to entice the viewer to look across to it. An attractive tree at the back added to the effect.

Taking away the square look is achieved in two ways. First of all, there is a circular motif, repeated in the quadrant of paving, the lawn and then the paved feature. This also allows for a good variation in the width of the borders and plenty of room for some tall plants in the back. Combined with the climbers on the fences, this will completely obscure the preponderance of woodwork which seemed so overpowering before any planting was done. It will also, of course, effectively reduce the noise of the trains running just behind the back fence.

Note that the materials have been kept as uniform as possible. It's a mistake to mix them too much in a small garden, so the paving used outside the dining-room doors is the same as that in the utility area and the same paving blocks used to make the circular feature have been introduced to edge the paved quadrant. Because the next-door garden was on a higher level, we were forced to build a retaining wall at the edge of the utility area. To avoid using yet another material, we bought a few bricks from the builders so that they matched the house.

The planting is fairly simple. We used only plants that are freely available at the garden centre, but we made quite sure each one would work for its living by providing a display over as long a period as possible.

A separate vegetable and fruit garden was really impossible in the space, so we have contented ourselves with mostly trained fruit on the fences and vegetables mixed in with the flowers. It works very well.

Obviously it's impossible to include all the features we would have liked. The garden is just too small. So to give you a taste of other planners' ideas, we visited a couple of gardens that had been designed by professional designers. If you feel you simply can't face doing it yourself, this is, of course, a way out. Many good garden centres employ landscape designers who will either visit your site and then provide a plan or, a little cheaper, will work from your rough drawings and photographs. Most gardening magazines offer this service too.

A small plot
This garden was much the same size as ours – 12 × 9 metres (40 × 29 feet) – and just as square. In fact the main principles of the design are much the same. Again the designer has looked to curved paving and lawn to reduce the squareness of the plot and he too has restricted the hard materials to brick and paving slabs. Note the use of the brick edging around the central bed and the edge of the paved area, and the inclusion

A difficult small garden on a slope. The problem has been cheaply and effectively solved by using wooden stakes to retain the soil, creating a series of terraces. In addition, an informal flight of steps has been made using logs as risers, with pounded soil covered with shredded bark as the treads.

HEDGE ——

COMPOST

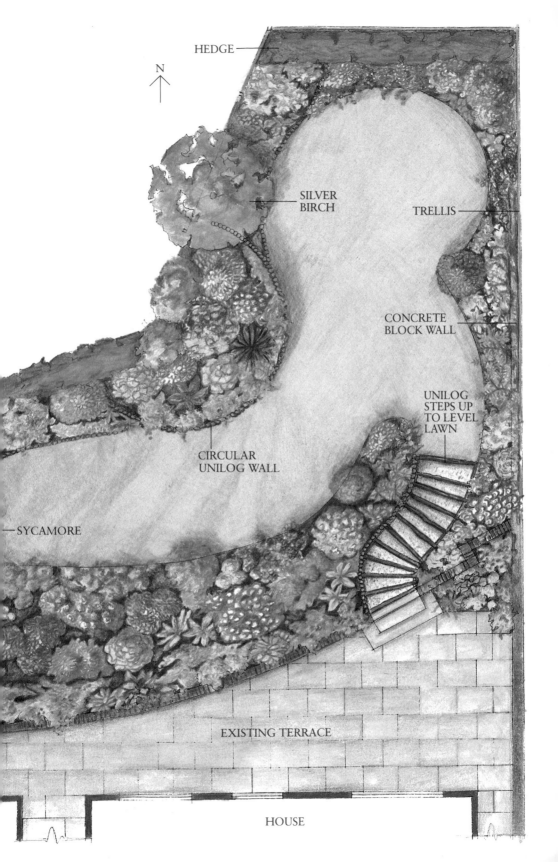

HEDGE

N

SILVER
BIRCH

TRELLIS

CONCRETE
BLOCK WALL

UNILOG
STEPS UP
TO LEVEL
LAWN

CIRCULAR
UNILOG WALL

SYCAMORE

EXISTING TERRACE

HOUSE

of the same bricks in the random paving pattern.

He has added interest by including a pool made with a plastic liner. It's informal in design and this has permitted the inclusion of a couple of rock outcrops that can be planted with alpine plants, which goes some way towards satisfying his client's passion for plants.

The small greenhouse is also a clue to an interested gardener. The octagonal shape is ideally suited to a small plot because it can be sited almost anywhere without looking out of place.

Again the fences have been covered with climbers, and further provision for some upward planting has been provided by the wooden pergola over the patio.

The circular bed in the centre of the lawn is gravelled and planted with alpine plants – a clever way to disguise a very obtrusive manhole cover.

A problem garden

Now here was a real headache. This is a garden ideally suited to a gardener with one leg considerably longer than the other! Before grading work started, the slope in one place was almost vertical and nowhere was there a level spot. It's also a very peculiar shape and measures 18 × 20 metres (58 × 66 feet) down the straight sides.

Obviously there was a lot of terracing to do and a lot of steps to build. To have done it all in stone or brick would not only have looked overpoweringly hard but it would have greatly exceeded the budget too.

The solution was to make the whole garden very informal. So the retaining walls have been made with lengths of logs driven into the bank and very firmly secured. The steps are made with the same material infilled with gravel. It's a cheap and very effective answer to a difficult problem.

Retaining the soil and actually increasing the slope of the banks in places has made it possible to provide at least an area of level lawn and a paved patio. So the garden can be used as well as looked at.

Because of the difficulty in cultivating the steep banks, most of them have been planted with low-maintenance shrubs underplanted with ground cover. Eventually there will be very little work to do, and it will always be a garden that can be enjoyed.

STARTING WORK

With the plan committed to paper, the real work can now begin. It'll be a relief to get rid of some of that rubbish.

Generally most of it can be put into plastic bags and carted down to the tip in the boot of the car. If you've been unlucky enough to be landed with all the builders' rubble from the whole estate, you may well need a skip. They can be hired by the day reasonably cheaply but, before you do so, it's as well to collect all the rubbish into one big pile. I know that means handling it twice, but it could take some time to unearth some of the buried 'treasure' and you won't want to do that with a skip sitting in the driveway clocking up money. Get the thing in, filled and out again as fast as you can!

Before you get rid of anything, make quite sure you can't put it to good use. If, for example, you have a slope away from the house, you may need to build up the base under the patio. To do that with concrete is expensive and all that old hardcore will do just as well.

The budget

There can't be many folk who move into a new house and find they've got money to spare! With conflicting pressures on the budget from carpets, curtains, the telephone, a new cooker and all that, the garden often has to come low down on the list of priorities. So, some careful planning is generally necessary.

Bear in mind that, even though you may have planned the finished garden, it doesn't all have to be done at once.

If you're really strapped for cash, you may, for example, decide just to cover the whole lot with grass for a year and leave it at that. Or there's an even better idea. Spend the grass-seed money on a few pounds of seed potatoes. They'll at least cover the area with green and, at the same time, they'll be effectively cleaning your land of weeds and helping to break up heavy soil. Then, when you harvest them, tot up the money

STARTING WORK

It's often best in the first year to fill the borders with cheap hardy annuals raised from seed.

you've saved and you'll find you can afford the grass seed and the paving slabs for the patio as well!

That patio is, of course, one of the most expensive items in the new garden. And there's no doubt that most of us, especially younger 'first-timers', will want a dry, hard place to eat outside, entertain friends to an al fresco barbecue or just to lie in the sun. But you can still avoid spending a fortune.

If you've bought a new house, you'll *have* to set the paving on a concrete base. I'll explain all about the reasons why later on (see page 63). So all you have to do is to make a slightly better job of the base and use that in the first year. Provided you get the levels right, you can easily cover it with paving slabs later on.

Planting is something to do slowly anyway. Often I've seen gardens of people with larger budgets and more enthusiasm than is good for them. They've had the garden 'laid out' and then gone down to the garden centre in April, on the first really sunny weekend of the year, and they've been seduced into buying everything that's in flower. They then spend the next ten years wondering why their garden only looks good in April!

The point is that you do really need to know a little about plants before you commit yourself to filling every available space. None the less, I accept that you don't want to spend months looking out at bare earth, so some colour and interest must be provided. This is what I'd do.

In the first year, buy a few packets of hardy annual seeds. Make sure the packet labels them 'hardy annuals' because half-hardies won't come up. They can be sown directly in the soil outside and, because they're so easy to grow, success is almost guaranteed (see page 131). They'll provide a show of colour from about May through to November, giving you the whole summer to get to know a few plants and, perhaps, to save some money to buy them.

In the meantime, make regular trips to garden centres, nurseries and gardens open to the public. All will give you a fascinating day out and you'll soon start noticing plants you wouldn't want to be without. Take a notebook with you and note the name and a brief description to aid your memory later on.

Of course, one thing that puts off many new gardeners is Latin names. Some of them, I agree, are a bit tortuous, but there's certainly no need to be worried about them. I do assure you that once you start to learn a few they come fairly easily.

30

And there's a tremendous sense of superiority to be enjoyed when you can spout a few Latin names in the right company!

Another great way to fill your garden with cheap plants is to get to know other keen gardeners. If you have a gardening club in the area, it's well worth joining it. Gardeners are amongst the kindest and most enthusiastic folk in the world and they'll be eager to press you to accept plants they've raised themselves from seeds and cuttings, or to dig up a bit from their gardens. Later on, once you get into it, you'll want to do the same thing – guaranteed!

Tools and equipment

You simply can't make a good job of building anything, especially a garden, without the right tools. What's more, I am firmly of the opinion that it's a false economy to buy cheap tools. So you can, I'm afraid, expect a pretty hefty outlay on tools and equipment for the garden. But, if you do it sensibly, there's still no need to give the bank manager apoplexy!

Bear in mind that many of the tools you need for the construction work can be hired. Small-tool hire shops have proliferated over the last few years and now it's possible in most towns to hire everything from a trowel to a tower crane at a fraction of the cost of buying it. Again, even the tools you *must* buy need not all be bought at once. This is what I'd suggest.

These tools will probably be necessary when you're building the garden but can be hired at a fraction of the cost of buying.

Spade

Buy this first and spend as much on it as you possibly can. You'll use it more than any other tool and if you buy a good one it'll last you a lifetime – literally. If you can run to stainless steel, do so even if you have to stretch every limit possible. It'll serve you well for ever and it'll be a perfect pleasure to use. Make sure you buy a size that suits you. Small men or slight women will be much better off with a smaller border spade than a bigger one. Above all, buy one that has been forged from steel, rather than pressed. The pressed ones are much cheaper and could, with luck, last you about a week!

Fork

Another tool you can't really do without. Again, it's worth buying a good, forged steel fork but stainless steel is an unnecessary luxury. The same rules about size and quality apply, of course.

Rake

The final member of the trio of tools you can't really do without. You'll use it extensively in the construction of the garden and it will be in constant use every season from February to November, so it's worth getting a good one. Avoid those that look like a strip of metal with nails driven through. A solid forged job is what you want and generally it's best to go for one with 12 teeth. Again, stainless steel is unnecessary.

Shovel

When it comes to mixing concrete, you'll need a shovel. A spade is set at the wrong angle to be comfortable and you certainly won't want to be shovelling concrete with a stainless steel spade! There will be little use for it afterwards, so it's best to hire.

Hoes

There are two types of hoe, with a few odd variations you'll see from time to time. The Dutch hoe is used for general weeding – it's the one you push while walking backwards. The swan-necked or draw hoe is used for hacking out larger weeds and for making drills for seeds. Both are useful but certainly not essential. In small gardens, most of the weeding is best done by hand-pulling anyway and drills can just as well be drawn with a stick. Wait until you can easily afford them.

Trowel

A planting trowel is certainly useful, especially where the soil is gritty or contains fragments of glass or to save your hands from getting too weathered. I plant most of my small plants with my fingers but I must confess they're not fit to be seen in delicate company! Remember that trowels do have a habit of getting lost and, being small, they're easy to clean so stainless steel is not necessary, though a favourite Christmas present for new gardeners.

If you're laying paving or building walls, you will need a bricklayer's trowel and ideally, a pointing trowel too. These are best hired unless you have other work for them.

Lawn edger

Unnecessary. It's just as easy to do the job with a spade.

Secateurs

You'll certainly need them eventually, but not in the first year.

Shears

A pair of hedging shears and another to cut the edges of the lawn will be useful later on, but both can certainly wait.

Sprayer

You'll use a pressure sprayer later on but initially it's probably better to hire one. The only thing you'll need it for at the construction stage is weed-killing and after that you probably won't use it for some time.

Knife

Absolutely indispensable. Buy a strong garden knife, small enough to go into your pocket without dragging your trousers off. At the same time buy a pocket carborundum stone to keep it sharp. A blunt knife is a useless embarrassment and far more dangerous than a sharp one.

Spirit-level

Indispensable in the construction stages, but expensive unless you use it for other do-it-yourself jobs. A 90-centimetre (3-foot) level is most useful and can be hired quite easily.

Straight-edge

For many of the construction jobs in the garden you'll need a 3-metre (9- to 10-foot) straight-edge. It's simply a piece of wood, about 7.5 × 2.5 centimetres (3 × 1 inches) thick, planed dead straight. You should be able to get the local timber merchant to machine-plane it. If you're intending to keep it for years, buy a length of hardwood since softwood will twist when it gets damp. You can, when the garden's finished, make saw-cuts at intervals to turn it into a useful planting board.

Club-hammer

A club-hammer is essential for paving and walling and, since you're likely to damage the handle a bit when paving (see page 68), it's only fair that you should buy rather than hire it. It'll come in very useful later and is not too expensive.

Brick bolster

You'll certainly need this to cut paving and walling slabs, but it can be hired, since you won't use it afterwards.

Wheelbarrow

If you have concrete and paving or large amounts of soil to

shift, a wheelbarrow is essential. There are many different designs available, some of them quite expensive. But there still isn't one better than the builders' 'navvy barrow' which is also one of the cheapest. Buy it from the builders' merchant and make sure it has a pneumatic tyre for easy wheeling. And if you use it for wheeling concrete, make certain it's clean enough to eat out of afterwards.

Boards

When you're building the garden, wide boards are very useful indeed. If the soil is soft, they can be put down to facilitate walking and the wheeling of barrows without damaging the soil and with half the effort. Scaffold planks are ideal and can be cheaply hired. But hang on to all the old pieces of wood you come across and make a portable path a bit like a tank-track by cutting them into 60-centimetre (2-foot) lengths and joining them together with nylon string stapled at the ends. You will find it invaluable for spanning wet soil without damaging it later on.

Lawnmower

This is one of the most expensive items you'll have to buy. If your garden is large and the budget runs to it, it's worthwhile buying a petrol-engined cylinder mower which will last many years. But the very cheap electric machines make a perfectly good job provided you expect them to last no more than about five to seven years. The points to remember are that a cylinder mower will make a finer job of the mowing but does not cope so well as a rotary with long grass. And mowers that don't pick up the cuttings are a real pain because the grass gets trodden into the house and the poor old gardener gets trodden down!

Hose
I'll be going on at length about watering new plants later. Suffice it to say now that you'll need to put on a lot of water so buy a good-quality hose.

Weed control

If the plot is infested with perennial weeds, it'll pay hands down to get rid of them before you turn a spade of soil. If you do this job right at the start, you'll save yourself literally months of hand-weeding.

The easiest way is to spray the lot with a glyphosate weedkiller (Tumbleweed or Roundup). It does a marvellous job, but it's by no means cheap, so it's important to use it economically. Funnily enough, my own experience has been that it also does a far *better* job when used in moderation.

First of all, choose a windless day. This is extremely important if your neighbours already have plants in their gardens. One whiff of this stuff drifting over the fence and onto their plants will knock them off too and that's not the best way to become 'Popular Neighbour of the Week'!

Also make sure that it's not going to rain for at least six hours after spraying. Mix up the chemical strictly according to the makers' instructions (an extra slurp for luck is definitely *not* a good idea), and put it into a pressure sprayer. If your garden is any size at all, I would invest in one of these because you'll find a lot of use for it later. They can, however, be hired quite easily from a small-tool hire shop.

The makers do actually recommend putting it on with a watering can, but that's frankly not good advice. The weedkiller acts when it's absorbed through the leaves and transported through the plant's system to the roots. There it stops them storing food, so after a couple of weeks the plant dies. The point is that the small droplets put on with a sprayer will stick to the leaves by surface tension. But if the droplets are too large and too many they just run off into the soil where the chemical is inactivated. You'll get a poorer kill at much higher cost.

After spraying, you'll just have to contain your enthusiasm to start digging. It's essential to leave the weeds to absorb the weedkiller fully. In the summer, a couple of weeks is ample time, but in winter you'll have to wait three to four. The weeds

Starting with a weed-free garden will save hours of work later. Modern weedkillers will do an effective job.

will start to turn brown when the damage is done.

Some of the weeds that have a running root system, or storage organs below ground, like couch-grass, ground elder and bindweed, may need two or even three applications. This is not because the weedkiller is not completely effective, but because some of the roots may not have leaves above ground when you spray. So if you find, young growths coming through after spraying, you'll have to go over the plot again, just to make sure. It really is worth while.

Getting to know your soil

It's absolutely vital, now, to get to know your soil. You'll probably begin to feel pretty enthusiastic and dying to get some plants into the borders. But unless you have some idea of the stuff they're going to grow in, you could be wasting your money. And with some plants, that could be a small fortune.

The first job is to dig a hole. A favourite trick of some builders is to leave the site looking neat and tidy by bulldozing a layer of soil over the top. But that soil can hide a multitude of sins! A hole about 60 centimetres (2 feet) deep reveals all.

Let me, first of all, paint the worst picture possible. You're unlikely to find all the disadvantages, so this way you may be able to count a blessing or two!

Imagine that the top layer of soil is yellow or grey and very sticky indeed. Underneath this is a solid layer of stone-hard soil mixed liberally with concrete, while below that is a layer of fine, crumbly brown earth. I regret to say that this is not as uncommon as you may think.

What has happened is this. The builders have used your plot to site the concrete mixer. Every night its residue of concrete has been emptied on the ground and this has hardened into a solid sheet. To make matters worse, excavators, dumper-trucks and wheelbarrows have trundled over the soil endlessly, compacting it into a hard, airless block.

Meantime, the footings for the house have been dug and the clay subsoil heaped in one corner. Once the building is finished, that subsoil is used to 'tidy up' the site, covering all the debris and mess of the whole operation.

What you are left with is a lifeless clay 'topsoil' overlying a solid rock-hard pan with the real topsoil underneath. Even if plants could grow in the clay, they could never root through the concrete to find comfort in the topsoil.

Now I must say that most modern developers have learnt this particular lesson and are a bit more careful. Many now use the garden as part of the sales package and nearly all are aware that buyers expect a much higher standard than of old. None the less, if you buy before the house is completed, it's well worth pointing out your interest in gardening and insisting on a better deal outside.

If you are faced with this worst of all situations, you have little alternative. The subsoil must be carted off and dumped. That hard pan *must* be broken up and the proper topsoil unearthed. I would love to be able to recommend a short-cut but I don't believe there is one.

Generally you'll find a much happier situation, though I must say that the hard pan caused by overcompaction is all too often in evidence. It must go, and the way to do that is by double-digging. But, before you start, there are two more tests to make to familiarize yourself properly with your soil.

Start by simply handling some of the topsoil. If, when it's moist, you can mould it into a ball like Plasticine, you have a heavy clay. Now you'll hear a lot of depressing advice about the difficulties of clay soil that is more or less designed to put you off for ever. Ignore it. I can tell you this; if you treat it with respect and are prepared to work at it, you'll grow much better plants in it than ever you would in sand.

If, on the other hand, the soil feels gritty when rubbed and will not hold together, there is a high sand content. This type of soil is easier to work than clay, but it's much hungrier and could well cost you more in fertilizer and manure.

If it feels silky when rubbed, the soil is silt, which should be treated very much like clay, or, unusually, you may find a very high organic content indicating a peaty soil.

Finally, if the soil appears dry and crumbly and greyish in appearance, you are gardening on chalk. In this case you'll often be able to see pieces of white, free chalk in the soil. It's poor, dry and hungry stuff and severely restricting on the types of plants you can grow but, treated in the right way, it will still provide you with a fine garden.

Of course, these are the extremes and what you will usually find is a mixture. These soils are called 'loams'. If there is a higher proportion of clay, it's a 'heavy loam', while more sand makes it a 'light loam', and, if you're really lucky, you get the happy 'medium loam'.

The final test is for the chemical content of the soil. Very keen gardeners will want to know exactly how much of the main plant nutrients already exist in their land, and to find out you can send a sample away for analysis. Frankly, for the first-

Testing the soil is cheap and easy to do. It really is essential before buying plants.

timer, that's going over the top slightly, though there is one exception. It really is absolutely vital to discover whether you garden on an acid or a chalky soil.

All plants are sensitive to the amount of lime in the soil and some so much so that they will simply die if the balance is wrong. Since a lime-test kit costs very little and is simplicity itself to use, it really is folly to buy any plants at all without knowing which will like your soil.

The simplest kits consist of a test tube into which you place a sample of your soil which has previously been air-dried. You then add a measured amount of distilled water plus a chemical provided in the kit. After a while, the soil settles to the bottom of the tube and a coloured liquid is left on top. This colour is compared with a chart to tell you the state of the soil.

The acidity is measured in terms of 'pH'. The scientific explanation of the symbol is complicated and unnecessary to understand. I never have! Suffice it to know that a pH of 7 is neutral, any figure below this being acid and any above alkaline.

Of course, to make use of these figures you need to know which plants like acid soils and which alkaline. Well, most test kits do include a list of plants and their preferences, but to make it really simple use this rule of thumb.

Most vegetables like a chalky soil so, if the pH is below 6.5, add lime to the land in the spring. The exception here is potatoes, which like an acid soil, so leave out the tatie land.

Most ornamentals either prefer or will tolerate a neutral-to-acid soil, so only add lime if the pH is very low – say below 5.0.

You will have realized that I have only talked about *raising* the pH and not about *lowering* it. This is because, while it is very easy to make soil more chalky simply by adding lime, the reverse is very difficult indeed. You can add acid peat until you're blue in the face (and red in the bank balance!) but the soil will always revert back to being chalky. While there are ways of growing acid-loving plants in chalky soil, the best bet, certainly at the outset, is to grow those plants that will do well in your soil. Instead of failing with rhododendrons, grow the beautiful lilacs instead; rather than fail with pieris, succeed with photinia. There are *always* plants that will like your soil, whatever it is.

Soil improvement

Unless you're very lucky indeed, your soil will need to be

improved and 'livened up' a bit if you're to be successful with plants.

The key to improving most soils is organic matter – anything that will rot down really. Nature, of course, provides organic matter in the form of falling leaves, dying plants and animals and animal dung. Everything is recycled time and again. We need to do much the same thing but, because we expect much more from our plot of land than Nature ever intended, we must use much more.

All organic matter has the effect of improving water-holding on dry soils and assisting drainage on heavy ones. It 'opens up' the soil, assisting the free passage of air and allowing young roots to work their way through the air spaces. Much organic matter contains plant foods and it also provides a home and a source of energy for millions of soil organisms that are absolutely vital to plant growth. There are several sources of organic matter.

Manure

Animal manure is by far the best soil conditioner and generally the cheapest too. It also contains quite a lot of plant food, so you'll save on fertilizer if you use it regularly. If you live in a country area where cattle are common, you'll have no problems getting hold of a trailer-load of muck quite cheaply. In the city, it's more difficult. But, even in urban areas, there's usually a riding stable or at least the odd pony or two where

There is a very wide range of superb lime-loving plants that will be much more successful on chalky soil. The lilacs are a fine substitute for rhododendrons.

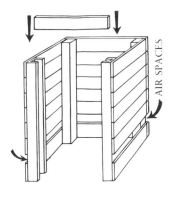

It's not difficult to knock up a compost container from old floorboards, available cheaply from a demolition contractor.

you can buy horse manure by the bag.

Whichever animal it comes from, all manure must be rotted for at least six months and preferably a year before use. Horse manure, particularly, is very hot when fresh and will scorch plant roots severely.

Spent mushroom compost
This is quite readily available and is a darned good soil conditioner, with one proviso. It consists of well-rotted horse manure mixed with peat but it also includes a small amount of lime. That's fine for the vegetable plot and perfectly good in borders where you're growing lime-loving plants. But, if you're blessed with a neutral or acid soil and wish to grow acid-lovers, then avoid mushroom compost. It contains very little in the way of plant food, so you'll have to add that in the form of fertilizer.

Other alternatives
It would be true to say that anything that will rot down will improve the soil, so there are many local alternatives that can be used. Seaweed is a wonderful soil conditioner and also contains a lot of plant food. Brewers will sometimes let you have spent hops which not only do the soil a power of good but also smell great! Woollen mills throw out any amount of waste which will all rot down to improve the soil. But make quite sure it *is* wool or cotton and not a man-made fibre.

In a new garden, you naturally won't have had the opportunity of making your own organic matter in the compost heap, but you'll start collecting compostable material straightaway, so it's a good idea to invest in a container. You can buy plastic or wooden ones at the garden centre or you can make your own. All you need really is a wooden box about 75 centimetres (2½ feet) square by 90 centimetres (3 feet) tall with a detachable front.

Special treatments
Different soils require slightly different methods of cultivation so it's as well to make a note of the basic rules.

But first of all, there's one rule that applies whether your soil is a light sand or heavy clay. Never try to cultivate it when it's soaking wet. You should even avoid walking on it if you can because, if you do, you'll force the particles together, driving out the air and making it a very inhospitable medium for plant roots.

It's not quite so bad on light soils, of course, but on heavy land, slopping about in mud will cause it to turn to concrete when it gets dry. So if you can't avoid walking on it, use boards to spread your weight. Mind you, it can be pretty frustrating for the gardener pacing the living room, glowering out of the window at soaking wet soil and itching to get at it. There is a solution that's very practical in a small garden and will enable you to get on when you want to.

It pays hands down to invest in a big sheet of clear polythene to cover the next bit of soil you want to work on. Not only will it keep it dry but, early in the season, it'll warm it up too, so you'll be able to get planting or sowing that much sooner.

Note that I have suggested *clear* polythene. The black sheeting is excellent if you want to suppress weeds, especially if you can keep it there for a long time. In the end, excluding the light will conquer even the most persistent weeds. It will also keep the weather off the soil, of course, but it does nothing to warm it up.

Types of Soil
Clay

Clay is without doubt the most difficult soil initially, because when it's wet, it's a sticky, boggy morass, and when it's dry, it's as hard as concrete, and neither of these states is exactly hospitable to plants. That's the bad news. The good news is that, with a fair bit of hard work, a clay soil will grow far better plants than a very light, sandy soil ever can.

The main problem with heavy clay soils (and with silt soils) is very bad drainage. If your soil is really heavy and wet, you may have to install a drainage system, but fortunately that's an extreme and you're unlikely to be that unlucky.

The best way to improve an averagely sticky clay or silt soil is to start by double-digging it (digging the soil to two spades' depth) and working in both coarse grit – about a barrowload to every 2 or 3 square metres (1 or 3½ square feet) – and organic matter well mixed through into all levels of the soil. The grit will open up the soil and allow air and water to pass more freely through it. The organic matter helps to open up the soil too, but in the case of well-made garden compost, or well-rotted animal manure, it also contains essential plant nutrients and provides a home for the millions of soil organisms that are vital to plant growth. When you've finished double-digging, spread a thick layer of organic matter over the area. It will get worked into the soil by the rain and the worms.

If you don't have any garden compost or a ready source of animal manure, you can use spent mushroom compost or one of the many alternatives available at the garden centre.

By adding all this organic matter and grit to the soil you are raising your borders above the level of your lawn, which will also help them to drain more freely.

When you dig heavy clay, you need to get your timing just right. In the early stages, before you've 'tamed' it with organic matter, you'll have to catch it between the times when it is dry and hard as a rock and the times when it has become thoroughly waterlogged and you're knee-deep in mud. The best way is to dig it over roughly in the autumn – ideally when it's drying out but still moist – and leave it for the winter frosts to work on. As it dries out it cracks, and when water gets into those cracks and freezes it forces them wider apart, breaking the soil down into smaller and smaller clods. With a bit of luck and few good hard frosts, you will find that in the spring you need only rake it down.

Incidentally, you should *never* walk on heavy soil when it is wet, since you are simply compounding the problems it suffers. If for some reason you simply have to walk on the soil, you should always put down wide scaffolding planks to spread your weight.

Planting as much as you possibly can also helps heavy soil, because the plants' roots open it up as they grow, and even after the plants have been removed, in the case of annuals, or indeed vegetable crops, the remaining roots still perform that service. So if you can, aim to keep the soil covered with plants all the time.

Sand
On first acquaintance, and compared to heavy clay soils, sandy soils are a doddle to cultivate. Free-draining, they are workable when other types of soil are still waterlogged, they warm up quickly in spring which is ideal for raising early crops, and they are very easy to dig over in preparation for planting. But every Eden has its serpent, and in the case of sandy soils it's the fact that they dry out very quickly, losing not only moisture but valuable plant nutrients too. For that reason they demand large amounts of organic matter which help retain moisture in the soil, and plant nutrients in the form of fertilizers every year. However, since organic matter will work its way through the thin topsoil very quickly and into the subsoil, it is a waste of time – and compost – to dig it in

too deeply. Either dig it into the very top of the soil or simply spread it over the surface and allow the elements and the worms to work it in for you. Applying organic matter this way – as a mulch – has another advantage. Because sandy soils lose moisture through surface evaporation as well as through free drainage, covering the surface with a mulch helps to prevent that happening.

Chalk

Chalky soils have many of the same advantages and problems as sand – they are very free-draining and are rarely too wet to work, but they lose water and nutrients very rapidly. They have an additional problem in that the layer of topsoil is usually shallow and chalky soils are always very alkaline, which limits the range of plants that will grow happily in them. The way to improve a chalky soil is much the same as with sand – add lots of organic matter and fertilizer, and keep the surface of the soil covered as far as possible to prevent evaporation. If you can use organic matter that is acidic, like peat, well-rotted manure, garden compost or grass cuttings, for digging in and mulching, you will help, though only in a small way, to counteract the alkalinity of the soil.

Medium loam

If you are lucky enough to have medium loam, even though it won't need lots of work to improve it, it will still benefit from an annual dose of manure or compost. Soil is like life – what you get out of it depends to a large extent on what you put into it.

Fertilizers

All plants need feeding regularly, but you don't need a degree in chemistry to do it. Until you get specialized, two bags, or at most three, are all you'll need.

If you're intending to plant trees, shrubs, fruit trees or herbaceous plants any time between October and March, use a handful of bonemeal around each plant. This will just supply phosphate which is all that's needed at that time of year to get the roots going.

All the rest of your plants will be happy with Growmore, which is a cheap general fertilizer that contains all the major plant food necessary. Use it when planting ornamental plants and fruit in the growing season between March and October, again at about a handful per plant or, for small bedding plants,

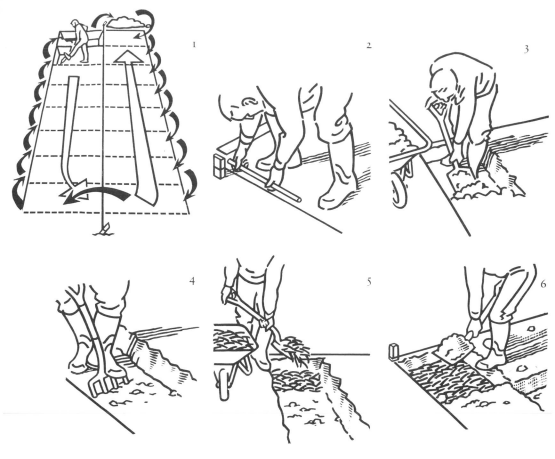

1. A large plot is best divided into two.

2. Mark out each trench exactly 60 cm (2 ft) wide to ensure level digging.

3. Remove the soil one spade deep from the first trench and cart it to the final trench.

4. Break up the subsoil to the depth of the fork.

5. Put bulky organic matter in the bottom and refill the trench halfway, throwing the soil forward from the next trench.

6. Add another layer of manure and completely fill the trench. Continue working down the plot in the same way.

about two handfuls per square metre (square yard). For vegetables, rake in a couple of handfuls per square metre before sowing or planting.

You'll get by perfectly happily with that formula but, if you want to be just a little more sophisticated, I would suggest that you use a rose fertilizer for all trees, shrubs and roses and also for fruit trees and bushes. It's just designed that little bit more for the job.

Double-digging

In the ornamental part of the garden, double-digging need only be done once in the life of the garden. In the vegetable plot, it's rare that it should be necessary more than once every six or seven years. All of which is just as well, because there's no hiding that it's hard work!

If you have been bequeathed that hard pan below the surface, I'm afraid there's no alternative. Even under the lawn area it will cause problems with drainage that will make your grass a quagmire in wet weather.

It's a good excuse to treat yourself to a really good spade

– stainless steel if you can run to it – and also make a scraper out of a bit of scrap wood. That fits into your back pocket and should be used regularly. You'll also need two canes or sticks 60 centimetres (2 feet) long and a garden line. Bear in mind, too, that when you get down to it you should go slowly and, when you feel you've had enough, take a rest, or you'll find yourself on your back for a week, cursing your luck.

Divide the whole plot into two equal halves with the garden line. The idea is to dig across half the plot at a time.

Measure the first trench using the 60-centimetre (2-foot) cane and dig out the topsoil to the depth of the spade. This first lot must be carted or thrown onto the very end of the second half of the plot. That way it will be waiting for you ready to refill the last trench when you get to it.

After digging out the first trench, get into it and just fork over the bottom. There's no need to turn the soil over – just put the fork in to its full depth and lift the soil to break it up.

Most books will now tell you to put a layer of manure, compost or peat into the bottom of the trench. Well, that's fine if you have unlimited supplies, but few of us have. I would refill the trench at least half full and then put a bit of organic matter in where the plants will be able to reach it. I also like to put a layer on the top when the trench is refilled.

The refilling is done with the soil from the second trench which is just thrown forward. But before digging it, mark out its 60-centimetre (2-foot) width with the other cane. This is quite important because it means that you refill the first trench with exactly the same amount of soil you dug out of it, so keeping the digging level.

Then simply continue in this way down the plot until you get to the end, then turn round and work back.

Single-digging is sufficient for most situations. Here the soil is dug only one spade deep and any manure put in the bottom of the trench.

Single-digging

In nine cases out of ten, this is all that's necessary. Here, you leave the subsoil alone and just turn over the topsoil. It's still unwise to get carried away and rush at it because you're almost bound to be using muscles you never knew you had!

The easiest way is to dig out a trench right across the plot, one spade wide and one deep, throwing it evenly behind you. Then you work the soil forwards each time to refill the trench in front. When you get to the end, you'll be able to find enough soil from that which you threw back to refill the last trench.

It's a good idea to use manure or some other organic matter. Just put it in the bottom of each trench before you refill.

FENCES AND HEDGES

Ideally, the 'hard' landscaping should be done first. Jobs like paving, walling and fencing can cause havoc to existing features because it's hard to avoid wheeling barrows over the soil and slopping a bit of cement. Much better to get all that kind of work over and done with before the cultivations begin. Generally the first job is to define your boundary.

Fence or hedge?

If you have plenty of room and a little patience, a hedge is certainly the best bet. A 'living fence' looks soft and makes an ideal background for the plants in the borders. In exposed areas, hedges make the very best windbreaks too. But even a formal, clipped hedge will take up about 1–2 metres (4 feet) of growing room all round the garden and this is generally too much in a small plot.

Fences which may look hard initially can soon be softened with plants.

Fences, on the other hand, take up little space and do have the great advantage of providing instant privacy. They may look a bit stark at first, but they can soon be softened by the use of climbing plants trained on wires fixed to the posts.

Mind you, a fence can cause problems too, and it's well worth making a good job of putting it up in the first place to avoid trouble later on. While it is certainly possible to remove and replace a rotten post, it's quite a big job and the cause of many a lost temper!

Posts generally rot at ground level, where conditions are ideal for the fungi that live on the wood. This is generally a big problem when posts are concreted into the ground. Not only does the post often rot quicker, but you're left with that massive chunk of concrete to remove before you can get the new one back in its place. It really is a headache.

But don't despair. Relatively recent developments in do-it-yourself fencing have done away with most of the problems. If you spend just a little more and follow the rules, your fence will last for many decades.

Panel fencing

There's no doubt that panel fencing is much the better bet for the do-it-yourselfer. It's not difficult to put up if you have a bit of help, there are many different styles to choose from, and modern panels are much stronger and will last a lot longer than was once the case.

When you choose panels, sort out the strongest you can find. There are still a few thin, interwoven types available and they're definitely a false economy. You may have to spend a little more on good-quality panels but they'll last much longer.

It's rare that you'll find them treated with preservative under pressure, which is the very best thing. That way they last for ever, but make sure they have at least been dipped in preservative. Painting it on afterwards is not nearly so effective. It is possible to buy posts that have been treated under pressure and they are well worth the little extra money.

Fixing the posts

There are four methods of anchoring the posts into the soil and you must decide which to use before putting in your order. First of all, they can simply be put into a hole and held firm with hardcore and gravel rammed in around them. This method has the advantage that water can percolate down through the filling and will not rest around the post at soil level where it causes rotting. It requires quite a knack to get the posts firm and exactly in place, but it's a good method if you can do it.

Alternatively, you can concrete posts in. Using wet concrete which needs only gentle tamping, it's easier to get the posts exactly positioned, and this method will certainly hold even the longest fence posts firm. But it does have the snag that posts tend to rot at soil level. To reduce the risk to a minimum, put a little waterproofing agent into the mix, bring the top of the finished concrete slightly above soil level and slope it away from the post so that it will shed water.

Bear in mind that with both these methods, you'll need posts at least 60 centimetres (2 feet) longer than the panels.

The modern method of fixing is to use special sockets welded to long spikes which can be driven into the ground with a sledge-hammer. They have two great advantages. First, there are no holes to dig, so the fence can be put up much faster. Secondly, and even more important, the socket also holds the post clear of the ground so it's unlikely to rot.

However, as you would imagine, there are disadvantages

The easiest way to erect fencing is to drive special post sockets into the ground but it's difficult to get the posts dead straight this way.

too. First, it's quite difficult to drive the spikes in accurately. Some manufacturers have made the sockets adjustable, so there is a certain amount of leeway, but even so, it's very difficult to get a perfect result. Secondly, I'm also not at all happy about their stability. With a fence below 1.5 metres (5 feet) high, in solid, level soil, they're fine. But higher fences, especially in made-up or unlevel soil, tend to wave about in the breeze.

The real McCoy, as far as I'm concerned, is a combination of the two best methods – a socket that concretes into the ground. These are available and will give you the best of all worlds.

If you decide to use any of these special fixings, the posts need be only 15 centimetres (6 inches) longer than the panels.

While you're ordering, you'll also need a supply of special brackets to fix the panels to the posts. They are a *great* advance on the old method of nailing through the side rail of the panel (which always has a habit of splitting), and well worth a little extra outlay. You'll want fixing screws too, and, if you're using concrete, some ballast and cement.

Building the fence

The first thing is to measure your boundary accurately, and that's a lot more important than you may appreciate. Nothing gets folk more worked up than the thought that their neighbour may be pinching a little bit of their land. I have known full-scale feuds between neighbours over no more than an inch of soil.

And once you've decided on the dividing line, remember that your fence must go *your* side of that line. It's also customary to give your neighbour the 'smooth' side of the fence. All panel fences have one side with struts and one side without and, though I know of no legal requirement, it seems that it's normal practice to put the struts on your side. But, whatever you do, when you come to fix the panels, make sure you get them all the same way round. I know it sounds impossible, but I once finished a fence only to find that I'd put just one panel in the wrong way round! And it's a devil of a job to get it out again.

Mark out the line with a garden line made with strong nylon twine and then set the first post. If you are driving in spikes, simply bang the spike down so that the base-plate rests on the ground, slot in the post and, if it's adjustable, tighten up the nuts.

If you're ramming in hardcore, you'll need to dig a hole about 45 centimetres (18 inches) deep and as narrow as you can make it. Put the post in, put a little hardcore round it and ram it down. Gradually fill to the top, ramming as you go. It's important with this method to check regularly with a spirit-level that the post is upright both ways.

Concreting the posts in is easier. Use a mix of 6 parts by volume ballast to 1 part Portland cement with a little waterproofing liquid added to the water. Make the mix as dry as you can, but workable. Again, dig a hole 45 centimetres (18 inches) deep and as narrow as you can and put a little concrete in the bottom of the hole before setting the post. This is important because it means that the post will be totally encased in waterproof concrete which will stop water rising up through it and rotting it. Put the post in the centre and fill round with concrete, ramming and checking for straightness as you go.

When the concrete is at the required height, make sure you slope the top of it so that water will run away from the post, to avoid rotting.

If you're using one of the sockets that can be concreted in, the hole can be a bit shallower – say about 30 centimetres (1 foot) deep – provided the soil is firm. Then, fix the socket to the post before you put it into the ground. That way you can make sure, with the spirit-level, that the socket is in the right position to ensure that the post is upright.

The golden rule with fencing is to put posts and panels up together as you go. It really is virtually impossible to put all the posts in first and then hope to fit the panels afterwards. You only need to be a little bit out, and you'll have to start cutting panels or nailing strips on. Much better to be on the safe side.

So if you are working with the special spikes, the next job is to fix the panel to the post. You can nail it on, but the special fixing brackets now supplied by some manufacturers are much better.

Make sure that the panel is at least 7.5 centimetres (3 inches) off the ground to avoid rotting. I do this with a couple of bricks underneath the panel, then pack these with bits of wood to get each panel exactly right.

If you're concreting posts in, or ramming in hardcore, you'll find it easier to dig the second hole before the panel is fixed. The best way is to measure the distance either with the capping strip supplied for the panels or, if they're nailed on and not

1. Fix the special sockets to the posts.

2. Check that the post is upright, fill round the socket with concrete and tamp down hard.

3. Fix the panels to the posts. They can be nailed, but brackets are better.

4. Ensure that the post is upright; hold it in place with a spare post.

supplied separately, with the panel itself. Then fix the panel as before, supporting the loose end on a brick packed with pieces of wood to bring it dead level.

Now the second post is fixed to the other end of the panel in exactly the same way as the first. Be careful to ensure that the second post is at exactly the right height. If the panel is levelled before fixing, you can do this by measuring from the top of the panel to the top of the post. I carry a 5-centimetre (2-inch) piece of wood in my pocket for the purpose.

If the posts are concreted in, you'll need to support each panel until the concrete is hard. This can be done with the fencing posts you haven't yet used. Just bang a nail in so that it projects at the end and lean it against the panel so that the nail hooks over it. Check again that the posts are level and leave it like this for at least 24 hours. When you get to the end of the job, you'll naturally have to find a few spare bits of wood to use as props.

At the end of the run, you'll find that the last panel won't fit. If it does, someone, somewhere, is certainly watching over you! Ordinary mortals will have to do some cutting.

Start by carefully measuring the space you need to fill. Then lever off the slats on one end of the panel. A big screwdriver and a claw-hammer will generally do the trick quite easily.

Mark the extent of the new size and nail the two struts back on again in the new position. You'll find you need to do this on a hard surface; a scaffold plank resting on the soil will do well. If the panel is more than half its original size, you'll need to shift the centre struts in the same way too, just to make it look uniform.

With the struts nailed on to their new position, the excess bit of panel can be cut off and discarded and the new-sized piece fixed in the space.

All that remains is to nail the caps onto the posts with a couple of 5-centimetre (2-inch) nails apiece and, if they come separately, the capping strips on the panels.

Most 'coffee-table' garden designers treat panel fencing with a grand contempt, but I must say that I agree with them on one point only. The colour – usually a vivid orange – is pretty revolting and not at all an attractive background for plants. However, there are several stains that are harmless to plants and will give the effect of instant weathering. Your builders' merchant or do-it-yourself store will stock a range of different colours which, for my money, make all the difference.

Stepped fencing

If your garden slopes, you'll have to make special provisions. Obviously you can't allow the panels to follow the line of the slope, or the posts will go in at an angle! So the panels have to be 'stepped' at intervals.

It's a good idea to work out the extent of the slope before ordering the panels. This is because each 'step' will require a longer post, so you need to know how many there'll be. You can do this with a straight-edge, a spirit-level and a number of pegs. Start at the highest end and put the straight-edge on the ground. The other end should rest on a peg which is hammered in until it's level. On a long garden you may need several pegs, with the height of the last one from the ground indicating the extent of the slope.

Ideally, each step should not exceed about 15 centimetres (6 inches) or the space under the panel will be too great. Starting at the lowest point, set the first panels in the normal way until you find you have to dig out soil to keep the panel level. Then, step up 15 centimetres (6 inches). When you reach this stage, don't forget that you'll need a post 15 centimetres (6 inches) longer than you've been using.

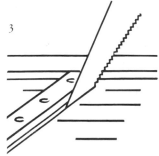

4

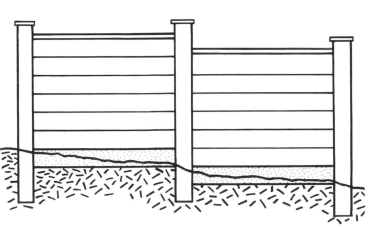

1. Remove the end struts from a complete panel, levering them up with a screwdriver.
2. Measure the required length and re-nail the struts in position both sides.
3. Saw off the excess and the panel will fit exactly.
4. On sloping ground, fencing must be stepped. Fill in the holes at the bottom with gravel boards.

Gravel boards

If you step up, you'll have a gap underneath the fence of 15 centimetres (6 inches) at one end of the panel, tapering down to nothing at the other. This space can be filled with a gravel board. Indeed, I like to use gravel boards in any case. Remember that it's invariably the bottom of the panel that rots first, because it's here that rain and soil splash up or soil gets piled against the panel. If rotting occurs on the panel, you have a major and an expensive job on your hands. But the gravel board is only 15 centimetres (6 inches) wide and easy and cheap to replace.

If you have concreted the posts into the ground, or used the rammed hardcore method, just dig out sufficiently to enable the 15 × 2.5 × 180-centimetre (6-inch × 1-inch × 6-foot) board to slide under the panel. It is fixed by nailing a 2.5 × 4-centimetre (1 × 1½-inch) block onto the post and then nailing the gravel board to the block.

If you have used metal sockets, the job is complicated by the fact that the socket prevents you nailing into the post. In this case fix the gravel board with a couple of metal brackets from the panel to the top of the board. You can buy brackets at most ironmongers or builders' merchants.

Other types of fencing

The cheapest fence I ever put up was one of the most attractive and durable. I made it with second-hand timber bought from the demolition contractor's yard for a fraction of the cost of proper fencing. You need for the posts 7.5 × 7.5-centimetre (3 × 3-inch) floor joists; for the rails, 7.5 × 5-centimetre (3 × 2-inch) joists; plus floorboarding at whatever size you can get hold of.

The posts are put in as previously described, about 2.5 metres (8 to 9 feet) apart, and the rails bolted on with 15-centimetre (6-inch) coach bolts. If you're a competent carpenter, you may prefer to make proper half joints, but it's not really necessary. The only thing to watch is that, if your posts have been set right up to the edge of your boundary, you must bolt the rails on your side of the fence or you'll be trespassing on your neighbour's land.

Then simply cut the floorboards to the required lengths and nail them on. It's best to put a small gap of about 2.5 centimetres (1 inch) between each board. This looks better and also filters the wind through. Naturally, the fence will need treating with a preservative afterwards.

The lower fence at the side is made from hazel wattles, while the taller one is home-made using old floorboards from the demolition contractor.

Paling fences are put up in much the same way. You can buy palings at most timber merchants or do-it-yourself stores and they look quite attractive, though naturally they have their limitations. Over about 120 centimetres (4 feet) high they begin to look wrong and they also offer no privacy.

Wattle fencing makes a very attractive boundary and a good windbreak in country gardens.

Nothing could be simpler to put up. Just drive round posts into the ground at the required distances and wire the panels to them. The great limitation of wattle fencing is that it will rarely last more than about ten years.

Trellis

Square or diamond-shaped trellis makes an attractive fence within the garden, its openness creating a much softer effect. It can be used to support plants, of course, yet still allows a glimpse through, here and there, adding to the illusion of extra space.

Trellis can also be used to good effect to top panel fencing, adding height without increasing the 'boxed-in' effect. This is the way we shut out the dreaded chemical factory which provided the 'view' from our Birmingham garden. The panel manufacturers generally make square trellis panels to fit their fencing and in various heights, normally increasing in 30-centimetre (1-foot) increments. Naturally the posts must be long enough to take the extra trellis which is simply placed on top and nailed through the side struts to the posts.

This square trellis has the advantage of being thicker than normal diamond trellis which is not really suitable for use as fencing. That is intended to be fixed to battens on a wall where it will receive less buffeting from winds and can be fixed at closer intervals.

It's also possible to buy tailor-made panels to fit any particular location. These panels are made in traditional styles and are very beautiful indeed. Unfortunately, so is the price! However, with care, a competent do-it-yourselfer could make his or her own.

Making rectangular panels is straightforward, provided you remember to drill the thin lathes before nailing or screwing through them. Curves require patience. You'll find that if you make saw-cuts about three quarters of the way through the lathe about 2.5 centimetres (1 inch) apart, you'll be able to bend them sufficiently. Naturally the bend should

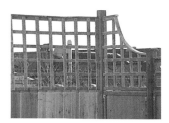

Trellis makes a useful extension to the fence without increasing the 'closed-in' effect. Note the attractive curve where the fence changes height.

be such that the cuts are on the inside of the curve and so close up rather than open. You can buy ready-made mouldings and wooden balls to embellish the trellis from the better timber merchants.

Gates

In a large garden a gate can be a delightful feature. There's something of a sense of mystery about a closed gate and the view immediately after opening it should reflect that. What's more, a half-open, or a wrought-iron gate with the glimpse of a beautiful border beyond tempts you to walk on to discover further delights. Alas, all this is somewhat fanciful in a small garden.

Generally, modern gardens can be seen in their entirety at a glance and there is little scope for mystery or surprise. In this case, make the gate relatively unobtrusive by using the same materials as the fence.

Gates in walls can be made of wrought iron. If you do use one, plan for some bulky planting beyond, which will add to the illusion of space and also provide privacy.

Hanging a gate is a simple and straightforward operation. Fix the hinges to the gate first, then put a piece of wood at least 2.5 centimetres (1 inch) thick on the ground between the gateposts to allow clearance beneath the gate when it's fixed. Offer it up to the gatepost and screw the hinges to the post.

It's very important, though, to make sure that the gatepost itself is strong and well anchored. There are few things more annoying than having to struggle to lift a gate off the ground before it can be opened. Try doing it with an armful of parcels!

Wrought-iron gates are often fixed directly to a wall. In this case it's necessary to hack out a hole with a masonry drill and cold chisel. Make it plenty big enough to take both the hinge fixing and a generous amount of cement and use sharp sand mixed 3:1 with cement for a really strong job. Allow at least three days for the cement to harden before hanging the gate.

If you have young children, you should also make sure that the latch is fitted at a height they can't reach. It saves an awful lot of worry, especially if you live near a busy road.

Sometimes there's a temptation to emulate the 'stately homes' by making an imposing entrance to the garden of a small house. You've seen them too, with impressive stone pillars topped by pineapples or recumbent lions. While I strongly believe that gardens are personal things and no one should set themselves up as arbiters of good or bad 'taste', let

A wrought-iron gate will not provide privacy but gives an attractive glimpse of the garden beyond.

me just urge you to think carefully before doing anything quite as grand. A sense of proportion is a wonderful thing!

Hedging

There's nothing quite like a good hedge to set off a garden, but there are two things you *must* have – space and patience. Whatever the advertisements in the Sunday papers may say, it will take at least three and probably five years for any hedge to reach 2 metres (6 feet) and it will take up a considerable area all round the garden. But if you can do it, then I urge you to have a go.

There are two broad categories of hedging – formal and informal. Basically a formal hedge is one that will stand clipping and can therefore be kept more compact. An informal hedge is simply a line of shrubs allowed to grow more or less naturally with just a little pruning from time to time. They take up much more room, depending on the one you choose, but they do have the great advantage that they will flower in season.

Before you choose a hedging plant, ask yourself what you're expecting of it. You're likely, for example, to want it to shield your garden from the view of passers-by or from the neighbours. A little privacy in the garden, after all, is a pretty necessary thing. In that case, you'll need something that will grow as fast as possible and to at least 2 metres (6 feet). Ideally it should also be evergreen or at least thick enough to protect you from view in the winter.

You may need a hedge to protect your garden from winds. If you do, you'll have to worry in the early stages about a windbreak to protect the windbreak! But more of that later. Make sure, in any case, that the plants you choose are hardy enough to do the job.

Finally, you may be anxious to keep out wandering dogs, cats or children. Indeed, you may even want to keep them in! So your choice then might be a plant equipped with the discouragement of fierce thorns. There are hedging plants available that would keep out an elephant, let alone the ginger tom from next door.

The main criterion, of course, will be aesthetic, so it's a good idea to go along to a few mature gardens to see what the plant looks like ten or more years after planting.

Formal hedges

Clipped hedges will be the choice of most first-time gardeners because they take up much less room. First of all, don't, for heaven's sake, be worried about all the work they entail. Ever since the appearance in garden centres of a chemical that slows down the growth of hedges, gardeners have got the impression that they take hours and hours of maintenance. In fact, most need clipping once a year and others, at the most, three times. And with shears or electric clippers, it's easy work and a great pleasure. Don't be worried about the Latin names either. The first one on my list is a real off-putter!

Leyland's Cypress (Cupressocyparis leylandii)
This is more often simply called 'Leylandii'. It's probably the most reviled conifer in recent times and, in my view, quite wrongly. One reason is that there are several different 'strains' of 'Leylandii', some of which are pretty indifferent. However, most nurserymen now stick to two types which are more compact and make excellent hedges, so the looser, floppier 'Leylandii' hedges of the past are no more.

Certainly it has been very widely planted because of its fast growth, so plant snobs should perhaps look for something less common. Nevertheless, it's a first-rate plant. After a year establishing itself, it will grow 60 to 90 centimetres (2 to 3 feet) a year to produce a good, matt background for border plants. And it can be clipped very hard, provided you start early in the life of the plants. I've seen hedges 2.5 metres (8 feet) tall and only 60 centimetres (2 feet) wide at the base, narrowing to 15 centimetres (6 inches) at the top – stunning!

There is also a bright golden form called 'Castlewellan Gold' which grows very nearly as fast and certainly brightens the place up. Some folk plant the green and gold alternately to give a kind of mottled effect. I don't like it but that's no reason why you shouldn't.

Plant both kinds 90 centimetres (3 feet) apart.

Western Red Cedar (Thuja plicata)
In my view, one of the best of hedging conifers. There's a variety called 'Atrovirens' which, for some reason, is grown widely in France but not so much here. It is available, however, and makes a lovely bright, fresh green hedge. It's not quite so fast as 'Leylandii', growing about 46 to 76 centimetres (1½ to 2½ feet) a year, but well worth the wait.

Thujas have one other great advantage too. They will shoot again from inside the plant if the outside gets scorched from wind or cold. So if your hedge turns brown and dead on the outside in a very hard winter, you can be happy that it will come back eventually.

Plant 90 centimetres (3 feet) apart.

Yew (Taxus baccata)
The real aristocrat of conifer hedges. It's slower growing but will make about 30 centimetres (1 foot) a year for the first five or six years. None the less, you'll need a little patience for a fully established, thick hedge. But if ever a hedge was worth waiting for, this is it. It forms a dense, impenetrable, matt green wall which can be clipped to perfection. It's hardy, tolerant of most garden soils and will live for a thousand years!

Plant 60 centimetres (2 feet) apart.

Beech (Fagus sylvatica)
Often a more realistic hedge than the conifers because of the cost. Buy bare-rooted plants in autumn and you'll do it a *lot* cheaper. Though not evergreen, beech retains its dead leaves all winter until the new ones push them off in the spring. This gives a superb russet brown screen, which makes a pleasant winter difference to the fresh green of the spring and summer. It will put on about 30 to 46 centimetres (1 to 1½ feet) of growth a year once established. One word of warning: like the conifers it should not be trimmed until it has reached its required height.

If it has a snag, it's that it really requires a light, well-drained soil. If yours isn't, you'd be well advised to grow the similar hornbeam instead. There is also a copper-leaved variety which is perhaps very slightly slower in growth and a bit more expensive, but looks splendid.

Plant 60 centimetres (2 feet) apart.

Hornbeam (Carpinus betulus)
A less demanding plant than beech, but with much the same appearance though lacking just a little sparkle. The dead leaves in winter don't have quite as bright a russet colour and the new foliage is perhaps not quite so fresh-looking. Still, a much better bet on heavy soil.

Plant 60 centimetres (2 feet) apart.

Laurel (Prunus laurocerasus 'Rotundifolia')
This, in my view, makes a really striking hedge. The bright, glossy green leaves are quite big so they sparkle dramatically in the sun. There's something very pleasing about the sight of

A row of Leyland's cypress makes an attractive, fast-growing hedge which can be closely clipped.

a well-grown, vigorous, healthy bush and laurel always seem to look that way. It will grow about 30 to 46 centimetres (1 to 1½ feet) a year and requires trimming only once. But then it's a secateur job rather than shears I'm afraid. If you cut through the leaves with shears, the jagged scars look ugly. It has the one other disadvantage that it's expensive – but well worth saving for.

Plant 90 centimetres (3 feet) apart.

Hawthorn (Crataegus monogyna)

This is a common field hedge, but I include it here because it's one of the cheapest and can make a very good animal-proof hedge. However, it *must* be cut back hard after planting and about halfway each year to keep it bushy at the bottom.

Plant 30 centimetres (1 foot) apart.

Beech is one of the best garden hedges. It isn't evergreen but it retains its old, russet-coloured leaves all winter.

Privet (Ligustrum ovalifolium)

I include this only to say don't grow it unless you have a very large garden. It makes a wonderful, fast-growing hedge, but it's so hungry it will rob the soil of all water and plant food for a couple of metres (yards) around it. That's just too much competition for most plants. There is also a yellow form which is, alas, just as greedy.

If buying a stately home, plant 30 centimetres (1 foot) apart.

Informal hedges

Since an informal hedge is simply a line of shrubs, you could, I suppose, use almost anything you like. However, as these will take up a lot of space, it's a lucky gardener who can indulge in one. My list is fairly short for that reason.

Barberry (Berberis)

If you want to keep all-comers out of your garden, *Berberis julianae* will certainly stop a nuclear missile! The thorns are such that nothing goes near, let alone through. It's evergreen and sports marvellous yellow flowers in spring, but it's a bit painful to prune.

Barberries make attractive, animal-proof hedges which, though generally grown informally, can also be clipped.

B. *stenophylla* is often grown as hedging and produces large, graceful, arching branches covered in yellow flowers in April. The spines are not quite so painful.

B. *thunbergii* 'Atropurpurea' has red foliage and yellow flowers in spring.

Plant 90 centimetres (3 feet) apart.

Laurustinus (Viburnum tinus)

A popular winter-flowering evergreen which will form a bushy hedge up to about 1.8 metres (6 feet) high. The large heads of flowers start as pink buds and open to white. They appear continuously from late autumn to early spring. A really excellent hedge even in shade. The variety 'Eve Price' is one of the best.

Plant 90 centimetres (3 feet) apart.

Roses (Rosa rugosa)

Often advertised as a wonderful flowering hedge, but leaves

For a low-growing hedge, lavender, with its grey, aromatic foliage and blue summer flowers, is hard to beat.

a lot to be desired in my opinion. Straggly in growth and fairly sparse in flower, not evergreen and prone to pest and disease attack, it's one advertisement not to be taken in by.

Low-growing hedges

Sometimes, a hedge is used not for screening or shelter, but simply as a decorative edging to a path or border. Often herb gardens are set out in a formal way using a close-clipped, dwarf hedge to mark the separate beds. If you're really ambitious, you could make a smaller version of the Elizabethan 'knot-garden'. This attractive floral feature looks at home even in modern gardens. Naturally, the hedge must be dwarf and it must respond to heavy clipping.

Box (Buxus sempervirens 'Suffruticosa'*)*

The edging box makes a perfect dwarf hedge with its dark, shiny leaves which respond well to clipping. It roots easily from cuttings just stuck in the ground, so you can save money by buying a couple of plants and raising the rest yourself. This is the most popular plant for knot gardens and formal herb gardens.

Plant 15 centimetres (6 inches) apart.

Lavender (Lavandula angustifolia)

One of the most attractive dwarf hedges, with smoky grey foliage and masses of insect-attracting blue flowers in summer. Go for the more compact varieties like 'Hidcote' or 'Munstead' and trim the plants over after flowering to prevent them becoming straggly.

Plant 30 centimetres (1 foot) apart.

Cotton lavender (Santolina chamaecyparissus)

The dense, silvery foliage alone makes this plant worth while and the bright, lemon-yellow flowers are a welcome summer bonus. Again, trim back after flowering.

Plant 30 centimetres (1 foot) apart.

Planting hedges

Obviously, the name of the game with hedges is fast growth, so it's worth going to town over the preparation of the soil.

Mark out the line and dig a trench at least 60 centimetres (2 feet) wide, throwing the soil out to one side. Fork over the bottom to break up the subsoil and then put in a good layer of organic matter. Ideally, use well-rotted manure; if you can't get hold of it, you'll have to use one of the alternatives. Put back half the soil and then add another layer of organic matter. Then completely refill and spread a bit more organic material on the top. You'll find, of course, that the top of the planting line is now well above the surrounding soil, so preferably leave it to settle for a few weeks.

The best time for planting is in the autumn. The soil will be warm then and the plants will make some roots before the cold weather sets in. They'll be on their marks then for a fast start in the spring. What's more, in the autumn you can buy plants either bare-rooted or root-wrapped, which is quite a bit cheaper than buying them in containers. Before planting, dust the soil with bonemeal, using about two handfuls per metre (yard) run.

Once the soil is prepared, the plants are easy to put in by cutting a slit with a spade.

Whichever plants you use, set them at the appropriate distances apart and exactly at the level they grew on the nursery. With small, bare-rooted plants, I just cut a slit with the spade, whack the roots in with a flick of the wrist, to make sure they hang downwards, remove the spade and put my boot on the roots. It really is as easy as that. Root-wrapped plants will require a larger hole.

If you do buy plants out of the dormant season they'll have to be in containers, and here there's one very important point to watch. It's a strange fact that, once the roots of a plant fill the container and then start going round the bottom of the pot, they tend to continue to do so – just as if they get dizzy and can't stop.

They will also continue the habit once they get into the soil. This means that they fail to spread out to provide proper anchorage. So it has been known for some plants, particularly conifers, to reach 1.8 to 2.5 metres (6 to 8 feet) and then just blow over. On inspection, the roots have been like a corkscrew, offering little or no anchorage.

So check the root systems of container-grown plants when you're planting and, if they have started to encircle the pot, gently tease them out before putting them in the ground.

Pruning
After planting hawthorn and privet, it's best to cut them back hard – to within about 5 centimetres (2 inches) of the ground. This may seem like defeating the objective, but it will give you a much bushier, closer hedge, with branches and foliage right down to the base. I would also cut back each year's growth by about a third every autumn until the plants have reached

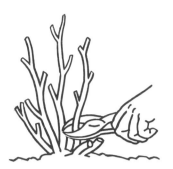

To encourage bushy growth right down at ground level, it's best to prune some hedging plants really hard.

the required height. Then trim as needed to keep them tidy; start in May or June, depending on growth.

Beech and hornbeam should not have their tops cut back until they reach the required final height. However, the sides can be lightly trimmed after the second season after planting.

Conifers must have their sides trimmed back early in their lives. Start cutting back lightly in the second season, continually trimming back rampant growth. If you don't, the inside of the plant will go bare and you'll have lost your chance. Don't cut back the tops until they've reached the required height.

The one exception here is yew, which seems to thrive on cutting back. If you've got the patience, cut back about a third of the current season's growth each year. The best time to prune conifers is the early part of August.

Windbreaks

If your hedge is to be used as a windbreak, you'll have to protect it in the early years. Conifers are particularly susceptible to wind damage, which dehydrates them and turns them brown. Ideally, erect a screen made of plastic windbreak material on the windward side. Unfortunately, windbreaks need strong supports and they don't look so pretty while they're up – which should be about 18 months if you plant in the autumn. But you could lose your plants if you don't protect them.

Aftercare

In the early stages, water is absolutely essential, especially if the plants were container-grown. Check regularly and make sure they never go dry.

Hedges often get neglected when the fertilizer bag's going round. Like all plants, they need feeding and an annual dose of fertilizer will make all the difference to their speed of growth. They'll certainly repay you.

Use an organic or a rose fertilizer applied in late February at about two handfuls every metre (yard) run of hedge.

Hedges can attract wildlife but can also harbour pests and diseases. On balance, I would clean out any rubbish that collects at the bottom of the hedge each autumn – after first carefully checking for signs of hedgehogs!

PAVING

Before you start to lay any kind of paving, there are two things you *must* get right. Neglect either of them and your paving will be a thorn in your flesh for ever more. What's more, you must studiously ignore all the advice you'll get (oh, yes you will!) about short cuts. Paving is expensive, and it's hard work. The only way to do it is the right way – first time.

The first golden rule is to get your levels right. Take meticulous care about this job because 'as near as dammit' simply won't do. At best you'll have a patio that's swimming in water. At worst you'll find damp creeping inside the house and rotting the carpets.

Secondly, make quite sure that the base is solid. This is especially important in new gardens, where the footings of the house have been dug out with an oversized mechanical shovel. After the walls are built, the shovel then pushes the soil back into the trench where it will continue to settle for a considerable time.

Paving slabs look very attractive when laid in an entirely random pattern.

You may have seen the local council pavers laying slabs on sand when they repair the pavement. But remember that they're doing it on soil that has been compacted for many years. Unless yours has too, you *must* use something more substantial. Otherwise the slabs will sink unevenly, and they'll tip up all over the place, creating highly dangerous 'trips', and you'll find yourself starting again.

Rectangular paving

Rectangular slabs certainly constitute the most popular form of paving and with good reason. For the do-it-yourselfer, they're about the easiest to lay, there's a vast range to choose from and they suit modern architecture and materials extremely well. You won't think they're cheap until you begin to compare them with other materials, when they begin to look very attractive indeed!

The easiest way to lay them is in straight lines and, if you choose square slabs, nothing could be easier. This looks fine on a small area and is the pattern we chose for our small quadrant of paving outside the patio doors. On a larger area, you may choose to use slabs of varying sizes laid in a 'random' pattern to eliminate the 'tram-line' effect. It's a softer finish which will harmonize well with plants.

If you decide to do it this way, you must either work out a pattern of paving on paper first and order the appropriate amount of slabs or simply work it out as you go along. The latter way you get a *really* random effect, but you must be careful how you order. If there are three or four different sizes, make sure you order equal *areas* of each size rather than equal numbers. Otherwise you'll find you finish up with far too many larger sizes.

If you're paving in a shady part of the garden, it's a good idea to use a slab with a non-slip finish. Without sun, slabs tend to get a thin covering of green algae which makes them very slippery and dangerous.

You may also need to do a bit of cutting. If you've been blessed with inspection covers where you intend to pave, you can expect to have to cut the paving round them. In this case, it could save some money to buy paving slabs that will cut easily with a hammer and brick bolster. While an angle grinder will cut through any slab, they have to be hired and you'll have to buy at least one disc however little cutting you need to do.

Getting the levels

This is the most important part of the job and even more so if the paving runs alongside the house. It's well worth taking the time and trouble over it.

Start by finding the damp-proof course (DPC) on the house. This is a waterproof membrane built into the house wall to stop rising damp. On modern houses it's easily recognized as a wider course of mortar between the bricks. Some older houses use a row of blue engineering bricks which are, of course, even easier to see. Whichever way it's done, the top level of the finished paving must come at least two courses of bricks, 15–18 centimetres (6–7 inches) below the DPC to cope with flash floods and rains splashing up from the paving above the DPC.

Now cut yourself some decent pegs. They'll need to be about 30–45 centimetres (1–1½ feet) long with a clean square top. Mark a clear line on each peg 8 centimetres (3 inches) from the top to give a guide for the level of the concrete base.

After marking out the shape of the paved area, bang the first peg into the ground 30 centimetres (1 foot) away from the house wall. Using a spirit-level, make sure the top finishes exactly two courses of bricks below the DPC. Then, using a straight-edge and spirit-level, put in a line of pegs about 1.2 metres (4 feet) apart and also 30 centimetres (1 foot) from the wall, all at exactly the same level as the first.

The second row of pegs must be slightly lower than the first. It's important to ensure that water runs away from the house, so the paving must slope slightly. Make the second row about 1.2 metres (4 feet) from the first and set the pegs about 13 millimetres (½ inch) lower. You can do this by putting a 13-millimetre (½-inch) thick piece of wood on the second peg as

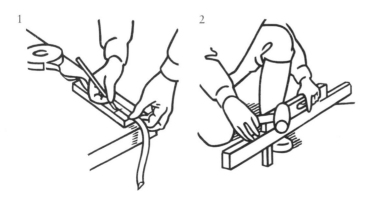

1. Cut pegs and mark them with a clear line 7.5 cm (3 in) from the top.
2. Level the first peg so that it's two courses of bricks below the damp-proof course.

you level it. Get it exactly level with the first peg, remove the block and it will be 13 millimetres (½ inch) lower. The second row can then be put in, checking the level against the first peg in the row and, using the bit of wood, with the other pegs in row one. A third and possibly fourth row of pegs follow, depending on the width of the patio.

When the pegs are all in, make quite sure that you put the work area strictly out of bounds to the rest of the family. Those pegs are very easy to trip over, causing injury and upsetting your levels too! As it is, you're bound to trip over one or two yourself before you finish the job!

Making the base

Generally there will be quite a bit of digging out to do to allow a good thickness of concrete for the base. You'll need at least 8 centimetres (3 inches) so the soil must be dug out to that depth below the line marked on the pegs.

When you're digging, try not to go too deep so that you have to refill, but, if you do, fill up either with hardcore or concrete. If you put soil back into the hollows, you'll only increase the sinkage problem. The same rule applies, of course, if the soil is too low in the first place. It must be made up with some hard material which is not subject to settlement. If you're moving into a house on an estate development, you'll almost certainly find plenty of hardcore about.

The base should always be made with concrete unless you're certain that the site has been compacted and undisturbed for years. You may, for example, wish to pave an existing gravel path, in which case the concrete base is unnecessary.

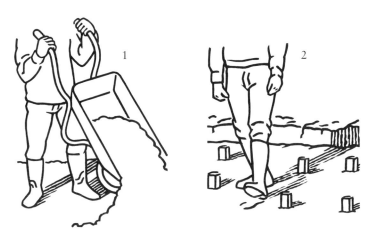

1. Mix the ballast and cement dry and spread it on the site.
2. Tread it down hard making sure it comes up to the marks on the pegs.

In fact, laying the base is not as arduous as it sounds. It's perfectly OK to mix the concrete dry, which is much less of a back-break than using wet concrete.

What I do is this. Put four shovels of ballast into a wheelbarrow and cover it with half a shovel of cement. Mix that about a bit in the barrow and then add another four shovels of ballast and a half of cement. Another little mix and top it off with two shovels of ballast.

Then wheel the lot to where you want it, tip it and rake it out. All this moving about will mix the ingredients together quite enough. Tread it down firmly by walking all over every little bit with your weight on your heels and then just level the top with the rake, so that the concrete comes to the mark on the pegs. And that's it. It won't be long before the moisture from below creeps up and that from above works down, to harden up the whole thing. The one exception to this rule is when you've opted to delay the paving and to use the concrete base as the patio initially, as suggested before (see page 30). In this case, you'll need to provide a wooden 'shuttering' to edge the patio. Set this level across the house and with a slight slope away from it. Make the concrete wet enough to work and level it with a board spanning the shuttering.

1. Start near the wall and set out five heaps of mortar for the first slab.

Laying the slabs

Now for the exciting bit. The slabs are laid on mortar, using a mixture of builders' sand and cement. Mix three parts of sand to one of cement and make it a fairly dry mix. It's not difficult to imagine what happens when the mortar is too wet. You place the slab on top of it and the whole lot instantly collapses to below the required height. It *must* be stiff enough to support the weight of the slabs.

Start with a slab at one end of the area and, if you're paving next to the house, it should be one of the rows nearest the wall. Take a lot of trouble over this first slab because it will set the pattern for all the rest.

Put down five little mounds of mortar, one for each corner of the slab and one in the middle. Make them 10 centimetres (4 inches) high to allow plenty of tapping down. Now rest the slab gently on top of the piles in roughly the right position. It needs to run exactly parallel to the wall and you should exercise a little caution – pessimism if you like. At the end of the job, you'll be pleased you started off looking on the black side!

Say you get that first slab just 3 millimetres (⅛ inch) out of

2. Carefully lay the first slab on the heaps of mortar.

1. Take extra trouble to get the first slab square with the house and level with the pegs.
2. Now the remainder of the slabs are laid in the same way, butting them up against each other.

3. The easiest way to cut slabs is with an angle grinder which you can hire.

line with the wall. Well, if the slab is 60 centimetres (2 feet) long and the whole paved area is 6 metres (20 feet), you'll be 10 times that amount out of line by the time you get to the end. So take care to get it right.

To make sure, set the slab 2.5 centimetres (1 inch) away from the wall. Wrap one end of a bricklayer's line round a brick and fix it so that it runs along the back line of the slab. Hold it in place with another brick resting on the slab. Take the line to the other end of the paving and hold it exactly 2.5 centimetres (1 inch) away from the wall. It should then run exactly along the back edge of the slab. If it doesn't, tap the slab into line and check again.

Now check for level by putting a straight-edge onto the top of the slab and the nearest peg. Tap the slab down until the straight-edge lies flush along the surface of the slab. Repeat the process with other pegs you can reach to make quite certain the slab is level all ways. Then recheck the line against the wall and you can feel satisfied you've got it right. After that first one it's all plain sailing.

The tapping down is best done with the handle of a club-hammer (or 'lump' hammer in some parts of the country). Never use the metal head or you'll damage the surface of the slabs and could crack them. Constant use will certainly ruin the handle but it will be neither difficult nor expensive to replace.

With the first slab in place, there's no need now to check for line again, because you simply butt the next slab up against it and continue in that way. However, it is always necessary to check for level. Do it from pegs in both directions for each slab you lay.

If you're laying slabs in a purely random pattern which has not been worked out in advance, you'll have to think a couple of slabs ahead each time. Try to avoid long 'tram-lines'. As soon as you see a line between two rows of slabs becoming too long, make sure you break it by putting a slab across it. This does take a bit of thought, but it's great fun to work out!

Cutting slabs

Unless you're very lucky (or perhaps very clever!) you'll almost certainly have to cut a slab or two. It may be right at the end to make it fit in, or you may have to cut around an inspection cover or a downpipe.

Most precast slabs are not difficult to cut in straight lines with a brick bolster and club-hammer. But if you have any fancy cutting to do, you'll be well advised to hire an angle grinder.

To cut by hand, measure the slab and mark the surface side with the edge of the bolster. Then turn the slab on its edge and make a nick in the edge both sides of the slab. You can afford to be a bit heavy-handed with this nick because the slab is unlikely to break. Turn the slab so that the back is facing you and you'll be able to mark the back by joining the two nicks.

Now lean the slab against your leg and start to tap a nick in the surface with the bolster. Turn it round and do the back, tapping fairly gently. Then tap the front again, and continue in this way until the slab cracks in half. The art lies in how hard you tap but it doesn't take too long to get used to it. It doesn't actually hurt your leg either, though it looks as though it should!

Our quadrant of paving proved a bit more difficult. Here, every one of the slabs at the edge had to be cut at an angle. Rather than face the frustration and expense of several broken slabs, we hired an angle grinder. This is a machine, generally

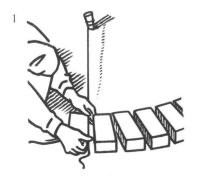

1. When putting in a brick trim, make sure all the bricks face into the centre of the circle.
2. They too, should be levelled to the nearest peg.

electric, with a rotating disc at one end. The hire shop will stock special discs for cutting stone. When you go to hire the tool, make sure you also hire a pair of goggles and, if you haven't any, some strong gloves.

Do the cutting outside, because you'll create a very great deal of dust and possibly bits of grit. Then just mark the slab and cut to the mark with the disc. Since discs are quite expensive and don't last too long, it's best to cut a quarter of the way through on each side and then to tap the slab along the line of the cut with a club-hammer until it breaks. If the cut edge is going to be seen, though, as it might if the slab is on the front of a step for example, it's best to make a clean cut straight through from the surface side of the slab.

A brick trim

The edge of the paving can be made more attractive by installing a brick trim. If you do decide to do this, as we did, it's best to put it in first, before laying the paving. You must make sure you use special paving bricks since those used for wall-building will flake when they freeze. We chose the same blocks used for the circular feature (see pages 72–5).

If the edge of the paving is straight, laying out the brick edging is straightforward. But if it's circular like ours, you need to be careful to set the bricks not only in a perfect circle but also so that each brick is positioned so that it faces exactly into the centre of the circle.

When you marked out the quadrant, you will have done so

Keep off the paving for a few days to allow it to harden and then clean off any dried mortar. The quadrant shape here is ideal for a few chairs and a table outside the patio doors.

with a cane at the centre and a piece of string (see page 24). The same set-up can be used to position the bricks, so make sure you leave the cane in. Tie a knot in the string at the required radius and line up each brick so that the knot is at the furthest end of the brick and the string runs exactly down the centre. Then each brick can be set on a bed of mortar and tapped down to the correct level exactly as for laying paving slabs.

The hardness of the paving can be softened by planting. Where you have left holes, cut through the concrete base and remove it and the soil beneath. Refill with good compost before planting.

Planting pockets

So far, I have recommended butting the slabs up against each other and paving the whole area. This is the way it should normally be done for a patio or path which will receive constant use. But if you can leave spaces for plants here and there, in those parts of the patio that don't get so much use, the paved area takes on a much softer look.

Certainly you should leave out a few slabs near to the wall so that you can grow climbers up against it. And wherever you feel you won't actually be tripping over them, leave pockets for other plants in the main area too.

Of course, it would be too much of a fiddle to try to leave areas of soil at exactly the right spot when you're putting down the base. So cover the whole area with the dry concrete mix and, once you've laid a pit of paving and left your hole for plants, chop out the concrete (not a difficult job with dry concrete), remove the soil as deeply as you can and replace with compost.

You'll need a well-drained mix for most plants, so use something like 3 parts good garden soil, 2 parts coir compost to 1 part coarse grit. Bear in mind that there's little plant food in this so you'll have to liquid feed from time to time.

Another way to soften the paving is to grow plants in the cracks between the slabs. There are many alpine plants that will thrive in this kind of situation, though you should avoid areas that will get a lot of wear. To leave space for plants, simply set the slabs slightly further apart and brush compost in between them. There's no need to hack out the concrete and indeed this would be an impossible task. For alpines, there will be plenty of growing space between and under the slabs.

When you've filled up all the cracks, get a few packets of alpine seeds, mix them with sharp sand and just brush them across the paving. They'll fall down between the cracks and germinate without much difficulty.

For a list of plants suitable for growing in paving, see pages 106–9.

Laying paving blocks

Several manufacturers now make paving blocks or brick paviors which will provide another interesting paving texture. There are two methods of laying them depending mainly on the area to be covered and, more important, the amount of weight the paving will have to bear. A garden path that will only be used to walk on can be laid by hand and tamped down with a club-hammer or a baulk of wood. If it's a driveway you intend to tackle, you'll have to pay more attention to the base and you'll need to hire a machine to tamp the blocks down. Laying garden paths in blocks or paviors is actually great fun but there's a bit of work to do before laying can begin. Start by deciding on the width of the path by laying out a few blocks loose, just to ensure that your measurements are correct. Put them so that there's about 6 millimetres (¼ inch) between them and then make the width of the path equal to an exact number of blocks, so eliminating or at least dramatically reducing the amount of cutting necessary.

The blocks are laid on a bed of sharp sand, so the first necessity is to install an edge to the path to stop the sand drifting out. This can be done with wood, made permanent by 'backing-up' with a fillet of concrete behind. Use 8 × 2.5-centimetre (3 × 1-inch) timber fixed to pegs driven into the ground at intervals. Make sure the pegs go *outside* the path area or they'll impede the blocks when you lay them. If you want to curve the path it helps to make a series of sawcuts in the edging, on the inside of the curve. Make them about 5 centimetres (2 inches) apart and halfway through the wood – then bending becomes very much easier. Naturally the edgings should be levelled with a spirit-level as they are put in.

If your soil is firm and has been undisturbed, you may get away without a proper foundation. Much better put in at least 5 centimetres (2 inches) though, just in case. Use dry ballast and cement as suggested for the patio base (page 66). As you'll need 5 centimetres (2 inches) of sand plus the depth of the blocks (normally 6 centimetres (2¼ inches)) you'll have to dig out about 16 centimetres (6¼ inches).

Put in the dry mix of ballast and cement and then cover that with sharp sand. You should wet it so that it's uniformly moist and then compact it well. Either use a garden roller or tread all over it. Afterwards rake it roughly level with a garden rake.

The final levelling is done with a notched board which you'll need to make. It should be a little wider than the path, with the notches cut at exactly path width and 2 centimetres (¾ inch) less than the depth of the block. So if the blocks are 6 centimetres (2¼ inches) thick, the notch should be 4 centimetres (1½ inches) deep so that the sand will finish 4 centimetres (1½ inches) below the level of the wooden edging. This will allow for the blocks settling 2 centimetres (¾ inch) when they're tamped down.

Lay out the first few rows of blocks as far as you can reach, bedding them down with a piece of wood and a club-hammer as you go. When you need to walk or kneel on the blocks you've laid, use a board across the whole width. If you need to cut blocks, you'll find it quite easy with a brick bolster.

When all the blocks are laid, cover the path with a shallow layer of sharp sand and brush it well into the cracks. If the blocks have not bedded down to the level of the top of the edging boards, you may have to go over the path with a plank and a baulk of wood tamping them down further.

If you lay the blocks in this way they may well settle a little further but this shouldn't matter. Settlement should be fairly uniform but the odd slight hollow here and there in fact adds something to the charm. There shouldn't be any problem with water lying on the surface since it will normally seep down between the blocks.

If you're laying a driveway, you'll have to take a lot more trouble. Here it's best to use precast concrete edgings, set in concrete, rather than relying on the wooden edging. When setting them, make sure you allow for a slope away from the house to remove excess water in wet weather.

The preparation also has to be more thorough. Here, the base should be at least 10 centimetres (4 inches) deep, preferably overlying a layer of rammed hardcore. It helps to lay the blocks herringbone fashion which forms a stronger bond, and they will have to be firmed with a machine. What you need is a flat-bed vibrator which you can hire from most

1

3

2

4

1. For block paving, the sand should be levelled with a notched board, using the shuttering for level.
2. Place the blocks in position and tap them down a little with the handle of a club-hammer.
3. Sweep fine sand between the blocks to hold them firm.
4. Put a board across and tamp down using a fencing post. More sand may then be needed.

small-tool hire shops. This will vibrate the blocks down very much firmer and there should be no problem of sinkage even if cars use the driveway.

Making a circular feature

Paving blocks laid in a circle make a very attractive feature and are not difficult to lay. Since the sunniest part of our garden was actually away from the house, we decided on a circular area of paving as a spot for sunbathing and as the main feature of the scheme. A wooden bench would make a pleasant sitting-out spot and a large, brightly planted urn would attract the eye across the garden to increase its apparent size.

Generally this kind of feature would be away from the house, so levels will depend upon the lie of the surrounding soil rather than on the damp-proof course. The method of laying the paving blocks is much the same as described for areas with straight edges, except that it's necessary to overcome the difficulty of making a circular edging.

Mark out the circle with a centre peg and a piece of string. Put pegs around the edge of the circle to mark the perimeter and also to set the levels. Before putting the pegs in, make a couple of marks on them. The first should be 4 centimetres (1½ inches) from the top and the second 9 centimetres (3½ inches) down. The centre peg should be tapped down so that the top finishes about 2.5 centimetres (1 inch) below the level of the soil. Level the pegs round the edge so that they're about 13 to 25 millimetres (½ to 1 inch) lower than the centre peg, to provide a fall.

Dig out sufficient soil to allow an 8-centimetre (3-inch) base of dry concrete which should reach the lowest mark on the pegs. This is tamped down hard as described before. Then cover with a 5-centimetre (2-inch) layer of sharp sand which should be consolidated and raked roughly level with the higher mark. Remove the centre peg and replace it with one of the blocks. The top of this block should be level with the top of the sand.

Now you'll need some lengths of straight timber about 2.5 × 4 centimetres (1 × 1½ inches). Roofing lathes are ideal and they're stocked by any timber merchant. These are cut into about 90-centimetre (3-foot) lengths and set around the edge of the circle, exactly level with the top marks on the pegs. Bed them in the sand and pack sand around them so that they won't move. Now, with a straight-edge resting on the centre block at one end, and on the roofing lathes at the other, you

PAVING

1. After digging out, pegging and laying the sand, bed some lathes into the sand at the correct level and pack more sand round them.
2. Remove the centre peg and replace with a stone block. The sand can then be levelled with a straight edge.
3. Starting in the middle, lay the blocks out on the sand in a series of circles. It's best to stand on a board.
4. When the circle is completed, put a flexible shuttering round the edge and secure with strong pegs.
5. Brush fine sharp sand into the spaces between the blocks. This will be worked down around the blocks to hold them firm.
6. Vibrate the blocks down with a flat-bed vibrator which can be hired quite easily. Then remove the shuttering and replace with concrete.

can scrape the sand level. In fact, if the area is anything but very small, this is really a two-person job.

Now put a wide board on the sand to work on, remove the centre stone and replace the sand at the required level. Then set the stones in circular fashion. You'll see that you need special sizes for the centre part of the circle where the radius is small.

When all the stones are laid, put in the edging. This is made with 10-centimetre (4-inch) wide strips of 3-millimetre (⅛-inch) plywood. They will easily bend around the stone circle and can be held in place with pegs. Don't skimp on the number of pegs you use or the plywood may belly outwards – one every 90 centimetres (3 feet) is the minimum. There's no need to worry about the levels of the edging this time – it's only a temporary measure.

Now brush sharp sand into the joints and tamp the blocks down as before. Using a flat-bed vibrator is much to be preferred to hand tamping if the area is large.

The blocks should sink by about 2 centimetres (¾ inch) as before. After consolidating, remove the plywood edging and put a fillet of concrete around the edge to hold the sand permanently. This is made with 6 to 1 ballast and cement mixed fairly wet and trowelled down to leave it finishing at least 2.5 centimetres (1 inch) below the level of the blocks.

You may decide to install a circular block feature in an existing lawn. If you do, the turf will serve to retain the sand and there's no need for a concrete edging.

Building walls

This is a more difficult task than paving, needing a good eye and a fair amount of natural skill. Don't expect to emulate the brickies you have watched building the house. They were probably on piecework and going like a train! Take your time and stand back to cast a critical eye over your work quite often.

Choice of materials

Walls can be made out of brick or stone, but you must be careful in your choice. Above all, avoid materials that will flake in a hard frost. There are some bricks, like 'common flettons', for example, that are intended for inside walls only. They're cheap initially, but they'll last no more than a year or two. Ideally, use 'stock' bricks or at least 'sand-faced flettons' which are made for outdoor use. In fact, second-hand stock bricks can usually be bought from a demolition contractor at a fraction of the price of new ones and, because they are weathered, they look very attractive indeed.

As previously mentioned, it's a mistake to mix materials too much in a small garden. So if you're using paving slabs for a patio, make sure you buy the same kind of stone for the walling. Alternatively, you could match the brick of the house walls, as we did.

Foundations

For walls up to 90 centimetres (3 feet) high, the foundations should be twice the width of the wall and about 15 centimetres (6 inches) deep. Start by marking out the line of the proposed wall. If there are to be right-angles, mark them out carefully with a builder's square. Dig a trench at least 20 centimetres (8 inches) deep and twice the width of the wall. Set pegs at intervals along it and level them in with the spirit-level. The pegs should sit about 5 centimetres (2 inches) below soil level, so none of the concrete will be seen.

The foundations should be made with a fairly dry but workable mix of ballast and cement at 6 parts to 1 and brought up to the top of the pegs. Tamp it down firmly as you go, to

PAVING

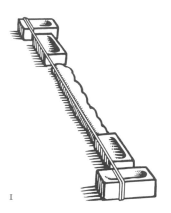

1

2

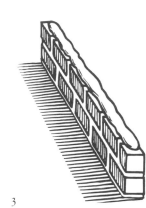

3

1. Start by setting the two end bricks and run a tight line along the top edge of the bricks.

2. The line will help align the rest of the bricks in that course. 'Butter' the ends with mortar before laying.

3. As successive courses are laid, the bricks must be 'bonded' for extra strength.

If the wall runs in two directions both runs must be put up together so that they are bonded at the corners.

eliminate air pockets. Then leave it to harden for several days before setting the bricks or stone blocks.

Laying the walling

Start by mixing up the mortar, using 3 parts builders' sand to 1 part of masonry cement. This is a slightly more flexible cement than Portland cement and will prevent cracking when the wall expands and contracts as temperatures alter. The mix should be quite sloppy if you're laying bricks, but drier for stone. It's easier to lay bricks with fairly wet mortar; while any excess which falls onto the face of a brick wall will easily scrape off the smooth surface, it sticks to the rougher face of stone and stains it.

Set the two ends of the wall first by putting down a shallow layer of mortar and tapping the block into it. Use either the blade of the trowel for bricks or the handle of a club-hammer if you're laying stone on drier mortar.

Now you need to run a bricklayer's line along the front edge of the bricks. I find the easiest way is to wrap it several times round a spare brick to hold it down each end. Put the line on top of the brick and hold it there with another spare brick rested on top. You may well find you need to move the bricks you've already laid, just to line them up exactly.

It's worth taking a lot of time and trouble over the end-bricks because they set the line and level for all the rest. Once the line is in position and nice and tight, you can then lay the rest of the course quite quickly. The line will give you the correct line and level, though it's worth checking for level both ways with the spirit-level every now and then, just to make sure.

Lay the whole line of mortar out now, and start placing the walling. If you're laying bricks, you'll find it quite easy to 'butter' one end with mortar before you lay each one. It can then be pushed up tight against the last one you laid, forming an instant mortar joint between the two. If you're laying stone blocks, you won't be able to do that. With drier mortar, it's difficult to get it to stick, so in this case simply set the block 13 millimetres (½ inch) away from the last block and point in with mortar after you've laid the whole row.

The mortar joints must be staggered to give strength and to look right. This means that if you're building a straight run of wall you'll have to start off every other course with half a brick. It's easy to cut them with a brick bolster and a hammer.

If the wall runs in two directions, you'll have a corner which will obviate the need for cutting bricks in half. The illustration on page 78 shows clearly why.

Some manufacturers supply 'jumpers' with their stone walling. These are stones twice the thickness of the rest which can be used here and there to good effect to give 'a random' look to the wall. Obviously, if you have a jumper in a course, it will push the line out of true, so just leave a space for it when you come to it and set it when the rest of the course is laid.

As you progress upwards, there is a great danger of allowing the wall to lean. It's not difficult to check a brick wall with the spirit-level put vertically on the smooth face of the wall. But stone walls with a rough face are more difficult.

Make sure you check each stone with the spirit-level *across* the run of the wall to avoid tilting and, every now and then, pause for a while, go to the end of the wall and squint down it to make sure it *looks* level. With stone walling, that's about all you can do. If you're worried that your eye is not too good, you can help yourself with a sighting post. Bang a post in near the end of the wall and level that with the spirit-level so that it's exactly upright. Then you can compare it with the line of the wall when you squint down it, and you should be able to get it dead level.

When the mortar is dry but not hard, you'll need to rake out the joints on the front of the wall, to slightly recess them. I use a small piece of wood, cut to just less than 13 millimetres (½ inch) and rounded at the end to give a neat recessed joint. When the raking out is complete, brush over the whole of the front of the wall with a soft brush to remove any excess mortar that may have stuck.

If you're building a double wall, it's a good idea to bond the two parts together for strength. Do this with a builder's 'butterfly' – a piece of wire bent to the shape of a pair of wings, which is bedded at intervals into the mortar of both walls.

If your wall is intended to retain soil, it's very important to remember to include drainage holes at the bottom. Otherwise water will build up behind the wall and, with nowhere to go, it could push the whole thing down. Just leave out half a block at about 2-metre (6-foot) intervals in the bottom course.

The tops of walls must be finished off with a coping. This is particularly important with brick walls because it prevents water being absorbed by the soft brick. If that happens, the bricks will flake in a hard frost. In fact, all walls, stone or brick, look much better with a coping, so it's worth doing in any case.

Manufacturers of walling stone always supply a special coping, made to just the right size. It should overlap the front of the walling by about 2.5 centimetres (1 inch).

For a single brick wall only 11 centimetres (4½ inches) thick, you'll need to use a similar type of stone or precast concrete coping. In our garden we used the same paving slabs used for the paved areas cut into 15-centimetre (6-inch) strips with the angle grinder. If the wall is low, this makes an ideal place to sit too. If your wall is double thickness you could use 23-centimetre (9-inch) bricks laid on edge.

Steps
Once you've mastered the technique for paving and walling, stone steps are not difficult because they're just a combination of the two. The walling is used for the 'risers' and the paving slabs for the steps themselves.

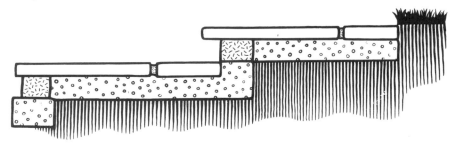

Decide first of all, the number and width of the steps. Check the height overall, using a straight-edge and spirit-level from the top of the slope as suggested for fencing (see page 51). The height of the risers can vary a little but you must be careful not to make steps dangerous. If the risers are too low, you'll create a series of 'trips' and you'll find your guests who are not used to them falling up them! On the other hand, risers that are too high are difficult to negotiate for some folk, especially older people and small children. About 13–18 centimetres (5–7 inches) is ideal.

When building the steps, always start at the bottom and, if they run onto the lawn, remember that the lowest tread should consist of a paving slab set into the lawn just about 2.5 centimetres (1 inch) below the turf level. That way you'll be able to run the mower over it without damage.

Put a 15-centimetre (6-inch) foundation behind the first tread and build a single wall on it. Then dig out behind to the required levels, fill in with a base of dry ballast and lay the

To build steps, use walling for the risers and paving slabs for the treads.

paving treads. The front of the slabs should overlap the walling by about 2.5 centimetres (1 inch), and there should be a continuous bed of mortar on the walling side, rather than the customary five mounds.

Then put another foundation behind the slabs and build the next riser. Note that you should never build the riser on top of the paving slab. In the case of even slight sinkage, that would tip the slab, making the steps very dangerous indeed.

Wooden steps

In an informal setting, wooden steps look very attractive and are much easier and cheaper to build. The risers can be made with either old railway sleepers (you'll find ads for them in the farming magazines), or chunks of logs. Either can be fixed by driving in a strong stake behind them at each end and nailing through.

The 'treads' are simply cut out of the soil and can be made attractive and mud-free with a thick layer of ornamental bark chips. You'll find those in various grades at the garden centre.

LAWNS

Britain has just about the best climate in the world for growing grass. All that rain does do us a *bit* of good really! So it's perhaps for this reason that the lawn is such a popular part of most English gardens.

Certainly a well-kept lawn does set off the garden well. It's the perfect foreground for flower borders and it makes a first-class surface for recreation and relaxation. If you have small children it does away with any worries about them injuring themselves when they fall over and, if you happen to be a sporty type, it's the ideal place for games like bowls or badminton, or for sharpening up your putting!

Mind you, our lawns are expected to put up with quite a lot of abuse. Lawn grass must be about the only plant in the world that's walked on regularly and also hard-pruned every week of the growing season and yet is still expected to look marvellous all the time. The amazing thing is that it will! But only if you start out on the right foot and you subsequently treat it well. When you think about it, it jolly well deserves a bit of extra tender loving care.

A good lawn makes a fine foreground for the mixed border.

LAWNS

Preparation

Whether you decide you want the finest of fine show lawns or simply an area that will take some hard wear, whether you intend to sow it or turf it, the preparation is exactly the same. There is a school of thought that claims that the preparation for turf need not be as thorough as for a seeded lawn, but that's just wishful thinking I'm afraid. The only way is the right way.

The first indication of what will be necessary will come when you dig that initial hole to find out about your soil (see page 36). If you come across the hard layer I've already warned about, you'll have to break it up. Leave it and your lawn will always be a soggy mess and the grass will never look happy. Even grass doesn't like to have wet feet.

Drainage

Once the layer is broken and drainage restored, you'll be able to assess the need for further measures. If the soil is heavy and still lies very wet, it will pay to do something about extra drainage. But that, I'm afraid, is not quite as easy as it sounds.

You'll read, in several books, instructions to lay drainage tiles to take away the excess water. Trouble is, where do you take it to? If you just divert it into the next-door garden you're likely to get something more than the odd black look, and if you dig a soak-away, as is sometimes suggested, you're still likely to get trouble. Bad drainage is caused by an impermeable subsoil, so the soakaway is going to be no better drained than the rest of the garden. Once it's filled with water, you're right back to square one!

Sometimes the local council will allow you to run garden drains into the storm drains, but you *must* ask them first. Even so, they will expect an expert job of linking them in and they'll probably send down an inspector to make sure it's up to standard, so you may well have to contract out that end of the job.

Of course, if you're lucky enough to have a ditch passing your door, then there's no problem, but that's pretty unlikely. However, there's normally no need to go to extraordinary lengths.

Grass doesn't need a very deep soil to grow perfectly well, so it is possible to improve the upper layer just enough to make a shallow depth acceptable to the grass. Some football clubs have actually laid their pitches on pure sand and they're growing very well indeed. And your lawn is unlikely to get that kind of wear!

The answer is to work into the soil a good dressing of coarse grit. Don't use sharp sand because on some soils that can do more harm than good, and *never* use builders' sand. How much you use will, of course, depend on how heavy the soil is. Generally a barrow-load every 1.6 to 2.5 square metres (2 to 3 square yards) will do.

That should make most soils acceptable to grass but, in severe cases, it may be worth going one step further. If the land is still really boggy, you put a 8-centimetre (3-inch) layer of coarse weathered ash or coarse grit over the whole area and then cover that with a further 8 centimetres (3 inches) of topsoil. That will raise the level of the lawn above the boggy area and will give excellent results. Naturally it has the disadvantage that it's expensive and a lot of extra work. But conditions would have to be really extreme to necessitate going to those lengths.

If the soil is very light, the reverse treatment is necessary. Now you'll need something in it to help retain as much moisture as possible.

Any organic material will do. Ideally dig in farmyard manure or well-rotted stable manure. Spent mushroom compost is excellent and generally quite cheap.

Of course, any organic material will eventually rot down in the soil and disappear. And under a lawn, it's not easy to replace because you have to get it below the level of the grass. So you may like to consider using one of the more permanent materials – perlite or vermiculite. These are minerals that have been expanded with heat to form porous particles. Both hold many times their own weight of water and will improve drainage and aeration at the same time.

I must say that I couldn't recommend using either for digging into the borders, for the simple reason that they're somewhat obtrusive. Vermiculite is a shiny fawn colour while perlite is glaringly brilliant white. Neither improve the look of the soil. But of course, underneath the lawn they won't be seen, and they'll certainly do a remarkably good job, virtually for ever.

Sloping gardens

If your garden is on a steep slope, you may consider terracing the lawn into a series of levels. This can look very attractive and should greatly increase the interest of the garden. But it's not quite as straightforward as it may seem. It isn't good enough simply to remove the topsoil from the upper part of the slope and transfer it to the lower half to level it off. That way, unless your topsoil is very deep, you're likely to leave the top part with only a very thin layer of topsoil over the subsoil.

Instead, the topsoil must be stripped off completely, the subsoil levelled and the topsoil replaced. It seems like an awful lot of work, but it's quite necessary I'm afraid.

Cultivation

Normally it's only necessary to single-dig the lawn area, working the organic matter into the bottom of each trench as you go.

If your garden is big, it's worth considering hiring a mechanical cultivator. This is also a good idea if your house is one of a row of new properties and the fences have not been erected. If you can get your new neighbours to club together you could almost certainly do the whole lot in a day, so it won't be expensive.

If you've had to double-dig the area to break up a solid layer, it's important now to leave it for a while to settle (it's also a very good excuse for a rest!) It depends a lot on the weather, but ideally you should allow at least three to four weeks. This could also give you the opportunity of creating what the old gardeners called a 'stale seed-bed'. I've no idea why it's called that, but it's a very useful technique.

Digging will have brought a lot of weed seeds to the surface where they'll germinate and compete with the grass seed, so the idea is to forestall them. Leave the land untouched until the weed seeds germinate and then, while they're still small, hoe them off and sow your grass. That will have dealt with the first flush so your grass will have a chance to get growing before any weeds that are blown in afterwards can germinate. It will also have allowed the soil to settle a bit more and, if the weed seeds germinate, you'll know that the soil is warm enough for the grass seed too.

Levelling

Lawns need not necessarily be dead flat. In fact, a certain amount of undulation in a bigger lawn adds a lot of interest. However, it's vital to make the undulations gentle and rolling so a lot will depend on the size of the area to be grassed. Obviously, the first consideration must be ease of cutting, so smaller areas may have to remain flat.

It's most important, when preparing the lawn for sowing or turfing, to eliminate any local bumps and dents. Small, low

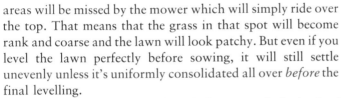

areas will be missed by the mower which will simply ride over the top. That means that the grass in that spot will become rank and coarse and the lawn will look patchy. But even if you level the lawn perfectly before sowing, it will still settle unevenly unless it's uniformly consolidated all over *before* the final levelling.

Start by roughly levelling the whole area with the back of a fork. Don't worry too much about local levels at this stage but make sure the level is generally as you want it. Then it must be evenly consolidated.

The last tool you want for this job is the garden roller. The effect of this is to push down the high bits and ride over the low areas. These will then sink further, making the lawn even more uneven than it was before. The only way to do it is with your feet. But here you may have yet another excuse for a day off, because you'll do more harm than good treading over the soil when it's wet. That breaks down the structure, destroying the drainage and rendering it airless. The rule is never to work the soil if it's wet enough to stick to your boots. Ideally, the top should by dry and crumbly.

Working systematically up and down, tread over every little bit with your weight on your heels. There's no doubt that this is an arduous task but one of the most important in the whole operation.

Before doing the final raking down, it's a good idea to scatter a little fertilizer over the area. This enables you to rake it into the surface whilst doing the final levelling and it means that the fertilizer will be dissolved and available to the young grass seedlings right from the start. Use Growmore applied at about a handful to each square metre (square yard). There's

1. To prepare the soil for seed or turf, start by roughly levelling with the back of a fork.
2. It's essential to consolidate the soil and the only way is by treading.
3. The difficult part is the final raking level. Take time and trouble.

no need to be too accurate at that low level, but make sure you don't overdo it or the young roots could scorch.

Now comes the delicate operation of final levelling. Of course, you can't learn the technique from a book. It's a matter of a good eye, a fine touch and a bit of practice. But there are a few points to note.

First of all, work just a little way in front of your feet, keeping the head of the rake almost horizontal to the ground. Don't stretch a long way forward and drag the soil towards you or you'll tend to pull it into ridges. It also pays, every now and then, to stand back from the work, crouch down and squint across the surface with your head as low as possible. That way, high and low spots show up much better.

If your soil is very stony, you'll find it's quite hard work pulling a pile of stones along all the time. So have a barrow handy and just shovel the piles off from time to time.

Turf or seed?

The choice between the two methods of making a lawn is generally made for you in your first garden – by the bank manager! Turf is considerably more expensive though it does, of course, have the great advantage of immediacy. You can use a turf lawn laid in spring or summer within about six weeks of laying – a little longer with autumn or winter laying. A spring-sown lawn is usable within about 10 weeks and an autumn-sown one not until well into the following spring. When I say 'usable' I mean you can walk on it. Hard wear should wait for six months, regardless of the method of making the lawn.

Of course, there's turf and turf and you need to be very careful about how you buy it. Alas, the turf industry is renowned for having more than its fair share of 'cowboys' and this makes it very difficult for the reputable traders. Of course it is possible to buy excellent turf advertised as 'parkland turf' but unfortunately that label seems to cover a multitude of different products.

The reputable turf grower will buy a field from a farmer, mow it, weed treat it, rake it, roll and feed it for about a year or even two. Then the turf is well worth having.

The cowboy buys a field and immediately cuts the turf, often with no treatment whatsoever. That often means that you're buying nothing more or less than cow-pasture. I've even seen it come complete with cow-pats! Often it's infested with weeds, what grass there is is coarse and tough and, because no rolling has gone on to flatten it out before cutting, the uneven ground produces turves that are thick one end and thin the other, and may be full of holes.

So try to see the turf before you buy. Sometimes this is claimed to be impossible for obvious reasons so, whatever you do, stress when you order that you want excellent quality and that if the turf is poor you won't accept delivery. But better still, spend about three times as much and buy 'cultivated turf'.

Now this really is the best quality you can buy and, if it means pawning the cat, it's well worth it! Here the grower buys a field and ploughs in the existing grass. He then carefully levels, fertilizes and sows a selected lawn-grass seed. Then, during the next couple of years, he rolls it, mows it, weed treats and feeds it just as if it were Gleneagles.

The turf you get as a result is *only* top-quality grass with not a weed in sight. It's green and healthy and each turf is cut to an exact thickness all over, making it a pleasure to lay. You can even choose whether you have a hard-wearing mixture of grasses or a super-fine one, though bear in mind here that the fine turf is not necessarily the best bet. Only choose it if you can give it a lot of time, trouble and expense in the future.

Starting with seed will give you all these advantages too, at a fraction of the cost. The only disadvantage, really, is that it takes longer to establish.

When choosing grass seed, think carefully about the conditions you can give it. These days there are plenty of different ready-mixed blends available.

First of all, consider the aspect. If your garden, or even part of it, is in heavy shade, ordinary grass-seed mixtures will not do. You must buy a mix made up specially for shady areas. You may have a mixture of conditions where you intend to grow grass – for example, a sunny, open spot surrounded by trees. Well, you'll just have to sow the two areas separately with two different mixtures. What's more, you'll need to cut the grass in the shady area less frequently.

Think about the kind of wear the grass will get. If you have two or three boisterous children who want to kick a ball about, you'll *have* to settle for a hard-wearing mixture, but if it's just normal wear, a finer grass will thrive.

But above all, consider the amount of subsequent management you can give the lawn. Really fine lawns do need a lot of maintenance and a fair bit of money spent on them. And, if they don't get it, they'll sulk and eventually revert back to coarser grasses.

Whether you're sowing seed or laying turf, it's a good idea to give it a flying start with a dressing of fertilizer.

My advice would be to buy a first-quality mixture containing no perennial rye-grass *only* if you are prepared to cut the lawn with a cylinder mower at least twice a week and preferably more, feed it twice a year, rake it, water it and weed treat it as necessary, and to use it just for gentle walking on. If you can't, the best bet in my view is to buy one of the newer strains of perennial rye-grass that have been bred especially for lawns. There are a few about. Perennial rye-grass has a bad reputation because the early breeding was done for cattle feeding and not for lawns. New varieties are shorter, much finer and very hard-wearing.

Sowing

The spring and the autumn are generally considered the best times to sow grass seed. I must say that I've done it every month from April to October with no ill effect and I wouldn't hesitate to sow during that period provided the weather is with you.

Naturally you wouldn't sow when the soil is soaking wet nor when it's bone dry. The ideal time is when the top has just dried out after a soaking. Then the seed will germinate quickly and once it's through you'll be able to water if the weather

turns dry. Try to avoid watering before germination because this has two ill effects. First, it tends to 'cap' the soil, forming a hard crust on the top which the seedlings have a difficult time breaking through. Secondly, it washes the seed into the lowest spots, so you'll get overcrowding in some places and sparse germination in others.

Its recommended that grass seed be sown at the rate of 60 grams per square metre (2 ounces per square yard) but I think that's a mite excessive. In fact I would go as far as cutting that rate in half, sowing only 30 grams (1 ounce). So, when you're buying, measure up the area in square metres (square yards) and buy 30 grams (1 ounce) for each.

Start by marking out the area to be sown. The best way is to set out a number of canes to mark the edges, but don't worry at this stage about being absolutely accurate. You'll have a better chance to get the edges right when you come to cut them out once the seed has established itself.

I don't believe it's necessary to go as far as to measure out square metres (square yards) with strings and canes and weighing out the seed. Simply stand with your legs stretched fairly widely apart. That should be roughly a metre (yard). Then lean forward as far as you can without tipping over and

To avoid disturbing the levels again, the best tool to rake in the seed is a spring-tine lawn rake.

scatter a couple of handfuls of seed in that area. You won't be far out. Even if the distribution of the seed is not as even as you would have liked, it will spread out evenly when you rake it in.

Alternatively, to be a little more accurate, measure out 1 square metre (1 square yard) and weigh up 30 grams (1 ounce) of seed to scatter over it. When you've seen what that looks like, you'll be able to judge by eye near enough.

When you're sowing, don't worry too much about restricting the seed exactly to the area you have marked out. It's best to go over the edges a little to ensure that you get a good 'take' of grass there to give you a good firm edge to cut later.

The best tool for raking the seed in is a spring-tine rake. If you haven't got one, it's worth buying because you'll certainly need it later. Aim to cover about half the seed. You'll find that this rake doesn't disturb the levels so much as the garden rake you used for the levelling.

Afterwards, there's no need to roll the lawn. Though this is sometimes recommended, it can have the effect of creating a hard crust on the surface of the soil, slowing down or even preventing germination.

After sowing grass seed, the word will quickly spread round the bird population that you offer the best free dinner in town and they'll descend upon you in droves. In fact, although it raises the blood pressure somewhat because whenever you look out of the window the garden is covered with hungry birds a-pecking, they rarely take more than their share. None the less, it's perhaps worth protecting it for a while.

A bit of netting laid over the surface will generally do.

Laying turf

Turfing can be done at any time of the year providing that the soil is in good enough condition. You can happily put it down in the middle of winter, except when the soil is frozen solid (when you wouldn't get the turf anyway), or when it's under a covering of snow. Unlike seed sowing, your timing is not really dependent on the soil temperature. Mind you, it'll take a bit longer to root in winter and if you choose the driest spell in the middle of summer, you'll have to water regularly, so it's best to choose your time if you can. Ideally, that's from the beginning of March to the end of May and the end of August to the beginning of January.

Order your turf by the square metre or yard and, when it arrives, stack it as near to the site as you can. You should be all ready to lay it then, because it won't want to be stacked rolled up for too long. Without light it will turn yellow in a couple of days in summer. At the same time, you should have to hand a good strong wheelbarrow to take the turves round to the back of the house, a few wide boards (scaffold planks can be hired and are ideal), a rake and an old knife. You'll also need a lawn sprinkler and a hose, especially if you're laying the turves in the summer.

There's no point in laying turf on soil that's bone dry, so if you're laying it in the summer and have had to wait for it to arrive, you may need to water first. Try to think ahead and put the sprinkler on for a couple of hours or so a day or two before turfing.

Start by laying out any curved edges. It's much easier to do it this way than to try to cut an edge later. If you lay out that edge, you can push and pull the turves into line with the rake and you can have a good look from time to time to make quite sure the curve suits your eye. It's surprising that what looks good on paper can sometimes appear quite out of place on the ground. And remember the golden rule – if it looks right, it *is* right.

When the edge is in position, just tap the turves down to get them in firm contact with the soil and to stop them moving about.

Now begin the turfing proper, starting preferably from a straight edge. Lay out the first row of turves and pull the ends of each turf into the one you've just laid, using the back of the rake. Try not to stretch the turves when laying them out because they're likely to shrink back to size, leaving ugly gaps between.

Then tap down each turf with the back of the rake. If you've levelled the ground properly to start with, you won't need to bash them down with a rammer as is sometimes recommended. Just a gentle tap to put them into intimate contact with the soil is all that's needed.

Now put one of your scaffold boards on the turf you've laid. You should make sure you never tread either on the turf or on the soil you're about to put it on. That way you make indentations with your feet and ruin all the hard work you did at the levelling stage. I find it's worth putting out two rows of boards plus a line to get you from the edge of the lawn over to the boards.

The second row of turves can now be put out. Most books will tell you to bond turves like bricks in a wall, but this is

1. When laying out the turves, always work off boards to avoid spoiling the levels.
2. Pull each turf into the previously laid one, using the back of the rake.
3. Tamp the turves down with the back of the rake to ensure good contact with the soil.
4. At the end of each row, lay the turf over the edging turf and cut off the excess.

absolutely unnecessary. If your borders are curved you'll do that automatically anyway, and even if they're not I can see no point in it at all. What you should do is again to pull the edges of the second row into the first with the back of the rake and then tamp down the whole row.

When you get to the end of each row you'll find that you need to cut the turf to fit. Simply lay the end of the turf over the edging turf you've already laid and cut off the excess with an old knife.

You may find that you can almost, but not quite, reach the end of the row with the last turf. In that case, lay it out and use a bit of one of the scraps you've cut off to fill in.

However good the turf may be, you're bound to find that from time to time there's either a very thin spot or even a hole.

This is often because there has been a stone underneath the turf just at the level of the cutter.

In the case of thin patches, they are best cut right out and the two bits of turf simply moved up together to fill the hole. If you come across a hole in the turf, just tear a piece off one of the scraps and stuff it in. It'll grow, however small it is, and, within a couple of days, you won't be able to see where it was.

When you've finished, take the boards off and get the sprinkler going. The weather doesn't have to be very dry or hot for the turves to start shrinking, so you can expect to need water right from the start. The only exception would be for turf laid in the winter or, of course, during rainy weather in spring or summer. But, in my experience, it *never* rains just as you've laid turf. That would be just too convenient!

The length of time taken for the turf to root will vary from about three days to three weeks depending on the weather. During that time it's vital to water regularly. Bear in mind that the only way the grass can get water is through you, and without it cracks will rapidly appear between the turves. If that happens, the only remedy is to brush a top-dressing between the turves to fill in the spaces. That's an awful lot of

After a few weeks the turf will have rooted. The first mowing should be with the cutters set as high as possible.

work and it looks *terrible*. So make sure the sprinkler goes round the lawn, leaving it on for no more than about half an hour at a time.

Until it has rooted, the turf does look a bit sorry for itself. The grass lies flat and has a bluish appearance. However, you'll soon see when it has managed to push out some roots, because it perks up noticeably. The grass starts to stand up and looks a fresh green again.

Immediate aftercare

Neither seeded nor turfed lawns should be cut until the grass is about 5 centimetres (2 inches) tall. The best thing to do then with a turfed lawn is to roll it by running the mower over it with the cutters held clear of the grass. If your mower is one of the light electric models you won't be able to do that, so try to borrow or even hire a light roller.

Then, after two days, cut the grass, first lifting the mower's cutters to their highest point. This will just top the grass and is sufficient for the first cut. For the second one, lower the cutters a little and put them lower still over the subsequent couple of cuts. This may seem like an awful nuisance, especially when you have to adjust the cutters with spanners. But, if you want to see the reason, just cut a bit of long grass very short. The result is a very yellow lawn which eventually turns an unhealthy-looking greenish-white. It will certainly recover after a few days but is a symptom of the harm done to the grass. In fact, you should also raise the cutters at the beginning of every season when the grass is long, even when the lawn is well established.

The final adjustment should leave the grass about 13 millimetres (½ inch) long. It's never a good thing to cut it too short, since this tends to encourage bare patches which are later colonized by moss and weeds.

A seeded lawn is treated in much the same way. Here, though, it's a good idea to go over it before the first cut, bucket in hand, removing any large stones that may have worked their way to the surface. They could cause untold damage to the mower and can, in fact, be quite dangerous.

Then try to roll it as before. This is even more desirable on a seeded lawn for two reasons. First, the roller will press down any stones too small to hand-pick. Secondly, and even more important, it will also bruise the young stems and encourage them to 'tiller'. This is really much the same process as pinching out the top of a plant to make it grow bushier. There are several small growth buds at the base of each grass stalk which will be encouraged to grow out rapidly when the stalk itself is bruised. So what will look like a very thin lawn at first, because it consists of a series of single-leafed plants, will quickly thicken up as each single leaf becomes a clump.

Despite starting with a 'stale seed-bed', you're quite likely to find several weeds thriving amongst the grass too. Well, you can forget most of them. Many will be annuals which will simply die out when you cut their tops off with the mower. A few may be perennials but most of those will be taller-growing plants, which again will not be able to survive regular cutting.

There may be one or two 'rosetted' weeds that grow close to the ground, like dandelions, buttercups or daisies. Because the mower misses them, they won't succumb. If you spot these, try first to pull them out. If you can't, either cut them off with a knife, or drop a tiny pinch of table salt right into the middle of the plant. Don't get any on the grass though, because it will kill that too. It's not a good idea to use weedkillers on young grass.

Feeding should not be necessary in the first year either. Leave that until the following spring and then use either Growmore or, for a rapid green-up, a proprietary lawn fertilizer.

A turfed lawn will already have a well-defined edge, though you will need to cut it a little deeper with a spade or edging iron later on when it has made good roots.

The edge of a seeded lawn will need cutting out afterwards. Don't be too impatient to do this job. It's important to allow the grass to make a good fibrous root system so that the edge is firm. It should be possible to cut the edges after about two months, but by this time the grass will have grown quite high because you won't have been able to get the mower over it right at the edges. Don't throw the clumps of grass away, but dig them in to the borders where the grass will help improve the soil structure.

All you need do during the first season is to cut the grass at least once a week, putting the cuttings on the compost heap, of course. Keep the sprinkler going round in dry weather and cut the edges with a pair of long-handled shears about every fourth cut.

GARDEN FEATURES

When you plan your garden, you're likely to want to include some kind of focal point – a feature around which the rest of the garden revolves. Or you may prefer to add it later. It could be an area to grow favourite plants, like a raised bed for acid-lovers or a scree-garden for alpines. You may want to liven up the garden with a pool or to add a barbecue for those al fresco parties.

What you must do is to ensure that it doesn't 'take over'. It's all too easy to allow a hobby horse to grow out of all proportion so that it dominates the whole garden. Obviously, the best way to get it in scale is to plan it right from the outset, but that's simply not how most gardens work.

Most of us find that, once the garden's built, there's a bit of a gap in our weekends and we look around for something else to add or some existing feature to improve. Half the fun of gardening is that your plot will be continually evolving. You never really finish.

So it's not a bad idea to plan the feature on paper first and then to stick a few canes in the garden and walk around them a few times trying to visualize what the completed thing will look like. It always pays in this job to take your time.

Pools

Moving water has a special attraction in the garden. It adds life and provides a home for a whole new range of plants that will not survive without water. And it will become a drinking fountain for all kinds of wildlife. In fact I would say that if you decide to garden your plot entirely organically, forgoing all chemical pesticides and fertilizers, a pool is essential. For then you'll need to attract birds and insect predators into your garden to keep the pests down. And a garden pool is a surefire way to do it.

But there's one very important factor to take into consideration before you start. If you have small children, your pool could be a death-trap. Yes, I know that sounds melodramatic, but small kids *have* been drowned in garden pools, even the shallowest kind. If you must have both moving water and children, there is a way round it which I'll cover later.

If you just want to provide a water-hole for birds and insects (and perhaps the odd small mammal), and your garden is small, you can make an attractive pool with half a wooden barrel. You can buy them at most garden centres these days. You may have to settle for one with holes in the bottom, since most are sold for plant containers. If so, buy a short length of dowelling of exactly the right size and just hammer a bit in to fill the hole. Don't glue it or paint it because that may stop it swelling when it gets wet.

You'll probably find that the whole barrel will leak like a sieve at first. That's because it has been allowed to dry out, but a good soaking will soon put matters right. Just keep filling it up with water and it will eventually become completely leakproof.

It's essential to sink it in the ground. Small pools always go green in the summer because the water heats up quickly. If you bury the pool, it keeps it cool and it will stay as clear as a bell.

When it's in, set it exactly level either with a spirit-level or just by filling it with water to the top. Firm the soil back around it and the job is almost done.

You'll need to plant with oxygenating weed, which is just planted in 2.5 centimetres (1 inch) of heavy soil at the bottom. I would also rest a couple of potted marginal plants, like irises or the sweet flag (*Acorus calamus*), on a brick or two at the edge so that the water just covers their roots.

You would even have room for a water-lily if you stick to one of the miniatures like *Nymphaea candida* or *N. laydekeri* 'Purpurata'. Ghastly Latin names, I know, but a good aquatic plant centre will be able to translate!

If you have small children, you could use the tub for a 'drown-proof' pool. Fit a small submersible pump in the bottom of the tub so that the top of the outlet pipe reaches just above the top of the barrel. Surround it with a few bricks and then pile some large cobbles around and on top of it. The top of the cobbles should be about level with the top of the tub.

If the pump has a spray nozzle on top, remove it and then fill the tub with water. Enough will get into it between the cobbles to allow the pump to bubble up a little jet of water over the cobbles. It sounds soothing and it looks good, without the slightest risk to your children.

You may wish to make a full-sized pool as the main feature in the garden and there's no doubt that it does add a lot of interest. It makes a real haven for all kinds of wildlife, from scudding water-boatmen to shimmering dragonflies. Where they come from always seems a mystery to me, but come they certainly do. By begging a little spawn from a neighbour with a pool, you could also introduce frogs. And they'll help solve your slug problem too.

An informal pool set in the grass is not difficult. Start by digging out a hole roughly like the drawing. You may not want to include a bog-garden area, in which case you simply make the left-hand side the same as the right. But I do urge you to fit in the bog-garden if you can, because it allows you to grow some wonderful plants you would otherwise find very difficult. Just take a look at the stand of candelabra primulas in the spring and you'll see what I mean!

It's essential to make the edges of the hole absolutely level all the way round. Otherwise you'll get large areas of the liner showing above the waterline. So, the first job is to set some level pegs all round the pool edge, levelling them exactly with the spirit-level.

The hole is lined with a waterproof butyl-rubber sheet but first you must guard against sharp stones working upwards to puncture it later. You can do this by lining the hole with a 5 centimetre (2-inch) layer of builders' sand pressed into the surface or, better still, with a special fibre sheet. You can buy this material at the aquatic specialists when you buy the liner.

When the sheet is in position, place the liner over the hole and weight the edges down with a few bricks. Then simply fill up with water. The weight of the water will gradually force the liner to the bottom of the hole, stretching it into place. You

If you use a liner, making a pool is a simple and relatively inexpensive affair. This cross-section shows the various levels required for a pool designed to attract wildlife and to incorporate a wet area to grow bog plants.

will have to go round folding it here and there as it fills, to make a neat job.

You may find, when the water reaches the top, that you have not been quite accurate with your levelling and the edge of the pool is lower at one point than another. In that case, simply lift the edge of the liner, push more soil underneath and pat it down.

When the liner is in place and levelled, the excess can be cut off, leaving an edge of about 15 centimetres (6 inches). Rake about 8 centimetres (3 inches) of soil over the top of this overlap and finally hold it down with turf.

The bottom of the pool is filled with a 8 centimetre (3-inch) layer of heavy garden soil. It makes the pool look like an ugly mud-hole at first, but it will settle in about 24 hours to leave the water reasonably clear. On the shallow side of the pool, make a sloping beach of large pebbles. Birds and small mammals find this invaluable when they come down for a drink. The bog-garden area is then filled right to the top with soil and the pool's ready for planting.

Plants for the pool

Your best plan when choosing plants is to get a catalogue from an aquatic specialist. There are several who sell mail-order, but there's nothing like paying them a visit to see what the plants look like 'in the flesh' if you can.

You will certainly need some 'oxygenating plants' which will add oxygen to the water, so helping to keep it clear. It's a good idea to buy a water-lily or two. Not only do they look marvellous, but they shade the water, which is another factor in keeping it crystal clear.

All kinds of marginal plants are worth while, especially since, apart from providing form and flower for the pool edge, they also make a home for insects like the beautiful dragon-flies.

Plant oxygenators either by fixing a weight to the clumps and throwing them in, or, better still, by pushing them into the mud at the bottom. A job for a sunny day!

Marginal plants are best planted in the soil but can be grown in their pots, provided they're covered with only a shallow depth of water.

Deep-water plants and water-lilies can be planted in the bottom of the pool if you can bear to get that wet and muddy. Alternatively, plant them in a special basket (obtainable from all aquatic plant centres) in heavy soil and lower them in on

a couple of strings held from either side of the pool. Some books suggest that they should be gradually lowered, setting them on bricks for a few days, lowering a little more, waiting a few days again, etc. This is in fact unnecessary. Just trim off the larger leaves and any dead or damaged growth and lower them straight to the bottom. But do make sure you don't 'drown' them by putting them deeper than they would naturally grow.

Bog plants, of course, are planted with a trowel in the normal way. But be sure you don't push the trowel through the liner!

Oxygenating plants

Pond-weed (Lagarosiphon major)
For a small pool, this is undoubtedly the one to go for. It will do the job without becoming over-vigorous and looks attractive under water.

For very shallow water or the mud at the water's edge

Marsh Marigold (Caltha palustris)
Bright glossy foliage topped by brilliant yellow buttercup flowers. The double form (*Caltha palustris* 'Plena') is even better, with more colourful flowers that last longer.

Lady's Smock (Cardamine pratensis 'Flore Pleno')
This is the double form of the well-known native, which I have recommended because it's not so rampant. It has small white or lilac flowers with yellow anthers in spring.

1. It's easy to make a pool from half a barrel. Start by sinking it into the ground.
2. It's essential to level it both ways so that the water comes level with the top all round.
3. Put a layer of heavy soil in the bottom, fill it with water and plant it up.

Golden Buttons (Cotula coronopifolia)
A small, spreading plant that is covered in yellow flowers all summer. Though short-lived it seeds itself freely.

Chameleon (Houttuynia cordata 'Chameleon'*)*
A superb foliage plant with leaves coloured green, cream and red. It runs freely so is only recommended for large areas.

Marginal plants

Sweet Flag (Acorus calamus 'Variegatus'*)*
A striking plant with brightly variegated, iris-like leaves. A bit vigorous for a small pool but easily controlled. Just lift it out and split it up.

When the planting has matured, an informal pool adds colour, interest and movement to the garden as well as attracting birds and insects.

Golden Club (Orontium aquaticum)
Well worth growing. The long, broad, waxy leaves glisten in the sunshine. The flowers are yellow and white and poker-like in May.

Bog Arum (Calla palustris)
This has glossy foliage and white flowers resembling the arum lily. It flowers in mid-summer and sometimes fruits too.

Iris (Iris laevigata)
One of the best of pool plants, this grows to about 45 centimetres (18 inches) tall and bears brilliant blue flowers in summer. There are several other forms with white or pink flowers and one with variegated foliage. If your pool is reasonably big, you'll have room for the yellow flag (*Iris pseudacorus*) and there is also a variegated variety of this species.

Pickerel Weed (Pontederia cordata)
Large clumps of handsome foliage with blue, delphinium-like flowers in late summer. Vigorous but easily divided.

Deep-water plants

Water Hawthorn (Aponogeton distachyos)
The attractive leaves float on the surface. The flowers are white with a black centre and appear over a long period through spring and summer.

Water Violet (Hottonia palustris)
This could also be classified as an oxygenator because it does that job as well. It has deep lavender flowers held 15 centimetres (6 inches) above the water.

Water-lilies

Nymphaea pygmaea
A tiny lily suitable for water up to 15 centimetres (6 inches) deep, so perfect for the wooden-tub pool if it's rested on a brick. There are white, yellow and red varieties.

Nymphaea 'Froebeli'
One of the best for a small pool 23 to 60 centimetres (9 inches to 2 feet) deep. The flowers are blood-red.

Nymphaea laydekeri
Another type for water 23 to 60 centimetres (9 inches to 2 feet) deep. There are varieties with crimson, pink and purple flowers.

Nymphaea 'Escarboucle'
Perhaps the best of all water-lilies. The large, bright red flowers are very freely produced. Needs water 30 to 90 centimetres (1 to 3 feet) deep.

Nymphaea 'James Brydon'
Another popular variety for water 30 to 90 centimetres (1 to 3 feet) deep. It has huge, globe-shaped flowers of rose pink.

Nymphaea marliacea
Again for deeper water, there are varieties with white, yellow, red and pink flowers.

Pumps and electricity in the garden
Though it's by no means essential, it's not at all difficult to circulate the water by means of a small submersible pump. If it's a fountain you're after, you have no more to do than place the pump in the pool at a level where the outlet will be above water, connect the electricity supply and turn on. Later you may feel you want to install a stream or a waterfall – but that's a subject for a book all on its own!

The one point I would make is this. Unless you are a very competent electrician, it's well worthwhile getting a qualified electrical contractor to install the electricity supply. As you can imagine, the fact that pumps are actually placed in water makes them potentially dangerous.

Scree-gardens
Modern gardens are, on the whole, too small for a full-scale rock-garden. Nonetheless, alpine plants are amongst the most beautiful of all, so it would be a pity if they were excluded from the scheme of things. There are several ways they can be incorporated in the design.

In the wild, most alpine plants live high up in the mountains, either wedged in crevices in rocks or growing in the gravel or 'scree' that collects at the bottoms of slopes. They therefore love cold, dry conditions and very good drainage. Indeed, it's quite difficult to get used to the idea that they will grow very

The large leaves of water-lilies help to shade the pool and therefore keep down green algae. They are available in a wide range of colours and for different sizes of pool.

happily in almost pure gravel with just a tiny amount of soil. What they hate is wet weather.

One way to grow them is in a stepping-stone path. This really is quite a good method for a small garden where paths, though necessary, are much begrudged because of the valuable space they occupy. This way they can be transformed into a floral feature that will delight you all the year round.

Of course, your scree-garden doesn't have to be in the form of a path. You can do the same thing by digging out a bed in the lawn perhaps, or, as I have done in my own garden, by making a circle of bricks with a path crossing the garden.

In a bed like that, you can also include some strategically placed rocks here and there. If you do, try to group them together to form natural-looking outcrops, rather than dotting them about. They never look quite natural that way.

Plants for the scree-garden
There are literally hundreds of alpine plants that will look good and do well in a scree-garden, so I will restrict myself to those that are easy to grow and rewarding. Once you start though, you'll find yourself wanting to collect more and more. There's no group of plants that is so notorious for getting the reluctant gardener hooked for life!

New Zealand Burr (Acaena)
These fairly vigorous carpeting plants will do well for a path but are perhaps too vigorous in the scree-bed. They form a

carpet of small blue-grey leaves topped by bristly brown seed-heads.

Yarrow (Achillea)

There are several alpine yarrows, with aromatic, finely cut foliage and attractive yellow flowers. One of the best is *Achillea* 'King Edward', which bears sulphur-yellow flowers from May to September.

Rock Jasmine (Androsace)

Beautiful dwarf cushion or mat-forming alpines with white or pink flowers. They don't like wet, so could be a bit difficult. If possible, grow them in a cleft between two bits of rock where drainage will be better.

Antennaria dioica 'Rosea'

A very hardy carpeter, also ideal for paving. It has small, silvery leaves and small flowers varying from white to deep pink.

Columbine (Aquilegia)

Delightful little plants, but make sure you buy alpine species or they'll be too big. I like *Aquilegia bertolonii*, with bright blue flowers. *A. discolor* is very tiny and has light blue flowers with creamy yellow cups. *A. scopulorum* is a bit bigger but has superb frilled foliage and flowers of light blue and primrose.

1. To make a scree path, start by installing a wooden shuttering at the edges.
2. Set the slabs on well-drained compost and tap them down level.
3. Brush coarse grit between the slabs for added drainage and to enhance the effect.
4. Plant alpine plants through the gravel between the slabs. They will soon spread to soften the hard lines of the paving.

107

Sandwort (Arenaria grandiflora)
Bright green, mossy mats of foliage dotted with white flowers in late spring and early summer.

Thrift (Armeria)
A well-known, cushion-forming plant with globular pink flowers.

Aubrieta (Aubrieta deltoidea)
A well-known plant used widely in walls, where it makes a striking display. It can be used in paths and paving but tends to sprawl. Cut it back hard after flowering to keep the plants compact. There are many colours available and it's easy to raise from seed.

Bellflower (Campanula)
There are several species of bellflower which make good scree plants though some of them can become invasive. One of the best is *Campanula cochlearifolia* (sometimes called fairies' thimbles) which forms mats of fresh green foliage topped by tubby bells in many shades of blue or white.

Sea Heath (Frankenia)
Small, heather-like plants with clusters of tiny pink flowers at their tips.

Everlasting Flower (Helichrysum bellidioides)
A prostrate carpeter that can be a bit invasive but is easily cut back. It has white, woolly foliage and small white flowers.

Mint (Mentha requienii)
The last thing you might expect here is mint, but this one has minute leaves studded with lavender flowers in spring, and is very aromatic. It's ideal in a cool place.

White Cup (Nierembergia repens)
After mint, one of the potato family! A creeper with underground stems that forms mats of narrow, emerald-green leaves covered in a profusion of small, cup-shaped white flowers in summer.

Pratia angulata
This is a mat-forming plant with fleshy, rounded leaves and delicate white, purple-streaked flowers.

Vegetable Sheep (Raoulia australis)
In fact, the name 'vegetable sheep' refers to another species of *Raoulia* but it's such a good name I couldn't resist attaching it to this one too. It refers to the fact that the tiny, silvery-white leaves make the plants look for all the world like sleeping sheep. This species is much smaller and forms mats of silvery-grey foliage covered in tiny yellow flowers in summer.

Pearlwort (Sagina glabra 'Aurea')
A creeping, moss-like plant with bright golden foliage.

Saxifrage (Saxifraga)
This is a great family and all are good in the scree-garden. They form carpets or low mounds, some with long spikes of flower, others studded with tiny stars of white, pink, red and yellow according to variety.

Stonecrop (Sedum)
A large group of plants with many species suitable for the scree-garden. One word of warning. I would avoid our native stonecrop, *Sedum acre*, which is sold widely in garden centres. It looks marvellous covered in bright yellow flowers, but it becomes a pernicious weed that you'll curse for years.

Houseleek (Sempervivum)
There are literally hundreds of varieties of these fascinating plants in cultivation, most of which are suitable for the scree-garden. They form mats of cactus-like rosettes which generally bear pink flowers.

Thyme (Thymus)
There are several creeping thymes. Many will become invasive so a path is the best spot. The flowers range from white, through pink to deep red, and the small leaves are variegated in some varieties. My favourites are the lemon-scented *Thymus × citriodorus* and the very pale pink *Thymus serpyllum* 'Annie Hall'.

There are, of course, many dwarf bulbs that can be used in the scree-garden to very good effect. They can remain in the ground and will poke their heads through carpeting alpines in the spring to give a welcome show of flower.

Pergolas

When they ran out of space in New York, what did they do? They went upwards. And that's exactly what we should be doing in our small gardens too. We should take every opportunity to put up structures that will carry plants skywards to give the garden a truly three-dimensional effect.

Where there's an entrance into the garden, it can be beautified with an arch over which roses and other climbers could be trained. Better still, develop the archway to form a covered walk, by building a pergola.

Kits are available at garden centres and these are undoubtedly the best bet. They're not expensive but, if the budget is tight, you could reduce the cost by buying second-hand timber from the demolition contractor and making your own.

The kits are extremely easy to erect. Here I would certainly use the metal sockets that are just driven into the soil. Unlike fencing panels, there is little or no wind resistance to worry about.

It's important to keep the pergola level, so the amount you drive in the metal spikes is critical. There are two alternatives.

Drive in the first spike and fix the post in it. Then measure the required distance for the next spike, using one of the pergola rails. Bang in the spike and put the post loosely in the socket. Then put a straight-edge on top of the posts and check for level with a spirit-level.

Because the posts are 2.4 metres (8 feet) high, that's not so easy, so you may prefer either to remove the first post and check the level of the tops of the sockets, or to measure 90

Pergolas are available in kit form and are easy to erect with just a hammer and screwdriver.

centimetres (3 feet) up each post, bang a nail halfway in and rest the straight-edge on that.

The side-rails can then be nailed on using galvanized nails, and the cross-bars are pre-joined so they simply slot over the top. Just like the fencing, make sure that you put the pergola up section by section as you go along. Putting all the posts in and hoping the cross-struts will fit is chancing your luck just a bit too much!

What you do with the posts now depends a bit on what you want to grow up the pergola. If it's to be roses, for example, you can train them up simply by tying them to the posts with string. But clematis needs different treatment. They climb by twisting their leaf stalks round anything they can find. They'll happily climb up a wire, but the pergola post is, of course, too thick.

The best bet is to fix a wire tightly top and bottom of the post, one on each side. Then force a piece of 2.5-centimetre (1-inch) thick wood under the wire to hold it away from the post so that the plant has room to get round it. Nail the piece of wood in place to stop it moving.

However, there's nothing to stop you having the best of both worlds and using the rose as an anchorage for the clematis so that you get the benefit of two sessions of flower. Other, more vigorous, twiners like honeysuckle would need to be grown on their own and the wire technique is ideal for them too.

PLANTING

Plants, of course, are what gardens and gardening are all about. Though the Japanese seem to get by with a few rocks and a patch of sand, I simply can't imagine such a thing as a garden without plants. What's more, however 'green' you may be now, I can guarantee that it will only take one season of gardening for you to become as enthusiastic about growing them as I am. But I have to admit that, to the newcomer, it can be a minefield!

You'll find lots of useful advice about planting the herbaceous border with monocotyledons or about the value of epiphytes in the pinetum, which is great when you don't know the difference between a bulb and a biennial! And, if you're building your first garden, there's not the slightest reason why you should.

So, if the old hands would just nod off to sleep for a few minutes, I'll explain!

Types of plants
If you look for them, of course you can find all kinds of complications in the field of garden plants. There are quite a few differences, for example, between botanical and horticultural definitions and many grey areas, over which august gentlemen with microscopes and Latin dictionaries have been arguing for generations. Well, you can forget all that for a start!

Gardeners, as opposed to plant collectors, have simplified the language considerably so it's not nearly as difficult as it looks at first sight. Here's my simple glossary.

Tree
Of course everyone knows what a tree is, but there are two distinct types sold in garden centres these days. A 'standard' or 'half-standard' tree has a clean stem up to about 1.8 metres (6 feet) or 1.2 metres (4 feet) respectively, with a 'crown' of

branches on the top. That's the traditional way of buying trees.

But these days, many trees are sold 'feathered'. That means that, though they still have a central stem, the side-branches have been left on to give the appearance of a large bush. With this type of tree, you can either grow it as it comes, leaving the side-branches on, or you can, at a later stage, prune it into a standard tree.

Most trees are deciduous, which means they lose their leaves in winter, while a few are evergreen, retaining their leaves.

Shrub

This is a woody plant that is grown as a bush rather than on a clean stem like a tree. All will grow in the garden for many years without dying down in the winter. Some shrubs are deciduous, losing their leaves in winter. There is an abundance of evergreen varieties. In fact the choice of evergreen shrubs is wider than that of evergreen trees. Typical shrubs you might find in the garden centre are flowering currant, forsythia and rhododendron.

Conifer

A plant that bears cones, but generally an evergreen with many small, hard, stem-like leaves. Conifers are typified by the tall, narrow hedging shrubs like the Lawson's cypress though not all are upright-growing. There are several useful conifers which will hug the ground too.

Rose

Again, we all know that roses are those prickly shrubs with the beautiful flowers that have for ever been the joy of young

1. A traditional standard or half-standard tree has a clean stem with a 'crown' of branches at the top.
2. A 'feathered' tree has been allowed to retain its side-branches. It can be grown like this or the bottom branches can be pruned back hard to make a traditional standard.

Above. A floribunda rose carries its blooms in clusters of smaller flowers. This is the very popular 'Iceberg'. *Opposite*. Hybrid tea roses have one bloom per stem. They are generally better shaped than floribundas. This is the popular 'Sunblest'.

women and a source of acute embarrassment to young men! There are many different types, which can again be conveniently classified.

Hybrid teas – medium-sized bushes with a long flowering period and generally one, perfectly shaped bloom per stem. *Floribundas* – again medium-sized, long-flowering bushes with clusters of flowers on the same stem. *Miniatures* – small plants like tiny floribundas. *Patio roses* – simply small bush roses bred for growing in pots but also at home in the border. *Climbers* – just like floribundas or hybrid teas in flower but with a climbing habit. *Ramblers* – a climbing or sprawling

habit and normally with just one or sometimes two flushes of flower. *Shrub roses* – these are very variable but generally make much bigger bushes with a shorter flowering period.

Climbers

As the name implies, these plants have a vigorous habit of growth and are used to cover fences or walls or to grow through trees and other shrubs. Most are perennial and shrubby, though there are a few herbaceous perennials and annuals. Examples of climbers are clematis, wisteria and honeysuckle.

Alpines

Plants from higher regions generally grown in the rock-garden. Examples are houseleeks and stonecrops.

Perennials

The word actually refers to plants that will live for many years, some dying down in winter but reappearing in spring. But in gardening terms it generally applies to herbaceous perennials. These are soft-stemmed plants, most of which die down in winter but come up again even bigger in spring. Unfortunately, they have a variety of other names too and which one is used depends upon the whim of the nursery or garden centre. They are known as perennials, hardy perennials, herbaceous perennials, hardy plants, border plants or hardy border plants. Examples are lupins, delphiniums and carnations. To complicate matters slightly, there are a few tender perennials grown too. These are plants that will live for a long time but need protection from frost, like geraniums.

Biennials

Plants that are planted one year, flower the next and are then pulled out. Examples are wallflowers and sweet williams. Botanically, some biennials are actually perennial but, since they flower best in the first year, they're grown as biennials, and all gardeners know them as biennials, so don't worry about it.

Annuals

Plants that flower in the same year that they're sown and then die. There are hardy annuals which will stand mild frosts so can be sown directly outside, and half-hardies which need starting inside and should not be planted out until all danger of frost has passed. They are sold in garden centres as 'bedding plants'.

Bulbs
Botanically, there are bulbs, corms, rhizomes and tubers, but I would lump them all together. They are all plants with fleshy storage organs below ground, and are often bought in a dry state. Remember that the bulk of spring and autumn-flowering bulbs are hardy so can be left in the ground for ever, where they'll multiply like mad, while most summer-flowerers are tender and have to be lifted each autumn. Hardies include daffodils, crocus and snowdrops, while the tender ones are things like dahlias and gladioli.

Patio plants
Some garden centres now sell what they call 'patio plants'. These are big, attractive plants in decorative pots. They're ideal for brightening up the patio, but bear in mind that some are not entirely hardy. Enquire and only buy the tender types if you can protect them from frost in winter.

Ericaceous plants
I include this category purely because it's a word still used sometimes by nurseries trying to blind you with science! It simply means 'acid-loving', so unless you *know* you have acid soil, don't buy them.

Planning the borders
What a headache! Here you are with the choice of literally thousands of plants, few of which you really know, and you somehow have to plant them in the right place. First of all you have to think about aspect – whether this particular plant likes sun or shade, wet or dry, acid or limy soil. They need to be positioned so that when they grow they exactly fill their allotted space, provide a show of colour all year round without one colour clashing with the other and they have to be planted according to their correct height and spread so that one doesn't hide or smother its neighbour. The number of different permutations is endless.

Put like that, it's enough to put you off for life, but fortunately it's not nearly as difficult as it sounds. Nonetheless, it's still worth finding out as much about plants as possible.

Get around to visit gardens open to the public, nurseries,

botanic gardens and garden centres, just to see as many plants as possible. The more you know about your plants, the more fun your garden will become.

But above all, take your time. I wouldn't expect to plant the whole garden in the first year or even the second, come to that. It's much better to buy slowly as you find plants you really can't live without (as you surely will) than to fill the whole garden in one go. While you're waiting, you can fill the borders with hardy annuals, which are the cheapest and most cheerful experience you'll ever treat yourself to, or with half-hardy bedding.

But when it comes to planning, how can you translate those magnificent herbaceous borders, shrubberies and rose gardens of the stately-home gardens to your own little semi-detached plot? Well, you don't have to.

All that grandiose stuff went out with debutantes. No one has the space or the money for it any more so we need to look for a different style of gardening. And the answer, in my opinion, lies in the old cottage gardens of our great-grand-fathers – well almost anyway.

They had much the same problem of lack of space as we do and their answer was to bung everything in the same border in what looked like a higgledy-piggledy fashion. Lupins and hollyhocks jostled with herbs for the medicine chest, while marigolds and roses fought for space with lettuces and beetroot. Every scrap of soil was used and it looked marvellous! We can use exactly the same technique in the gardens of modern houses. You don't have to have a thatched roof and a rustic porch to plant yourself a cottage garden! What's more, we have a much more exciting range of plants to choose from, including many improved varieties of those self-same plants our great-grandfathers grew. So the modern cottage garden can look even better than a chocolate-box.

Now I'm not suggesting that this kind of scheme is easy to perfect, especially if you are not well acquainted with the plants. But you'll be pleased to hear that there is a perfect let-out. You see, there's a whole range of plants that can be lifted and replanted *even when they're in full flower*. Nearly all the herbaceous perennials are so accommodating that they'll wilt for no more than a day or two and then recover to their previous glory. So, all you have to do is to plant your border as well as you can and then, if you find you've made a mistake, simply pour a bucket of water over the plant in the wrong position, lift it with as much root as possible and transplant it where it looks right. Then give it another bucket of water and it'll never look back!

However, I wouldn't like to recommend the same treatment for trees and shrubs. Mind you, if you find they're in the wrong place you can, with a bit of upheaval, lift and replant in the dormant season during autumn or early spring, but generally they like to get their roots down and establish themselves.

Still, when you think about it, that makes the job a lot easier. Herbaceous plants, alpines and bulbs can all be lifted in flower, and annuals and biennials will only be there for one season anyway, so all you really have to get right first time are the trees and shrubs. And if you make a mistake there, you can still rectify it at the small cost of slowing the plants' growth down a bit. I hope that sets your mind at rest a little!

Buying plants
Most garden centres and nurseries are a pretty respectable bunch and the trade in general is averse to ripping off its customers. What's more, most are aware of the need for good quality control and would rather throw away a bad plant than sell it. So all in all, you can expect a fair deal, even though you may be a bit in the dark about what you're buying. But they are all in the business of making a profit, so they are sometimes not quite as saintly as they would have you believe!

I have never, for example, seen a notice in a garden centre warning customers not to buy the expensive rhododendrons until they have tested their soil for lime. I have often seen garden centres selling frost-tender bedding plants in May when there is every likelihood of a cold snap. And, though most have made a big effort in the past ten years to upgrade quality, there are still a few who are happy to sell you rubbish. Inevitable I suppose.

My first rule when buying plants is perhaps the most difficult to adhere to. Never buy on impulse.

It's a well-known fact in the business that you can sell anything that's in flower. It's obvious, really, that plants become very difficult to resist when they are looking blooming beautiful. But resist them you must.

When you go plant shopping, take a good plant book or a comprehensive nurseryman's catalogue with you. Then you'll be able to look up that irresistible buy to see whether or not it will suit your soil, position and space. If it's not listed in your book, ask before you buy and, if they can't, or won't, tell you all the details, leave it where it is.

Assessing good quality is sometimes difficult. Often, the best plants are the smaller, less dramatic-looking ones and they are often the cheapest too!

It would be fair to say that buying herbaceous perennials is not really a problem. Almost anything you buy, so long as it's actually alive, will grow and flourish in most gardens in a fairly short time. But buying trees and shrubs takes more care.

First of all, look at the pot. If it's full of weeds, my advice would be to get in your car and go elsewhere. Obvious neglect almost certainly means that other important cultural practices have also been neglected, so the plants are likely not to have been fed and watered correctly, pruned or repotted. Have a special look at the bottom of the pot. If a mass of roots is showing through, the plant will be pot-bound and will take a long time to establish after planting and start into regrowth. That kind of garden centre doesn't deserve your business.

If you're buying in the spring or early summer, just lift the plant by its top-growth to make sure it's well rooted in the pot. If it looks as though you're going to pull it out of the compost, it has just been repotted and will suffer on transplanting.

When you've found the plants you want, sort through them to find the best of the bunch. This is not necessarily the tallest – in fact often the reverse is the case. I would always buy the *bushiest* plant in the row, making sure it's compact and well shaped and has no damage to the branches.

If you're buying climbers, reject those with a long length of bare stem and all the growth at the top. Look for the one with a number of shoots right at the bottom. Even if the top part of the plant looks dead, this is still the best one to go for. Conifers must never show any sign of brown foliage. This is often due to wind damage or to the pots freezing in winter and, with most conifers, it will not grow out.

Trees should be well shaped and have a good, well-balanced head if they are standards or half-standards. They should also be standing upright. Yes, I know that sounds pernickety but, if they have been growing on the slant, they haven't been fed and watered properly because the pot has not been level.

Sometimes, it may be better to buy trees and shrubs from a nursery rather than a garden centre. Most garden-centre plants are container-grown and are therefore generally restricted in size and more expensive. On the other hand, trees or shrubs grown in the field and lifted bare-rooted are in most cases bigger and cheaper. However, they can only be lifted and planted in the dormant season between November and the end of March. But, if you have the patience and are lucky enough to have a good, old-fashioned nursery within reasonable distance, you will almost always get a better bargain. Indeed, if you buy a hedge of one of the cheaper plants like quickthorn or privet, this may well be the *only* way to buy them.

In my view, fruit trees should also be bought from a specialist grower if possible. While many garden centres do sell a reasonable range of trees, a specialist will have a wider choice of varieties which will also be generally cheaper, and he'll be able to guarantee them free from disease. It's also much wiser to buy one-year-old or, at most, two-year-old trees. One-year-old apples and pears, for example, while costing less, will start to fruit much earlier than older trees you are likely to be offered in the garden centre.

Buying bulbs is generally easy since the quality overall is pretty good. However, it's as well to press each bulb and to reject any that feel spongy. Naturally, if you see any sign of disease or damage, leave them on the shelf.

A few bulbs really shouldn't be sold at all in the dry state. Two notable examples are hardy cyclamen and snowdrops. They are generally much too dry ever to grow and, once planted, that's the last you're likely to see of them! These are much better bought either from a nursery, which can guarantee to lift them and send them straight out, or in pots where you *know* they're growing.

Buying plants through mail-order is often fraught with problems and that's a pity because it's often a way to get hold of less usual varieties that garden centres don't stock. I certainly wouldn't advise against mail-order, provided you stick to a couple of basic rules.

First of all, never expect a bargain. The newspaper advertisements you will see offering plants at 30 for a penny ha'-penny are best used for wrapping the fish and chips. They will be tiny rooted cuttings and very difficult to get established.

Secondly, avoid ads that go into great eulogies about this wonderful new plant but don't tell you the proper Latin name of it. Instead they invent a fancy name of their own so you'll never really know what you're buying. The wonderful rose hedges are a perfect example. The artist's impression of a perfectly clipped hedge smothered in masses of marvellous blooms the size of a cabbage is misleading in the extreme. What you generally get is something very like the common wild rose that sprawls all over the garden and has a couple of fairly nondescript pink flowers for a few weeks every year – and of course absolutely nothing in winter.

Remember, too, that your rights are well protected. If you are not satisfied with the plants you receive, you should send them back immediately and demand they give you a refund.

But most mail-order nurseries are highly respectable places and are anxious to provide good quality and service. Naturally even they make mistakes from time to time though, so, if you're not satisfied, again at least give them a chance to put things right. Most will.

Finally, when you do find a mail-order nursery that sends you good-quality plants, well wrapped and at a fair price – stick with them.

Plants in pre-packs bought from department stores or supermarkets are another tricky proposition. Cheap they certainly are and some are quite good. But a store is the worst place in the world to keep plants, which deteriorate rapidly. So unless you can see the plant clearly through the plastic and it is obviously healthy and unshrivelled, it's best to leave it alone.

Just a word about bedding plants, though I have already hinted at the dangers. In most parts of the country, it's unwise to plant them outside until the first week in June, when all danger of frost should be past. Further north, it could be even later. This goes for all half-hardies, whether they be the boxed annuals or the perennials in pots, like geraniums or fuchsias.

Again, because of the rule that anything in flower will sell quickly, most summer bedding will be in flower when you buy it. Remember that in some cases this could mean that they'll finish earlier too, so it's sometimes a good idea to buy those that haven't started to flower yet.

Some important general planting rules

I'm afraid I tend to get a bit worked up on the subject of planting. The reason is that so many new gardeners spend a lot of money on plants and then, through carelessness, or more often through ignorance of the correct technique, allow them to die. It's a sorry fact, but a true one, that over half the trees and shrubs planted each year die in the first season. So bear with me if I chunter on and take care you follow the instructions to the letter!

First the general rules that apply to all plants.

Always plant at the right time of year. Most deciduous trees and shrubs (those that lose their leaves) will actually do better if they're planted in the autumn – from the end of October to about mid-December. The reason for this is that the soil is then warm from a summer of sunshine and it's unlikely at that time to dry out. What's more, as soon as leaves fall from deciduous plants they naturally put on a spurt of root growth. So they'll start growing immediately and get established before the real cold sets in. Then they'll be ready for a flying start in spring.

Of course, if deciduous trees and shrubs are bare-rooted instead of container-grown, they *must* be planted in the dormant season between the end of October and March.

Evergreen trees and shrubs are better planted either in September or in April or May. But if you do leave them until the spring, it's *vital* that you water them regularly if the weather turns dry.

Most herbaceous perennials can also be planted in the early autumn. But if you're in the least worried about their hardiness, leave it until the spring. I'm convinced that plants that are on the borderline of hardiness will stand a much better chance of survival if they are allowed to get established in the milder weather and then get the shock of a cold winter rather more slowly.

There are generally two planting times for bulbs, in the autumn for the spring-flowerers like daffs and crocus and in the spring for the summer-flowering types like lilies and gladioli. As I've already pointed out, there are some, like snowdrops and hardy cyclamen, that are best planted immediately after flowering, or from pots.

Most biennials can go in during the early autumn but always leave half-hardy bedding plants until the last frost is well and truly behind you. They're expensive and just not worth the risk of earlier planting.

In a new garden, soil improvement will generally be necessary for all plants. But it's folly just to dig a hole in uncultivated soil and add organic matter to the material you have dug out. However much you improve a small planting area, it will always be subject to problems, more especially on heavy soils.

If you dig a hole in otherwise uncultivated land, it tends to act like a sump, draining water from the soil around it and surrounding the roots with wet, cold earth. At best it will slow growth; at worst it will actually drown the roots and kill the tree.

So leave your planting until you've had the chance to cultivate the whole border (see pages 38–45).

But, even with the border cultivated, you may still have to add extra organic matter. If the land is heavy, it's likely to come out in large lumps which will be difficult or impossible to break down to a fine soil. Bear in mind that the roots need to be completely surrounded by soil with as few large air pockets as possible. If it's not fine enough to allow that, mix some moist organic matter with it.

Planting instructions always include the advice, 'add a handful of bonemeal'. I can't for the life of me think why. Certainly it's the stuff to use in winter when only the roots may be active, but at any other time of year the plant will need the full range of plant nutrients. So enrich the soil with either rose fertilizer or Growmore.

After planting, the *most* vital part of the whole operation is to water as and when it becomes necessary. With bare-rooted plants, in autumn it may not have to be done at all because the weather is likely to be wet anyway. But at any other time, and especially with pot-grown plants, it's *the difference between life and death*. Well, I warned you I was likely to get melodramatic, but it grieves me that the already high failure rate after planting rose in the drought year of 1976 to a staggering 90 per cent! That, for me, is enough evidence to show that most failures are due to nothing more than lack of water.

Watering doesn't mean a little sprinkle from the watering-can either. The soil around the plant must be *saturated*. If you just add a little, the roots tend to come to the surface in search of water and there, of course, they are even more at risk from hot sunshine. So put the hose on the roots until the soil is soaked right down to the lower levels, especially if you're planting in the summer.

Planting techniques

TREES

When all trees were sold bare-rooted, gardeners really had no choice but to plant either in autumn or in early spring. The autumn was considered the best time by many because the trees had a chance to get established before the winter frosts and so were well placed to take off in spring. The soil is still warm, for one thing, there is unlikely to be a prolonged dry spell and, once their leaves have fallen, most plants put their energies into a final spurt of root growth before closing down, as it were, for the winter. The only disadvantage of autumn planting is that a prolonged spell of really cold winter weather can kill off a few less hardy plants while they are still not properly established, though that applies more to shrubs and herbaceous perennials than to trees.

If you're planting bare-rooted trees, the old rules still apply, though you can plant any time up to March when the ground isn't either waterlogged or frozen. If you buy container-grown

Above left: When you start to fill in the hole, give the plant's roots some good topsoil from around the edge. Replace it with some of the surplus you have dug out.

Above right: Hammer the stake into the ground at an angle to avoid disturbing the rootball.

Left: Nailing the tree tie to the stake keeps it firmly in place. Use another hammer held firmly against the back of the stake to keep it rigid while you hammer in the nail.

125

trees, obviously you can plant at any time of year, though again it's easier in the autumn when drought is unlikely and you don't need to be quite so careful about frequent watering.

How to plant container-grown trees

By the time you've got round to buying your trees, you will have already prepared your borders by digging over the soil and improving it in whichever ways are necessary (see pages 38–45).

Before you actually start digging your hole, give the rootball of the tree, still in its container, a thorough soaking. Not only will this make it easier to remove the pot when the time comes, but it will also ensure that the roots and the soil around them are really moist before you plant them, something that's much harder to do once they're in the ground.

Dig a hole slightly bigger than the container. Check that it's deep enough by putting the container in the hole, then laying a bamboo cane, or even your spade, across it. If the cane rests on the soil on both sides *and* the top of the container touches it, the hole is deep enough.

If your soil is low on organic matter, add a few spadefuls of organic matter and a couple of handfuls of blood, fish and bonemeal to the pile of soil you've dug out. Then remove the tree carefully from its pot. If it's a thin, black polythene one, slice it off with a sharp knife. If it's a rigid, plastic pot and you've watered it thoroughly beforehand, the tree plus rootball should lift out fairly easily. Should it stick in its pot, try holding the trunk of the tree and twisting it very gently or try gently squeezing the sides of the pot just to loosen the soil. If all else fails, you'll have to cut the pot away using a Stanley knife or something similar. Put the rootball into the hole and make sure that the tree is facing the right way. Many trees have a pretty obvious front if you look at the shape, so make sure that's facing the point from which you'll be looking at it most often. Then start carefully shovelling in the soil. When you've filled the hole, firm the soil with the ball of your foot. The aim is to get rid of any large air pockets but not to compress the soil too tightly together, so go gently.

It's a very good idea to use the surplus soil to build a small retaining wall around the tree about 30 centimetres (1 foot) out from the trunk. When you give the tree a thorough soaking, that wall will help keep the water where you want it – directly over the rootball.

Staking

Almost all new trees need staking, but recent research has shown that short stakes – reaching only one third of the way up the trunk – are more efficient than the traditional, much longer ones. Allowing the top of the tree to sway about in the wind, it seems, thickens the base of the trunk and helps strengthen the root system.

Use a cane or a spade to check that the top of the rootball is level with the soil.

You'll need two stakes of 5 × 5 centimetres (2 × 2 inches) timber. To work out the length, measure the tree's trunk and divide by three and add 45 centimetres (18 inches) to hammer into the ground. Hammer the stakes in just outside the rootball on either side, then nail a cross-piece between them. Attach it to the trunk with a special plastic tree tie which has a collar to prevent it chafing. Whatever you do, don't use wire or nylon twine which will cut into the tree as it grows and either kill it or allow diseases in.

Alternatively, you can use just one stake, the same length as described above, and hammer it diagonally into the ground behind the tree and close to the trunk. Then use a tree tie in the same way.

Planting evergreens

Evergreens, like conifers, are best planted in September or left until April or even May. They are almost always supplied either in containers (in which case plant them as you would any container-grown tree) or 'rootballed' – that is, they have been dug up with a good ball of soil around the roots, which is then wrapped in sacking for delivery. Leave the sacking round the roots until the moment you are ready to plant – it not only protects them from damage but also stops the young roots on the outside of the rootball from drying out. When you have dug the correct-sized hole, remove the sacking, make sure the plant's at the right level and finish planting in the same way as before.

Planting bare-rooted trees

The key to success with bare-rooted trees is to make sure that the roots never dry out. The very small roots which take up essential nutrients, as well as water, will die if they're exposed to the sun or to drying winds for any length of time. This means that if the trees arrive at a time when you can't plant them right away, you must 'heel them in'. Dig a trench of about a spade's depth, throwing the soil forward. Lay the trees in the trench with the roots at the bottom and the trunk

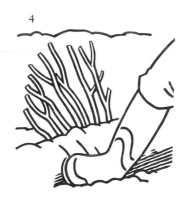

1. If bare-rooted plants cannot be planted straight away they should be heeled in. Dig a trench throwing the soil forward.
2. Put the roots of the plants in the trench, leaning them slightly against the soil you have dug out.
3. Dig another trench behind the plants, again throwing the soil forward to cover the roots.
4. Put your boot on the soil to firm it round the roots. In winter, plants can stay like this for some time.

leaning away from you, on to the soil you've thrown forward. Then cover the roots by digging another trench behind the first and throwing the soil forward on to them. When you're ready to plant, remove the trees to where you're going to plant them but keep the roots covered with sacking. Dig a hole wide enough to take the roots when they're spread out and deep enough for the soil, once the tree's planted, to be exactly level with the soil-mark on the trunk of the tree, which indicates the level at which it was grown at the nursery. Check this using a bamboo cane or a spade placed across the hole. Now take a stake one third the length of the trunk, plus 45 centimetres (18 inches), and hammer it well into the hole.

Before you plant, check the roots and if any are broken or damaged, cut them back cleanly with a sharp knife or secateurs. Put the tree in the hole, arranging the roots around the stake if need be, and then put in a little fine soil (mixed with blood, fish and bonemeal) over the roots. Hold the trunk of the tree firmly and jerk it up and down a few times, so that the soil settles in between the roots. Half-fill the hole and tread it firmly but gently with the ball of your foot. The aim, again, is to eliminate large air pockets in which the roots would dry out and die, but to avoid compressing the soil too much. Refill the hole completely and firm the soil with your foot. Fix the trunk to the stake with a special tree tie, and mulch around it with well-rotted compost or manure. Finally, mulch around the base of the tree with a thick layer of bark or compost, to prevent evaporation and competition from weeds.

CLIMBERS

The most important thing to remember when it comes to planting climbers is that the soil at the bottom of a fence or wall (and particularly a house wall where the overhanging eaves keep most of the rain off it) is very dry. So always add lots of organic matter to the planting hole and make sure that the climber itself is at least 30 centimetres (1 foot) away from the wall.

As for support, whether or not it's necessary depends on the type of climber. There are three main groups, the first of which encompasses the self-clingers like ivy, Virginia creeper and the climbing hydrangea. Initially, when they've just been planted, they'll need some help to get a grip, but tying the young stem to a bamboo cane which slopes up against the wall or fence is usually all that is necessary. Face them in the right direction and let them get on with it.

The second group, climbers and twiners, like honeysuckle, jasmine and clematis, which attach themselves by twining either their stems or their leaf stalks around something else, do need support. There are a number of alternatives.

The cheapest method for fences is to stretch horizontal wires between the fence posts, starting about 60 centimetres (2 feet) from the ground. Place them about 30 centimetres (1 foot) apart and secure them with staples. To make a mesh you then weave lengths of thinner wire vertically through these 30 centimetres (1 foot) apart, and secure them on the top and bottom horizontal wires.

To make a support system on a wall you can fix wooden battens 25 × 35 millimetres (1 × 1½ inches) to the wall first with Rawlplugs and screws, and then attach wires to them as described in the preceding paragraph. This lifts the wires clear of the wall, not only allowing twiners to get behind them, but also letting air circulate which helps prevent diseases like mildew on roses. Alternatively, you can, of course, use wooden or plastic trellising, fixed to the fence posts or the battens, but it's more expensive and, in the case of the plastic stuff, more obtrusive than the wires.

Climbers in the third group, which includes roses and wall shrubs like Moroccan broom (*Cytisus battandieri*), have no means of support, visible or otherwise, and so they do need to be tied. You could use a framework of wires or trellis, or you could support a large wall shrub by fixing a piece of chicken wire about 2 × 2 metres (6 × 6 feet) to the wall with special lead headed wall nails, and tie the stems to it. From

PLANTING

Above. Lead-headed nails are a convenient means of fixing some plants to the wall. *Below.* Most climbers can be fixed to the fence with horizontal wires. Strain them tight using a length of wood as a lever against a post.

only a few steps away, the wire will be invisible. You could use chicken wire for twining plants, but it would have to be fixed to battens, to allow space for the plant to grow through and behind the wire. Lead-headed nails have pliable flanges of metal on the top, which can be bent around wires or plant stems. These nails can also be very useful for fixing climbers that need support in only a few places (some climbing roses, for example) directly onto a wall, but if you find you're having to bang in more and more of them, one of the other methods is preferable.

SHRUBS
Shrubs are planted in exactly the same way as trees, though, of course, they don't need staking.

HERBACEOUS PLANTS
The principles of planting herbaceous plants are really much the same as for trees, shrubs and climbers: prepare the ground well, give the plants a really thorough soaking in their pots a few hours before you plant them and add a handful or two of organic rose fertilizer or a general-purpose feed like Growmore to the planting hole.

Place the plants, still in their pots, on the soil to see how they look. If they don't look right, it's easy to try some other grouping at this stage. In fact, most herbaceous plants are very easy-going even if you realize, after you've planted them, that they're in the wrong place. Provided that you give them a good soak before you dig them up and another afterwards, and keep them well watered until they've settled in, you can even move them in full flower: after looking a bit floppy for a day or two, they'll perk up again. Obviously, it's better if you don't have to do that, though.

If your soil wasn't too bad to start with and you've prepared it really well, you should be able, with a trowel, to make a hole just large enough to take the rootball, and firm it in. Once your plants are in, firm the soil around them with your knuckles (but without compressing it too much) and then give them a thorough watering.

ANNUALS
Half-hardy annuals bought from the garden centre should never be planted out until all danger of frost is past – which means the end of May for the South, early June for the Midlands, and even mid-June for the North and Scotland.

Prepare the top layer of soil before you plant, adding a little organic matter and some general-purpose organic or rose fertilizer, resisting the temptation to be too generous or you'll wind up with lots of lush leafy growth and not many flowers. Soak the plants well beforehand, and then remove them carefully from their trays. If they're in individual cells, simply plant as they are. If they're in one tray, remove the whole block and gently tear the plants apart or even cut them with a sharp knife if necessary. Although the object of using annuals, in part anyway, is to fill the gaps while shrubs and herbaceous plants are slowly growing, be careful not to plant them too close to the permanent subjects. If you do, they'll be competing with them for nutrients, moisture and light, which will slow down their rate of growth.

Hardy annuals are sown directly into the soil where you want them to flower, and you can start sowing as soon as the soil is dry enough to cultivate – in March or early April in a good year. If you have a heavy soil, it's well worth covering the area you plan to sow with annuals with a piece of clear polythene in the previous autumn. This not only prevents the soil from getting saturated by winter rains, but it also helps it to warm up earlier in spring.

Above left: Give climbers a good start on a chicken wire support by weaving the young growths, or leaf stalks, in and out.

Above: Building a small retaining wall of soil around newly planted shrubs or trees helps keep the water where it is most needed – directly above the rootball.

131

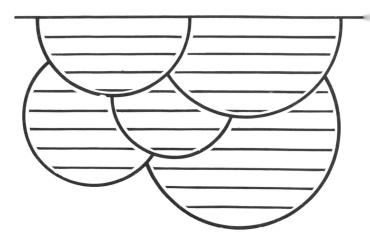

To sow hardy annuals in informal drifts, mark out the drifts first but then sow in straight drills within them. This helps sort the plants from the weeds at thinning time.

In mixed borders annuals look best in informal clumps or drifts, so scratch out a shape, free-hand, on the soil with a stick. Within that shape, it's a good idea to sow the seeds in straight lines about 15–20 centimetres (6–8 inches) apart, rather than to scatter them broadcast. Weed seeds germinate at the same time as the annuals, but if you've sown your seeds in straight lines, it's very easy to see which are weeds and which are not. Once they're thinned out and growing well, you're not aware of the straight lines at all.

Incidentally, if you have heavy clay soil, try making your seed drills a good bit wider and deeper than normal and filling them with fine seed compost. That is a far more hospitable environment for delicate, emerging roots than thick, wet clay. By the time the roots of the young plants have outgrown the drill, they are tough enough to cope with the clay.

After sowing your seeds, cover them lightly with soil (or seed compost in the case of heavy clay) by running a rake between the drills. Then tap the soil down gently with the back of the rake. Once the seedlings emerge, keep them free of weeds and, when they're big enough to handle, thin them out to 15–20 centimetres (6–8 inches) apart by removing all the seedlings in between. It's hard for first time gardeners to pull up and discard perfectly healthy seedlings, but it's essential. If you don't thin them out enough, you'll wind up with spindly, rather sickly plants.

You can start a few hardy annuals in small peat pots or modules (which are plastic trays divided into several cells) on a sunny windowsill in March, which means that when you plant them out in May they'll have a head start on the weeds.

Sow them in moist seed compost – two to a pot or cell if they're large seeds like lavatera or a small pinch sown centrally if they're smaller – then cover them to their own depth with seed compost or vermiculite (which you can buy from the garden centre). Cover the pots or trays with opaque polythene (those white bags they give you in supermarkets for frozen food are ideal) and put them in the airing cupboard, having first checked that it's not too hot for the variety you're sowing. Check the seed every day and when the first one germinates take the pot or tray out and stand it on a light windowsill. With large seeds, if both germinate, remove the weaker seedling. Where you've sown a small pinch of seed, leave the clump to grow and plant it out eventually as it is.

In a greenhouse you get light from all directions, but on a windowsill you get it from only one and so your seedlings will grow towards it, making them thin and spindly. You can help stop this by turning them regularly or, better still, making a light box – any good-sized cardboard box with the top and front removed and the remaining sides, back and bottom painted white. That will reflect the light around the seedlings and encourage sturdier, more even growth.

Gradually harden off your seedlings by putting the pots or trays outside on dry, mild days, at first bringing them in again at night. Plant them out in May at the recommended planting distance for the variety.

BULBS

Spring-flowering bulbs, which really are nature's reward for getting through the long, grey winter, should be planted from August onwards, though tulips shouldn't be planted until November since this helps avoid the fungus disease 'tulip fire'. Summer-flowering bulbs should be planted in spring because many of them are tender.

The one thing all bulbs hate is waterlogged soil – it rots

A good way to plant bulbs is to dig out a wide hole a little deeper than necessary, put in a layer of grit and then set the bulbs on that.

Lavatera trimestris 'Mont Blanc': just one packet of seeds sown in a large drift makes a stunning display.

them in no time – so if you have a heavy soil, always plant them on a thick layer of coarse grit. Make sure you plant them at the correct depth. A quick rule of thumb for bulbs is to plant them at three times their own depth at least, so that they have twice their own depth of soil on top of them. A bulb that's 2.5 centimetres (1 inch) deep, for example, needs to be planted in a hole at least 7.5 centimetres (3 inches) deep so that it has 5 centimetres (2 inches) of soil on top of it.

You can plant large bulbs, like tulips or daffodils, individually using a bulb planter or in a group in one large hole. That's certainly the best method for small bulbs. Again, in a mixed border, clumps or drifts of bulbs are much better than straight lines or singletons dotted about the place, and *en masse* they make much more of an impact too. You often read that the way to achieve a natural effect with bulbs is to throw a handful in the air and plant them where they land. But all too often 99 per cent of them fall in a huddle together, while the remaining 1 per cent land a step away. It's easier to draw an irregular shape on the soil with a stick – a rough kidney shape, for example – dig it out to the required depth and then place the individual bulbs pretty evenly within it.

If bulbs are to remain permanently in your borders, you need to plant them where they're unlikely to be disturbed. It's so easy, once all trace of them has disappeared in summer, to slice through them with the spade as you merrily dig away. One answer is to plant them around shrubs where you're unlikely to be digging anyway.

Another way is to plant them with your perennials so that they conveniently hide the dying foliage after they've flowered. If you're going to plant cranesbills – *Geranium* 'Johnson's Blue', for instance – intermingle them with small bulbs like crocuses or squills. In winter and spring, when the bulbs are growing and in flower, all you can see of the cranesbills are small brown tufts. By the time the bulbs have finished flowering, the cranesbills have started into growth, and by the time the bulbs' foliage is beginning to die off, the cranesbills' new fresh green leaves will hide it completely.

It's all too easy to forget about feeding bulbs but a handful or two of blood, fish and bonemeal, or a watering with a liquid plant food such as Phostrogen, once flowering is over will pay dividends with next year's flowers.

TREES

The trees you choose to plant will almost certainly be the largest living features in your borders, and to some extent will dictate the rest of the planting, so it is very important to choose the right trees and plant them in the right place. In a small garden you should naturally choose small trees avoiding the huge weeping willows or gigantic monkey puzzle trees you sometimes see dwarfing small front gardens.

Don't be put off though by trees described in the garden centre as reaching 10 metres (33 feet). That's really not as huge as it sounds.

In a very small garden you're unlikely to have room for more than two or three trees, so finding the right position for them is essential. Since they're going to be the tallest plants in your garden, and since you will certainly choose particularly attractive specimens, they will draw the eye, so you must make sure that they will draw it to where you want it to look. In the first time garden, for instance, we planted the very pretty ornamental crab apple, *Malus* 'Profusion', in the corner diagonally opposite the patio doors. That was part of the overall design, intended to swing the axis of the garden from the much shorter front-to-back axis to the diagonal one across the garden, and make the plot seem larger.

You can also use trees to screen a blot on the landscape. If you have a view of, say, an electricity pylon in the distance or an ugly tower block, a carefully sited tree can be used either to mask it completely or, if that's not possible, to conceal it partially and distract your eye so that you don't notice it quite as much.

Never plant vigorous trees closer to the house than 12 metres (40 feet) away. This is particularly important on clay soil where the withdrawal of water can cause soil shrinkage, which can damage the foundations and lead in turn to cracking and subsidence – extremely expensive problems to put right.

What tree?

Where space is at a premium, the trees and shrubs you choose really have to earn their keep. You can't afford to choose something that is lovely for a couple of weeks, and then for the rest of the season is just plain dull.

You want a tree with as many appealing qualities as you can get – very attractive new foliage, striking autumn colour, interesting variegated or coloured foliage through the summer, flowers, berries, superb bark, a good strong shape against the sky in winter. The shape of the tree is well worth thinking about. One with a broad head and large leaves, like some of the maple family – *Acer platanoides*, for instance – will create dense shade beneath it while a mountain ash (*Sorbus aucuparia*) with a much more open head and feathery leaves will provide the sort of dappled shade in which many plants thrive.

Talking of shade, aspect isn't such an important factor in your choice of trees as it is in the choice of most other plants. In the majority of gardens trees will soon grow above the shadows cast by garden walls and fences, so unless it's shaded by the house, of course, a tree in a north-facing border will get as much sun as in one facing south. Obviously, if your garden is in the shadow of tall buildings or large overhanging trees, any trees you plant won't grow into the sun, or at least not for a very long time, so bear that in mind when making your choice. In the lists of suitable trees that follow, all will thrive in sun or light shade, and those that will grow happily in a more shady spot are labelled accordingly.

Many trees will grow well in several different soil types, but they are listed in each category where appropriate, so that if you have a sandy soil, for example, you'll find our complete selection of suitable trees under that heading. Almost all the trees that will grow in clay, chalky soil and sandy soil will also do as well – if not better – in the elusive, slightly acid medium loam, so under that heading are listed those few small trees that will *only* give of their best in a good, rich, well-drained slightly acid loam.

Trees for clay soils

FOR VERY WET, HEAVY SOILS
'Golden' grey alder (Alnus incana 'Aurea')
It has soft golden leaves and stems and red-tinged catkins in spring. Its leaves become more green in the summer, but it has good autumn colour.

The paperbark maple (*Acer griseum*).

Approximate height and spread after five years 3 × 1.5 metres (10 × 5 feet); after 20 years 11.5 × 3.5 metres (38 × 12 feet).

Silver willow (Salix alba sericea, also known as S.a. argentea)
This makes a small, round-headed tree with long, slender, silvery leaves. In winter its bare stems form a delicate tracery against the sky. It responds well to pruning.

Approximate height and spread (if unpruned) after five years 3 × 1.5 metres (10 × 5 feet); after 20 years 5 × 2.5 metres (16 × 8 feet).

FOR MOIST CLAY SOILS
Maples (*Acer*)
Paperbark maple (Acer griseum)
This maple is a near-perfect tree for a small garden because it has so many good qualities – attractive, orange-buff foliage in spring, glorious red and scarlet autumn colour, and in winter, on wood that's at least three years old, the orange-brown bark peels away to reveal new cinnamon-coloured bark

beneath. Added to which, its ascending branches and rather open habit allow light to reach plants growing beneath it. It's also very slow-growing.

Approximate height and spread after five years 2 × 1.2 metres (6 × 4 feet); after 20 years 6 × 3 metres (20 × 10 feet).

Snake-bark maple (Acer capillipes)
Another small tree whose bark – grey-green with white veining – is one of its most attractive features. Its fresh green leaves are tinged red in spring and turn fiery orange-red in autumn.

Approximate height and spread after five years 3 × 1.5 metres (10 × 5 feet); after 20 years 7 × 5 metres (23 × 16 feet).

Acer negundo 'Flamingo'
It has leaves which are pink when they open and then turn green and white with a pink flush which gradually fades as they mature. The brightest and most attractive colouring is on new growth, so ideally the tree should be pruned every year, but since it can be quite difficult to prune something 4–5 metres (13–16 feet) tall, it is certainly easier to grow it as a shrub. Many nurseries supply it in both forms.

Average approximate height and spread (unpruned) after five years 3 × 2 metres (10 × 6 feet); after 20 years 6 × 5 metres (20 × 16 feet).

Acer pseudoplatanus 'Brilliantissimum'
This is a very slow-growing small tree about which opinions are sharply divided. Some people love its foliage, which opens deep shrimp-pink in spring, becoming paler flesh pink, then creamy-yellow and pale green before assuming its summer mid-green, and don't mind that it's actually rather dull for the rest of the season. Others think the spring pyrotechnics don't actually compensate for its lack of interest during the rest of the year. It's a matter of taste.

Approximate height and spread after five years 2.5 × 1.5 metres (8 × 5 feet); after 20 years 4.5 × 3.5 metres (14½ × 12 feet).

The Norway maples (*Acer platanoides*) are quite a bit bigger but fine for a medium-sized garden. Most will grow from about 20 to 25 feet (6–7 metres) in 10 years. That sounds much bigger than it actually is, so it's not a bad idea to go outside and check the height of a tree (perhaps comparing it to the house, which probably has eaves something like 20 to

25 feet (6–7 metres) high) to persuade yourself that you're not buying a monster!

A. 'Drummondii' has striking green foliage with a broad creamy-white margin.

A. 'Royal Red' makes a shapely tree with dark red leaves.

The 'golden sycamore' (*Acer* 'Worleei') is bigger but it keeps its yellow foliage until July, when it turns a fresh green.

Flowering thorn (Crataegus laevigata 'Paul's Double Scarlet', *also known as C.l.* 'Coccinea Plena')
This makes a small, round-headed tree and has dark pinky-red double flowers in late spring and early summer. It bears a few small, red berries in the autumn. Less widely available, though very attractive, is the double pink-flowered variety C.l. 'Rosea Flore Pleno'.

Approximate height and spread after five years 4 × 1.2 metres (13 × 4 feet); after 20 years 6 × 6 metres (20 × 20 feet).

Golden chain tree (Laburnum × watereri 'Vossii')
It has masses of bright golden flowers hanging in long bunches in May and June. Its green bark is also an attractive feature and its sharply ascending branches mean that you can usually grow plants underneath since they will get plenty of light. The only drawback with laburnum is that every part of it – not only the seeds – is poisonous, so it's not a tree to choose if you have small children or are planning to have some.

Approximate height and spread after five years 4 × 2 metres (13 × 6 feet); after 20 years 7 × 5 metres (23 × 16 feet).

Ornamental crab apples
(Malus)
You really are spoilt for choice here because so many varieties of ornamental crab are excellent for small gardens, what with masses of flowers in spring, in some cases attractively hued foliage, and bright-coloured fruits in autumn.

Japanese crab (Malus floribunda) is a stunning sight in spring when it has deep red buds, newly opened pale pink flowers and more mature blush-white ones all at the same time. It has a semi-weeping habit, and branches on mature specimens can almost reach the ground, as though they are bowed down under the weight of the flowers! In autumn it has small, cherry-like fruits.

Approximate height and spread after five years 4 × 1.5 metres (13 × 5 feet); after 20 years 8 × 6 metres (26 × 20 feet).

Malus hupehensis also flowers abundantly, and as a bonus its white flowers, which are pink in bud, are scented. In autumn it has small yellow fruits flushed with red.

Approximate height and spread after five years 3 × 1.2 metres (10 × 4 feet); after 20 years 6 × 4 metres (20 × 13 feet).

Malus sargentii is one of the smallest crabs. It has masses of scented white flowers (tinted yellow in bud) with golden stamens. In autumn it bears bright red, currant-like fruits and its leaves turn yellow.

Approximate height and spread after five years 1.5 metres × 70 centimetres (5 × 2½ feet); after 20 years 5 × 2 metres (16 × 6 feet).

Malus × adstringens 'Simcoe', a small but strong-growing tree, has coppery young foliage, large, purplish-pink flowers in abundance and purplish-red fruits in autumn.

Approximate height and spread after five years 2.5 × 1.5 metres (8 × 5 feet); after 20 years 4.5 × 2.5 metres (15 × 8 feet).

Malus × zumi 'Golden Hornet' has white flowers, followed by bright yellow fruits in autumn. For some reason birds prefer red and orange fruits to yellow, so these get left until well into the winter when everything else has gone. It's also useful as a pollinator for apple trees.

Approximate height and spread after five years 4 × 1.5 metres (13 × 5 feet); after 20 years 8 × 6 metres (26 × 20 feet).

Malus 'John Downie' is more upright in habit than 'Golden Hornet', has pink-budded white flowers and plenty of large orange fruits flushed with red which are the best for making jelly or wine.

Approximate height and spread after five years 4 × 1.5 metres (13 × 5 feet); after 20 years 8 × 6 metres (26 × 20 feet).

Malus × schiedeckeri 'Red Jade' is a small, weeping crab which has bright green leaves that turn yellow in autumn and blush-white flowers followed by small, bright red fruits.

Approximate height and spread after five years 2 × 1.5 metres (6 × 5 feet); after 20 years 3 × 5 metres (10 × 16 feet).

Malus 'Maypole'. This is one of a new breed of columnar trees introduced in the summer of 1989 and marketed under the name 'Ballerina trees' which are ideal for a confined space since they reach a height of only 2.5 m (8 feet) and a spread of about 30 centimetres (1 foot) in five years. 'Maypole' has purple-tinged foliage, cerise-pink flowers and a good group of dark red fruits in autumn. It also has three columnar cousins

The Japanese ornamental crab (*Malus floribunda*).

– 'Waltz', 'Polka' and 'Bolero' – which are surprisingly heavy-cropping apples. They're early-flowering, mid-season and late respectively and these are well worth considering because they need no pruning and so are extremely easy to look after. Although they are partially self-fertile, they will produce a much better crop if you plant two different varieties, and the ornamental crab 'Maypole' will pollinate all the rest.

Approximate height and spread after five years 2.5 metres × 30 centimetres (8 × 1 foot); after 20 years 7 metres (22 feet).

The following *Malus* hybrids are recommended for their coloured foliage.

Malus × moerlandsii 'Liset' has glossy, deep red leaves, deep crimson flowers and ox blood-red fruits.

Malus × moerlandsii 'Profusion' has coppery-crimson young foliage which slowly turns green, purplish-red flowers which fade to pink, and ox blood-red fruits.

Malus 'Royalty' is considered by some to be the best purple-leaved form since its wine-coloured foliage keeps its glossiness until it falls. It has large, mid-pink flowers and wine-red fruits.

Approximate height and spread after five years 4 × 1.5 metres (13 × 5 feet); after 20 years 8 × 6 metres (26 × 20 feet).

Malus 'Profusion'.

Flowering cherries, plums and peaches
(Prunus)
This species offers an even wider choice than the ornamental crabs, though you need to stop yourself being seduced by some of the spectacular, double-flowered varieties, like the 'boudoir' pink *Prunus* 'Kanzan', that you often see in streets and parks – the best place for them, some would say. Make sure that you choose one which will still have something to offer once the flowers have fallen after just a week or so and you've swept sackfuls of petals off the lawn.

Some breeders are now offering Japanese flowering cherries grafted on to dwarfing rootstocks, which means the final height and spread of the tree is reduced. Instead of *P.* 'Taoyame' ending up at 7 × 7 metres (23 × 23 feet) after 20 years, for example, it will reach only about 5 × 5 metres (16 × 16 feet). It's worth checking with the garden centre before you buy on which sort of rootstock your tree is grafted.

Purple-leaved plum (Prunus cerasifera 'Nigra') is at its best in spring when the new blood-red foliage provides a dramatic contrast to the pale pink flowers which appear at the same time, or even sometimes slightly before it. The foliage gradually darkens to purple through the summer.

Approximate height and spread after five years 3 × 1.5 metres (10 × 5 feet); after 20 years 8 × 4 metres (26 × 13 feet).

Prunus 'Accolade' is a superb small tree with a graceful, open, spreading habit. In early April its clusters of deep pink buds open into semi-double, hanging, light pink flowers up to 4 centimetres (1½ inches) across with fringed petals. It goes on flowering for weeks.

Approximate height and spread after five years 3.5 × 3 metres (12 × 10 feet); after 20 years 8 × 8 metres (26 × 26 feet).

Yoshino cherry (Prunus × yedoensis) also makes a graceful small tree with arching branches and masses of almond-scented, blush-white flowers in late March–early April. It also has good autumn colour.

Approximate height and spread after five years 3 × 2 metres (10 × 6 feet); after 20 years 7 × 5 metres (23 × 16 feet).

Sargent's cherry (Prunus sargentii), which eventually forms a rather flat-topped tree and scores on several counts. Not only does it have masses of single pink flowers in early spring, but its new leaves are coppery red when they first appear, turning first green, then, as early as September in some areas, brilliant vermilion and scarlet.

Approximate height and spread after five years 3.5 × 2.5 metres (12 × 8 feet); after 20 years 9 × 10 metres (30 × 32 feet).

Korean hill cherry 'Autumn Glory' (*Prunus verecunda* 'Autumn Glory') also scores heavily on several counts, with bronze-tinged new foliage, single white flowers and stunning autumn tints – deep purples and reds. It forms a spreading, dome-shaped tree and in winter its somewhat twisted stems make a delicate tracery against the sky.

Approximate height and spread after five years 2.5 × 2 metres (8 × 6 feet); after 20 years 8 × 9 metres (26 × 30 feet).

Tibetan cherry (Prunus serrula) has masses of small white flowers in May, but its main claim to fame is its superb, mahogany-coloured bark which peels away to reveal a surface as smooth and polished as that of fine antique furniture. It takes between five and ten years for this to develop.

Approximate height and spread after five years 4 × 2 metres (13 × 6 feet); after 20 years 7 × 4 metres (23 × 13 feet).

Autumn cherry (Prunus subhirtella 'Autumnalis') in fact

produces semi-double white flowers on bare stems from early autumn (November) intermittently right through the winter to April, depending on the weather. A really cold snap can delay the flowers, but a spell of mild weather will bring them out. It has quite good golden autumn colour too. There is also an attractive variety with pink flowers, *P.s.* 'Autumnalis Rosea'.

Approximate height and spread after five years 1.5 × 2 metres (5 × 6 feet); after 20 years 7 × 7 metres (23 × 23 feet).

Japanese flowering cherries
(*Prunus serrulata*)
Lombardy cherry (Prunus serrulata 'Amanogawa') makes a tall, narrow column of pale candy-pink flowers in spring and its foliage turns gold and flame in autumn. It's a very popular choice for small gardens because it is so narrow.

Approximate height and spread after five years 3 × 1 metre (10 × 3 feet); after 20 years 6 × 2.2 metres (20 × 6 feet).

Prunus 'Shirotae' *or* 'Mount Fuji' has fragrant, single or semi-double pure white flowers, very attractive against the fresh, light green leaves with their distinctive fringed edges in spring. It forms a wide-spreading tree, and in mature specimens some of the horizontal branches may touch the ground.

Great white cherry (Prunus 'Taihaku') produces single, pure white flowers up to 5 centimetres (2 inches) across, which are set off by the coppery-red young foliage in mid-spring. The leaves, which are exceptionally large, turn first green, then red and gold in autumn.

Approximate height and spread (for both trees) after five years 3.5 × 2.5 metres (12 × 8 feet); after 20 years 7 × 7 metres (23 × 23 feet).

Prunus 'Taoyame' is a small, slow-growing tree with a spreading habit. It has fragrant, semi-double, shell-pink flowers which fade to blush-white, and attractive coppery young foliage.

Approximate height and spread after five years 3 × 2 metres (10 × 6 feet); after 20 years 7 × 7 metres (23 × 23 feet).

Weeping cherries
Prunus × *yedoensis* 'Shidare Yoshino' has masses of pale pink flowers, fading to white, on branches that weep to the ground in early spring. *Prunus* × *yedoensis* 'Ivensii' has fragrant, snow-white flowers and a similar habit. They are not so easy to find as Cheal's weeping cherry (a name sometimes applied

Sargent's cherry (*Prunus sargentii*) in autumn.

to *Prunus subhirtella* 'Pendula Rosea' and sometimes to *Prunus* 'Kiku Shidare Sakura'), but specialist nurseries have them and they are well worth the extra effort involved in finding them. Cheal's weeping is also very prone to a fatal fungus infection so it's best avoided.

Approximate height and spread after five years 3 × 3 metres (10 × 10 feet); after 20 years 5 × 6 metres (16 × 20 feet).

Ornamental pears
(*Pyrus*)
Snow pear (Pyrus nivalis) takes its common name not only from the white flowers which it produces in abundance in spring, but also from the white 'wool' which covers the young leaves and shoots appearing at the same time. The foliage then becomes silver-grey. It's not widely available, but good specialist nurseries stock it.

Approximate height and spread after five years 3 × 2 metres (10 × 6 feet); after 20 years 7 × 5 metres (23 × 16 feet).

Willow-leaved pear (Pyrus salicifolia 'Pendula') has long, silvery willow-like leaves which are also covered in a silky white down until early in the summer. It does produce small white flowers in April, but it's grown primarily because of the silvery foliage it eventually forms.

Approximate height and spread after five years 2.5 × 2 metres (8 × 6 feet); after 20 years 4 × 3 metres (13 × 10 feet).

Rowan or mountain ash and whitebeam
(*Sorbus*)
Another family with many members worthy of garden room in a small plot, since they have flowers, pretty foliage, good autumn colour and berries.

Sorbus 'Joseph Rock' has clusters of small white flowers in spring and fresh green, feathery foliage which turns copper and gold in autumn when its yellow berries appear. Though it's a pyramid shape when young, its branches become more steeply ascending with age and it finally forms a tight, neat head. Look out, too, for *S*. 'Embley', which has superb autumn colour.

Approximate height and spread after five years 2.5 × 1.5 metres (8 × 5 feet); after 20 years 10 × 5 metres (32 × 16 feet).

Kashmir mountain ash (Sorbus cashmiriana) is a superb little tree, with very pale pink flowers in spring and beautiful, fern-like foliage which turns red in autumn. Its hanging clusters of pearl-white berries stay on the tree until well into the winter. It has a more open habit than 'Joseph Rock'.

Approximate height and spread after five years 2 × 2 metres (6 × 6 feet); after 20 years 4 × 4 metres (13 × 13 feet).

Sorbus vilmorinii makes a slightly larger tree than *S*.

The weeping willow-leaved pear (*Pyrus salicifolia* 'Pendula').

cashmiriana, with white flowers in spring and delicate ferny foliage which turns purplish-red in autumn. Its berries, which hang in clusters, start out a rosy red then fade slowly to pink, blush-white and finally white.

Approximate height and spread after five years 2.5 × 1.5 metres (8 × 5 feet); after 20 years 6 × 3 metres (20 × 10 feet).

Sorbus sargentiana comes into its own in autumn and winter when its large and attractive leaves, up to 30 centimetres (1 foot) long, take on superb autumn colour. It also has bright red fruits which are then replaced by large crimson buds, sticky like a horse chestnut's, on pale creamy-green stems.

Approximate height and spread after five years 2.5 × 1.5 metres (8 × 5 feet); after 20 years 6 × 3 metres (20 × 10 feet).

Whitebeam (*Sorbus aria* 'Lutescens') is a picture in the spring when it has white flowers and its new, silvery foliage is covered in creamy down. The leaves turn grey-green on top and grey below, which creates an attractive effect when the wind disturbs them. It sometimes has red-orange berries in autumn. If you can find its near-relative, *S. thibetica* 'John Mitchell', snap it up. Its leaves are twice the size and quite dramatic in spring.

Approximate height and spread after five years 3 × 2 metres (10 × 6 feet); after 20 years 12 × 8 metres (39 × 26 feet).

Trees for chalky soils
Chalky soils are usually rather shallow and, of course, alkaline, so lime haters, like the Canadian maples or the sweet gum (*Liquidambar styraciflua*), won't thrive. Even so, there are plenty of attractive trees to choose from.

Maples (*Acer*)
Acer negundo 'Flamingo': see under 'Trees for Clay Soils'.
Acer pseudoplatanus 'Brilliantissimum': see under 'Trees for Clay Soils'.

Birches (*Betula*)
Although our native silver birch (*Betula pendula*) is very beautiful, it's perhaps at its best grown with others in a group, and a very small garden simply doesn't have room for a copse! Incidentally, birches don't transplant well, so if you do want one of these trees buy a container-grown specimen, not a bare-rooted one.

Swedish birch (*Betula pendula* 'Laciniata') has deep-cut, feathery, light green foliage which turns yellow in autumn and, combined with its horizontal branches and hanging twigs, gives it an airy, delicate effect. Its stems soon become white.

Approximate height and spread after five years 6 × 1.5 metres (20 × 5 feet); after 20 years 12 × 5 metres (39 × 16 feet).

Purple-leaved birch (*Betula pendula* 'Purpurea') makes a smaller tree, with bright purple foliage in spring, which slowly ages to dark green, and purple catkins in winter.

Approximate height and spread after five years 4 × 1 metres (13 × 3 feet); after 20 years 8 × 2 metres (26 × 6 feet).

Himalayan birch (*Betula utilis jacquemontii*) stands out for its dazzling white stems under the peeling brown bark. It also has good autumn colour and large catkins in winter.

Approximate height and spread after five years 6 × 1.5 metres (20 × 5 feet); after 20 years 12 × 5 metres (39 × 16 feet).

Laburnum × watereri 'Vossii'; see under 'Trees for Clay Soils'.

Malus species: see under 'Trees for Clay Soils'.

Prunus species: see under 'Trees for Clay Soils'.

Pyrus species: see under 'Trees for Clay Soils'.

Golden false acacia (Robinia pseudoacacia 'Frisia')
Will grow in chalky soil that has been enriched with organic matter and is neither too thin nor too alkaline. It has wonderful feathery golden foliage, which appears quite late in the spring, and an attractive, open habit. Its branches are rather brittle, so it needs a spot sheltered from the wind. It is also notoriously difficult to get established, so always buy container-grown trees and make sure you plant it in the right place first time round!

Approximate height and spread after five years 3 × 2 metres (10 × 6 feet); after 20 years 12 × 6 metres (39 × 20 feet).

Whitebeam (*Sorbus aria* 'Lutescens'): see under 'Trees for Clay Soils'.

Trees for sandy soils
Although they have the same tendency to dry out as chalky soils, and some of the same trees will grow quite happily in them, some sandy soils are likely to be less alkaline, so there are additional trees that will grow well in them.

The Himalayan birch (*Betula utilis jacquemontii*) in winter.

Maples (*Acer*)
Acer griseum; *Acer negundo* 'Flamingo'; *Acer pseudoplatanus* 'Brilliantissimum': see under 'Trees for Clay Soils'.

Snowy mespilus (Amelanchier lamarckii)
Another superb small tree. It's smothered in small, white flowers in spring at the same time as the new leaves appear, tinged with bronze. In autumn these turn brilliant orange-red or yellow and, though the tree will grow on a slightly alkaline soil, the colouring is better on an acid soil.

Approximate height and spread after five years 4 × 3 metres (13 × 10 feet); after 20 years 7.5 × 6 metres (25 × 20 feet).

Birches (*Betula*): see under 'Trees for Chalky Soils'.

Katsura tree (Cercidiphyllum japonicum)
A fine tree with heart-shaped leaves which open a purplish-pink, turn first a sea-green in summer and then shades of smoky pink, red and yellow in autumn. Although it will grow on sandy soil, it will relish an annual mulch with organic matter. It dislikes windy conditions, so make sure that you find it a sheltered spot.
    Approximate height and spread after five years 5 × 3 metres (16 × 10 feet); after 20 years 10 × 7 metres (32 × 23 feet).

Golden honey locust (Gleditsia triacanthos 'Sunburst')
Has beautiful, bright golden, feathery foliage and makes a broadly spreading tree. Again, it will appreciate extra organic matter. It's one of the easiest-to-grow golden foliage trees.
    Approximate height and spread after five years 3 × 1.5 metres (10 × 5 feet); after 20 years 7 × 5 metres (23 × 16 feet).

Trees for slightly acid, medium loam
Almost all the trees already listed in the preceding sections will grow in slightly acid, medium loam, so the following will only do really well in this type of soil.

Golden Indian bean tree (Catalpa bignonioides 'Aurea')
This tree has the most beautiful, large, velvety, gold leaves which have a coppery tinge as they unfurl and keep their freshness throughout the summer. It is very slow-growing and eventually produces a small, spreading tree, as broad as it is high; or, if it's cut back regularly, it makes a wonderful shrub. You can buy trees grafted on to a 1.5 or 2 metre (5 or 6 foot) stem, to give height immediately.
    Approximate height and spread after five years 1.5 × 1.5 metres (5 × 5 feet); after 20 years 15 metres (50 feet).

BORDERS

The basic rule for first-time planting is: don't try to fight Nature – work with it instead. You can't make a shady garden sunny, for instance, but you can choose to grow shade-loving plants that are every bit as beautiful as the sun-lovers. And while of course there's plenty you can do to improve poor soil, you can't totally alter its character. A chalky soil, for instance, will never be a rich, acid loam.

You need to know, first of all, which way your garden faces, because that affects how much sun it gets and therefore which plants will thrive. If you get early morning sun on the back of your house, and lose it after midday, your garden faces east. If you get sun only in the afternoon, it faces west. If, as you stand with your back to the house, the sun rises to the left of your garden, travels over the garden and sets on the right – lucky you: your garden faces south. If the sun rises to the right, though, and travels across the garden in the opposite direction, the garden faces north. In midsummer, when the sun is at its highest in the sky, a north-facing garden gets quite a lot of sunlight, but in spring, autumn and winter, when the sun is much lower in the sky, the garden will be largely in the shadow of your own and your neighbours' houses. While a north-facing garden isn't ideal, there are so many superb plants that thrive in shade that if your garden didn't have any shade you would have to create some!

You need to look at surrounding features, too. Obviously, if there's a large sycamore or even an expanse of factory wall at the bottom of your west-facing garden, you're not going to get much of the afternoon sun which, theoretically, you could expect.

It's also absolutely essential to know what sort of soil you have – whether it's clay, sand, chalk or medium loam, whether it is acid or alkaline – and to learn which plants will grow well in it. One of the real joys of gardening is that for every plant that won't thrive in your soil, there are others, just as

beautiful, that will. If you have an alkaline limy soil, for example, you won't be able to grow rhododendrons or camellias, which need an acid soil, but you can grow shrubs like sweetly scented winter- and spring-flowering viburnums, lilac and mock orange (*Philadelphus*).

Bearing these two factors in mind, you can choose and plant your plants knowing that, all other things being equal, they will grow happily where you have put them.

Shade-lovers, like white bleeding heart (*Dicentra spectabilis* 'Alba'), ferns, hostas, euphorbias and the deep-rose-pink-flowered *Daphne retusa*, thrive in a woodland garden in early summer.

North-facing borders

Many new gardeners are daunted by the prospect of a shady, north-facing border but in fact, the truth is that there are many absolutely superb plants which will only give of their best in a shady spot. With a few exceptions, like some of the primula family, the blue poppy (*Meconopsis betonicifolia*) and some golden foliage plants like the golden elder (*Sambucus nigra* 'Aurea'), the shade-lovers are not as showy, not as brightly coloured as the sun-loving brigade, but theirs is a more subtle, quieter charm that remains appealing for longer.

Many shade-loving plants originate from moist, cool woodland, so their colours are paler – soft primrose yellow,

153

NORTH-FACING BORDERS

White Turk's-cap lilies (*Lilium martagon* 'Album') above plants with superb foliage like *Astrantia major*, the wine-red *Heuchera* 'Palace Purple' and the steel-blue *Hosta* 'Halcyon'.

pale pink, mauve and blue, as well as white – than those whose natural habitat is bright sunlight. They also tend to have large leaves to make the most of the available light which is needed in the plant's food-manufacturing process, and it's in the shady border that many plants, grown as much for their foliage as their flowers really thrive – things like plantain lilies (*Hosta*), elephant's ears (*Bergenia*), lungwort (*Pulmonaria*) and the dead nettle (*Lamium maculatum*).

Foliage is particularly important in a shady border since many woodlanders flower in spring before the trees come into leaf and take most of the light, and so you will be relying on foliage to provide a lot of summer colour and interest.

The use of shrubs and herbaceous plants with variegated foliage like the much-maligned green-and-gold spotted laurel (*Aucuba japonica* 'Variegata'), or the gold-splashed ivy (*Hedera helix* 'Goldheart'), the golden elder or Bowles' golden grass

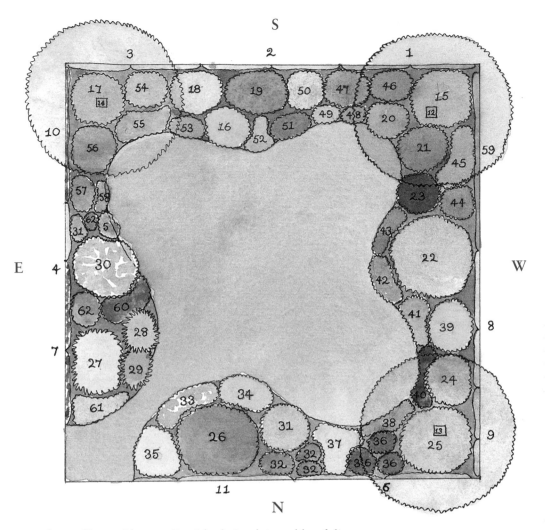

(*Milium effusum* 'Aureum') with their plain golden foliage really does seem to create a patch of sunshine in the shade. But plants with variegated and coloured foliage need enough plain greens around to point up the contrast and show them off to full advantage.

The actual design of the border is a matter of personal taste, but in this instance, since you are using plants which grow informally in their natural setting, it's probably better to adopt a similar informal style. Neat rows just wouldn't look right.

The density of the shade and the nature of the soil, particularly whether it's moist or dry, will make a deal of difference to what will grow well.

Another important factor is the acidity of the soil, so check it with a lime-test kit before planting. Don't try to make limey soil acid by adding organic matter – it doesn't work.

MOIST SHADE, ACID SOIL

The following plants must *have an acid soil.*

SHRUBS
Camellias
These exquisite flowering shrubs are often thought of as exotic and therefore tender, but in fact, as long as they are sheltered from icy north and east winds, they will grow very well in a north-facing border or in dappled shade. They produce masses of single, semi-double or double flowers in a whole range of colours from white through many shades of pink to blood-red, and even a few multicolours like the pink-and-white striped *Camellia japonica* 'Lady Vansittart'. They start flowering between February and April, depending on the variety, and keep their flowers for several weeks. Once the flowers have fallen, their elegant, glossy green leaves are attractive in their own right.

Good varieties include: white flowers – *Camellia japonica* 'Alba Plena'; pink flowers – the soft pink, semi-double *C.j.* 'Lady Clare', the clear, rich pink *C.j.* 'Leonard Messel' and perhaps the most widely grown and most popular of all *Camellia × williamsii* 'Donation', with an abundance of large, semi-double, clear pink flowers from February onwards; red flowers – the large, semi-double, deep crimson *C.j.* 'Mercury', and *C.j.* 'Adolphe Audusson' whose semi-double, blood-red flowers have conspicuous gold stamens.

Approximate height and spread of *japonica* types after five years 1×1 metres (3×3 feet); after ten years 1.5×1.5 metres (5×5 feet). *Williamsii* types grow larger – up to 3×1.5 metres (10×5 feet).

Checkerberry or wintergreen (Gaultheria procumbens)
A creeping, low-growing evergreen, providing good ground cover under larger, acid-loving shrubs. It has oval, green leaves, small, white flowers in summer, and bright red berries in autumn and winter. The berries and leaves both have the medicinal scent of wintergreen. It doesn't like heavy clay soils.

Approximate height and spread after five and ten years 10 centimetres $\times$ 1 metre (4 inches $\times$ 3 feet).

Pernettya mucronata
Although this dwarf evergreen is less well known than many other acid-lovers, it's well worth considering for a shady

border. It has very small, glossy, deep green leaves, masses of small, white flowers and the most beautiful berries in autumn, ranging in colour from pearly white through various shades of pink to red and purple. To ensure a good crop of berries, plant the shrubs in groups of three or four, making sure that there's at least one male among them. The sex of a pernettya is not instantly obvious, so ask at the garden centre for a guaranteed male form. Good varieties include: white berries – *Pernettya mucronata* 'Alba', 'Snow White'; pink berries – 'Sea Shell' (pale shell pink), 'Pink Pearl' (lilac-pink); red berries – 'Bell's Seedling' (dark red), 'Cherry Ripe' (bright red); purple berries – 'Mulberry Wine' (magenta ageing to deep purple).

Approximate height and spread after five years 50 × 80 centimetres (1½ × 2½ feet); after ten years 80 centimetres × 1.2 metres (2½ × 4 feet).

Pieris

These are perhaps the ideal evergreen shrubs for a very small garden because they really do earn their keep. In spring tassels of small white flowers, which are bell-shaped rather like those of lily-of-the-valley, open at the same time as the new foliage. The crowns of new, slender, spear-shaped leaves start out an almost unbelievably vivid shade of scarlet, slowly fading through pink, cream and pale green before acquiring their glossy summer mid-green. The clusters of small, red buds for next season's flowers, which form in the autumn, add brightness during the winter months.

There are many good varieties available, but look out for *Pieris formosa* 'Wakehurst', which has shorter, broader leaves than most but superb spring colour; *Pieris forestii* 'Forest Flame', one of the hardiest varieties, with particularly bright new foliage; and *Pieris japonica* 'Variegata' whose leaves are variegated with creamy white flushed with pink when they first open. The last named is more slow-growing than most and forms a smaller shrub – about two thirds the usual height and spread.

Approximate height and spread after five years 80 centimetres × 1 metre (2½ × 3 feet); after ten years 1.5 × 2 metres (5 × 6 feet).

Rhododendrons

These are without doubt among the most eye-catching of our flowering shrubs and there are literally hundreds of different ones to choose from. Most of them, though, grow much too

157

The acid-loving *Pieris forestii* 'Forest Flame' in spring.

large for a small garden and many have little more to offer in the way of interest once the large, brilliantly coloured flowers have faded. There are some excellent dwarf rhododendrons, however, worth considering for any border in dappled shade. Look out for 'Bluebird' with violet-blue flowers, 'Pink Drift' with lavender-pink flowers and aromatic, olive-green leaves, 'Scarlet Wonder' with trumpet-shaped, frilly, red flowers, and 'Moonstone' with rosy-crimson buds opening to a creamy pale primrose yellow. Also attractive is *Rhododendron yakushimanum* and its hybrids. *R. yakushimanum* itself is a real beauty – not only does it have masses of rose-pink buds, opening to apple-blossom-pink flowers which slowly fade to white, but its foliage is striking too. Its long, narrow, leathery leaves are silvery when they first appear, turning a really dark, glossy green on top, with woolly, brown undersides. Its many hybrids – like 'Doc' (light pink, fading to white), 'Grumpy' (pale yellow with a hint of pink, fading to white), 'Silver Sixpence' (creamy white with pale lemon spots) and 'Surrey Heath' (rose pink lightly tinged with orange) – have superb flowers in a range of striking colours, but none has the same beautiful foliage as the parent.

Approximate height and spread after five years 60 × 60 centimetres (2 × 2 feet); after ten years 80 centimetres × 1 metre (2 × 3 feet).

Azaleas

These plants are members of the same family as rhododendrons. Some of the deciduous kinds have almost neon-bright flowers in shades of orange, yellow and pink, while the foliage provides good autumn colour. Look for 'Koster's Brilliant Red' (vivid orange-red), 'Gibraltar' (dark red buds opening to flame-orange with a yellow flash), 'Coronation Lady' (salmon-pink with a bright orange flare).

Approximate height and spread after five years 1 × 1 metre (3 × 3 feet); after ten years 1.5 × 1.5 metres (5 × 5 feet).

The evergreen azaleas make small, rounded shrubs that are smothered in flowers in spring. Good varieties include: 'Blue Danube' (blue-violet), 'Mother's Day' (semi-double, bright red), 'Blaauw's Pink' (salmon pink), 'Hinomayo' (clear pink) and 'Palestrina' (pure white).

Approximate height and spread after five years 60 × 60 centimetres (2 × 2 feet); after ten years 80 centimetres × 1 metre (2½ × 3 feet).

OTHER PLANTS

There are very few herbaceous plants (or annuals or bulbs) which must have an acid soil to do well – most of those that dislike lime will grow happily in neutral to slightly acid soil.

An exception is the Himalayan blue poppy (*Meconopsis betonicifolia*) which needs a cool, rich, acid soil if it is to produce its best colouring. The flowers are a rich blue in summer and grow to a height of 90–120 centimetres (3–4 feet).

MOIST SHADE, AVERAGE SOIL

The following plants will thrive in moist shade on fertile, well-worked garden soil.

CLIMBERS

Clematis

Clematis like their heads in the sun and their roots in the shade. Some are suitable for north-facing walls or fences, though the majority do prefer a sunnier situation. They also do best in a limy soil, but will grow well enough in neutral or slightly acid conditions.

Good large-flowered varieties to look for include the widely available 'Nelly Moser' whose pale pink-mauve petals are striped with a deeper pink; the mauve-pink, free-flowering 'Comtesse de Bouchaud'; the pure white 'Marie Boisselot'; and the lavender-blue 'Mrs Cholmondeley'. Small-flowered varieties also do well on north walls – not the extremely rampant *Clematis montana*, unless you have masses of space, but varieties of *C. alpina*, for instance, which have nodding blue and white flowers in spring and are marvellous growing through evergreen shrubs like firethorn (*Pyracantha*). The late-flowering *C. viticella* varieties, with small flowers in wine-red, purple or white, are also good for growing through other shrubs. Most varieties should either be pruned back hard in winter to encourage better flowering or, in the case of *C. alpina*, should simply be pruned to keep them within their allotted space.

Flowers March to October (depending on the variety). Approximate height and spread 3–5 metres (10–16 feet).

Ivy (Hedera)

Probably the best evergreen climber for shade and tolerates all kinds of soil. One of the variegated kinds, like the small-leaved, bright gold and green 'Goldheart', or the much larger-leaved *Hedera colchica* 'Paddy's Pride', really would brighten up a dark wall or fence. If you want a plain green – as a background for variegated shrubs, perhaps – the glossy, dark green *H. hibernica* is ideal. Ivies are self-clinging, but may need some help when you first put them in.

Approximate height and spread after five years 4 × 4 metres (13 × 13 feet); after ten years 5 × 5 metres (16 × 16 feet).

Climbing hydrangea (Hydrangea petiolaris)

A marvellous climber for all soils, and for shade. It's worth growing simply for the masses of bright, fresh green leaves it produces each spring, but it also has large, flat heads of white flowers in early summer, which turn brown in autumn and remain, attractively, on the bare stems in winter.

Approximate height and spread after five years 1.5 × 2 metres (5 × 6 feet); after ten years 3 × 4 metres+ (10 × 16 feet+).

Honeysuckles (Lonicera)
They usually flower slightly better in sun (though, like clematis, they like their roots in moist shade) but a few varieties will thrive in shade where they're also less prone to aphid attack. *Lonicera × tellmanniana* has rich yellow flowers, flushed with red in bud, while *Lonicera × americana* has very sweetly scented flowers in summer which open white and slowly fade to yellow, flushed with pink. The gold-netted Japanese honeysuckle (*L. japonica* 'Aureo-reticulata') isn't as vigorous as *L. × americana* but has attractive semi-evergreen foliage as well as sweetly scented, small, yellow flowers in summer.

Flowers June to September. Approximate height and spread 3.5 × 8 metres (12 × 26 feet).

Virginia creeper (Parthenocissus)
Worth growing for its superb autumn colour, and if you make a point of seeking out *Parthenocissus henryana*, you will also get the benefit of its beautiful, dark, velvety green leaves deeply veined with silver and pink in summer. It's not as vigorous as some of the other Virginia creepers, but quite vigorous enough to cover a garden wall or fence in a couple of years. Like all its relatives, it's a self-clinger.

Approximate height and spread after five years 2.5 × 1.5 metres (8 × 5 feet); after ten years 5 × 3 metres (16 × 10 feet).

Roses
Roses usually need a sunny situation to do well, but there are several ramblers and climbers that will grow successfully on shady walls provided that they have a moist enough soil. Look for 'Morning Jewel' with bright pink flowers, the pearly, blush-white 'New Dawn', 'Pink Perpétue' with carmine pink flowers, the yellow-flowered 'Golden Showers' and the red 'Danse du Feu', all of which go on flowering throughout the summer.

Flowers June–October. Approximate height and spread 2.5 × 2 metres (8 × 6 feet).

SHRUBS
Japanese maples (Acer palmatum and A.p. 'Dissectum')
These are among the most beautiful small foliage shrubs there

Clematis 'Nelly Moser' does best in part-shade since too much sun causes the flower colour to fade.

are, with lovely leaves of bright green, in shades of red or purple, and even, in the case of one very recent introduction (*A.p.* 'Ukigumo'), variegated green, cream and pink. *Acer palmatum*'s leaves are, as its name suggests, hand-shaped, while *A.p.* 'Dissectum' has deeply dissected, feathery leaves. Many varieties have very good autumn colour, and most form very small, umbrella-shaped trees with an attractive outline in the winter months. Most will tolerate some lime but they must have shelter from cold winds and late spring frosts. They also need dappled shade: strong midday sun can scorch the foliage and cause quite serious damage. They are ideal focal points in a border.

Approximate height and spread after five years 80 centimetres × 1 metre (2½ × 3 feet); after ten years 1.2 × 1.5 metres (4 × 5 feet).

Spotted laurel (Aucuba japonica)
Much loved by the Victorians but out of fashion for many years, will grow happily in practically any type of soil, including a limy one, and will also tolerate deep shade. Female forms will produce clusters of bright red berries in autumn and keep them throughout the winter, but only if there is a male form nearby. Look for 'Crotonifolia' (male), which has large leaves speckled with gold, and 'Variegata' (female), whose smaller leaves are splashed with gold and yellow over about half their area. It grows quite large but you can cut it back, so it's a good choice for the back of a border or very shady corner.

Approximate height and spread after five years 1.2 × 1.2 metres (4 × 4 feet); after ten years 1.8 × 1.8 metres (5½ × 5½ feet).

The delicate foliage of the Japanese maple *Acer palmatum* 'Dissectum', seen here in a blaze of autumn colour, needs protection from direct sun; it's a superb feature shrub for a shady border.

Dogwood (Cornus)

Another excellent, accommodating shrub for small gardens since many varieties provide very attractive plain or variegated foliage in spring and summer, and vivid bark – scarlet or yellow – in the winter months. It will tolerate waterlogged soil and some lime, and though it does also grow in full sun, it will grow happily in shade. Good varieties to look out for include *Cornus alba* 'Elegantissima', which has beautiful pale green and white variegated foliage, and 'Spaethii' which has variegated gold and green leaves; both of these have brilliant red stems in winter. 'Westonbirt' is another attractive dogwood with fresh green foliage and the brightest red stems of all. *C. stolonifera* 'Flaviramea' has soft green foliage which turns yellow in autumn, revealing butter-yellow stems – a good contrast to the red-stemmed varieties. To get the best and brightest-coloured bark, you need to prune the stems hard back each spring which means that the shrub never grows bigger than the amount of growth it can make in one season.

Approximate height and spread after five years (if unpruned) 2.5 × 3 metres (8 × 10 feet); after ten years 2.5 × 4 metres (8 × 13 feet).

False castor-oil plant (Fatsia japonica)

Often thought of as a houseplant, but in fact it's extremely hardy and thrives in deep to medium shade. It's what's known as an architectural shrub because of the bold, dramatic shape of its large, handsome, glossy, evergreen leaves. In spring it produces spikes of creamy-white flowers rather like golf balls, which eventually turn into clusters of black berries. Removing these will encourage the plant to produce larger leaves. There is a variegated version, but it is nothing like as hardy as its plain green cousin.

Approximate height and spread after five years 1 × 1 metre (3 × 3 feet); after ten years 2 × 2 metres (6 × 6 feet).

Garrya elliptica

An evergreen, grown mainly for its long, pale, grey-green catkins in winter. Some people feel that the rather dull green foliage during the rest of the year is too high a price to pay, but if you want to grow one, make sure it's 'James Roof', the catkins of which are extra long.

Approximate height and spread after five years 2.5 × 1.5 metres (8 × 5 feet); after ten years 3.5 × 2.5 metres (12 × 8 feet).

Chinese witch hazel (Hamamelis mollis)
This shrub is grown for its sweetly scented, yellow, spider-like flowers which appear all up the bare stems in winter and early spring. They're followed by large, oval or even round leaves which have good autumn colour. The usual advice is to plant a scented winter flowerer like this one near a window or where you'll pass it frequently, but it's usually too cold to have windows open in winter and prominent places you pass frequently deserve something that's more spectacular in spring and summer too. Perhaps the most beautiful form is *H. m.* 'Pallida' which has silvery-yellow flowers and attractive lustrous leaves, while *H.* × 'Jelena' and *H.* 'Ruby Glow', which have coppery-orange and coppery-red flowers respectively, are also worth considering.

Approximate height and spread after five years 1.5 × 2 metres (5 × 6 feet); after ten years 3 × 4 metres (10 × 13 feet).

Hydrangeas
These are among the most spectacular summer-flowering shrubs. There are many different sorts, of which the best known are the 'mop-head' varieties, with large, round heads of flowers, and the 'lace-caps' which have flatter flowerheads. They're happy in medium shade and will grow on most moist soils, though the flower colour is affected by acidity or alkalinity – many forms are blue on acid soil and pink on limy soil. Look for *Hydrangea macrophylla* 'Hamburg' or 'Mme Emile Mouillère' (both 'mop-heads') and *H. m.* 'Mariesii Perfecta' or 'White Wave' which has white outer flowers and pink or blue central ones depending on the soil (all 'lace-caps').

Approximate height and spread after five years 1 × 1.2 metres (3 × 4 feet); after ten years 2 × 2 metres (6 × 6 feet).

Pachysandra terminalis
This plant is happiest on a neutral or acid soil and forms a carpet of serrated, diamond-shaped, light green leaves and spikes of small white flowers in mid-spring. It will thrive in deep shade, provided there's enough moisture. It can be a little invasive.

Approximate height and spread after five years 20 centi-metres × 1 metre (8 inches × 3 feet); after ten years 30 centimetres × 1.4 metres (1 × 5 feet).

Firethorn (Pyracantha)
An ideal shrub for training against a shady wall. It has glossy,

54. *Rodgersia podophylla*

3. *Hedera helix* 'Goldheart'

19. *Photinia* × 'Red Robin'

18. *Weigela florida* 'Variegata'

55. *Geranium nodosum*

The north-facing border shown in the plan on page 155 a year after planting.

16. *Berberis thunbergii* 'Aurea'

52. Bowles' golden grass

53. *Viola labradorica*

. *Lonicera tellmanniana*

50. *Brunnera macrophylla*

47. *Hosta* 'Honeybells'

1. *Hydrangea petiolaris*

12. *Prunus* 'Pink Shell'

49. *Hosta fortunei* 'Aurea'

46. *Rheum* 'Ace of Hearts'

51. *Heuchera* 'Palace Purple'

48. *Hosta* 'Buckshaw Blue'

20. *Sopraea* × *bumalda* 'Goldflame'

15. *Eleagnus pungens* 'Maculata'

evergreen leaves, white flowers in early summer, and yellow, orange or red berries in autumn. Good varieties include *Pyracantha coccinea* 'Mojave', with orange-red berries; *P.* 'Orange Glow', with very dark foliage and orange berries; and *P.* 'Soleil d'Or', with mid-green leaves and deep yellow berries.

Flowers May to June. Approximate height and spread after five years 2 × 1.2 metres (6 × 4 feet); after ten years 3.5 × 2 metres (12 × 6 feet).

Willow (Salix)
Another large family with many members worth considering for moist shade. Of the smaller-growing ones *Salix* 'Boydii', which has round, green leaves covered with woolly down when young, forms a gnarled-looking bush which never reaches more than 50 × 70 centimetres (1½ × 2½ feet) – ideal for the front of a border or even for a trough. Eventually reaching about twice the size but even more attractive is the woolly willow (*S. lanata*), with its grey leaves and small, yellowish-grey catkins which appear at the same time as the new leaves. *S. hastata* 'Wehrhahnii' has masses of large, silvery-white catkins on dark purplish stems and eventually forms a rounded, spreading bush approximately 1.2 × 1.2 metres (4 × 4 feet).

Of the medium-sized willows, the coyote willow (*S. exigua*) is a superb background shrub with very fine, long, silky, silver leaves, as well as pale yellow catkins in spring. It will reach 3–4 metres (10–13 feet) in ten years, but produces more attractive foliage if it's pruned hard back every three or four years.

Golden elder (Sambucus nigra 'Aurea'*)*
Elder adds a splash of brightness to a shady border. It produces its brightest-coloured foliage on new wood, so it's best pruned back hard each spring, which also limits its size to the amount of growth it can make in one season. Its showier relative, the golden cut-leaved elder (*Sambucus racemosa* 'Plumosa Aurea'), which has very deeply cut, divided foliage, needs more light, though it will thrive in dappled shade.

Approximate height and spread after five years (unpruned) 3 × 2 metres (10 × 6 feet); after ten years 4 × 3.5 metres (13 × 12 feet).

Christmas box (Sarcococca humilis)
A dwarf, evergreen, thicket-forming shrub that has narrow,

pointed, glossy green leaves and sweetly scented, small white flowers as early as February. It needs a rich soil, but will tolerate some alkalinity, and will grow in deep shade though not quite as well as it does with a little more light.

Approximate height and spread after five years 25 × 30 centimetres (10 × 12 inches); after ten years 50 × 40 centimetres (18 × 16 inches).

Skimmia

Another invaluable small evergreen shrub, provided it gets the right soil conditions – it won't tolerate any alkalinity and dislikes extremes of waterlogging and drought. It has shiny aromatic leaves, scented white flowers in late spring, and clusters of shiny red or white berries in autumn. To be sure of berries you need to plant at least one male with any number of females. Good varieties include *Skimmia japonica* 'Nymans' or 'Foremanii' (both female) and *S. j.* 'Rubella', a male form which has short, fat pokers of deep red buds which open to blush-white, sweetly scented flowers.

Approximate height and spread after five years 40 × 40 centimetres (16 × 16 inches); after ten years 60 × 60 centimetres (2 × 2 feet).

Snowberry (Symphoricarpos)

Another shrub grown primarily for its berries – not only white, but many shades of pink as well. Some forms produce lots of suckers which can be a nuisance, so make sure you go for a non-suckering variety like *S.* × *doorenbosii* 'Magic Berry', with small mauve-carmine berries, or *S.* × *d.* 'Mother of Pearl', which is a semi-weeping form with large, white, pink-tinged berries.

Approximate height and spread after five years 1.5 × 1 metre (5 × 3 feet); after ten years 2.5 × 2 metres (8 × 6 feet).

Viburnum

This family of plants has a member to suit practically every garden situation.

Viburnum davidii, which forms an attractive, low, spreading, evergreen shrub, has large, leathery, dark green, glossy leaves. The white flowers in June are followed by striking turquoise fruits, provided there is a male plant around to pollinate the female. It's not always easy to be sure you've got bushes of both sexes, but if you have enough room, plant at least three and so increase the odds!

54. *Rodgersia podophylla*

3. *Hedera helix* 'Goldheart'

18. *Weigela florida* 'Variegata'

19. *Photinia frazerii* 'Red Robin'

The north-facing border shown in the plan on page 155 five years after planting.

55. *Geranium nodosum*

53. *Viola labradorica*

52. Bowles' golden grass

16. *Berberis thunbergii* 'Aurea'

2. *Lonicera tellmanniana*

50. *Brunnera macrophylla*

1. *Hydrangea petiolaris*

12. *Prunus* 'Pink Shell'

46. *Rheum* 'Ace of Hearts'

49. *Hosta fortunei* 'Aurea'

48. *Hosta* 'Buckshaw Blue'

51. *Heuchera* 'Palace Purple'

47. *Hosta* 'Honeybells'

20. *Spiraea × bumalda* 'Goldflame'

15. *Eleagnus pungens* 'Maculata'

Approximate height and spread after five years 80 × 80 centimetres (2½ × 2½ feet); after ten years 1.2 × 1.2 metres (4 × 4 feet).

The guelder rose (Viburnum opulus) is even more accommodating – it will grow in waterlogged or dry soil and is tolerant of acidity and alkalinity. *Viburnum opulus* 'Sterile', the snowball shrub, produces, as its common name suggests, white snowball-like flowerheads in May or June. As its botanical name indicates, it doesn't bear any berries, whereas *V. o.* 'Notcutt's Variety' produces both white 'lace-cap' flowers not unlike those of the hydrangea and large clusters of translucent red berries in autumn. It's also worth thinking about the much smaller *V. o.* 'Compactum', which has white lace-cap flowers and red fruits but reaches only half the size of the other two. A viburnum that divides opinion sharply is *V. rhytidophyllum*, which makes a large shrub with huge, leathery, deeply veined leaves that have grey-brown, felty undersides which droop in cold weather. It has heads of buff white flowers, then red berries which eventually turn black. Some people think it's dull, others regard it as a striking, architectural shrub – an acquired taste perhaps, but good in a shady corner. It can grow quite a lot bigger than the other viburnums mentioned here.

Approximate height and spread after five years 1.5 × 1.5 metres (5 × 4 feet); after ten years 3 × 3 metres (10 × 10 feet).

HERBACEOUS PLANTS

Monkshood (Aconitum)

With its tall spikes of hooded, dark blue flowers and glossy, deeply divided leaves, this is a good choice for the back of a partially shaded border, though since it is poisonous in all its parts it is best avoided if you have small children. Good varieties include: *Aconitum napellus* 'Bressingham Spire', *A. carmichaelii* 'Arendsii' (both deep blue) or the shorter-growing, creamy-yellow-flowered *A. orientale*.

Flowers July to August. Approximate height and spread after five years 1 metre × 40 centimetres (3 feet × 16 inches).

Lady's mantle (Alchemilla mollis)

A star among herbaceous plants. Its fresh green leaves look like carefully folded fans as they open, and it carries sprays of tiny yellow-green flowers for months on end. It will grow practically anywhere – in sun or shade, in soil that is damp or dry, acid or alkaline. It seeds itself with alacrity in the crevices of paving, in walls and steps, but usually looks so good that you just leave it there.

Flowers June to August. Approximate height and spread 50 × 30 centimetres (1½ × 1 foot).

Japanese anemones (Anemone × hybrida)
They provide late summer–early autumn colour with their masses of tall pink or white flowering stems. Good varieties to look out for include *Anemone × hybrida* 'Queen Charlotte', with semi-double, rich pink flowers with gold stamens, and *A. × hybrida* 'Alba' or the tall *A. × hybrida* 'Honorine Jobert', both with large white flowers.

Flowers August to October. Approximate height and spread 50–100 × 35 centimetres (1½–3 feet × 15 inches).

Columbines (Aquilegia)
Beautiful cottage-garden plants with flowers in a whole range of colours from white and blue through pink, red and yellow. Many of the widely available hybrids like 'McKana' or 'Mrs Scott Elliott' have bi-colour flowers – white and red, pink and yellow, and so on. Their foliage, a little like that of the maidenhair fern, is also attractive. They like dappled shade under trees or shrubs.

Flowers May to August. Approximate height and spread 60 × 40 centimetres (2 feet × 16 inches).

Astilbes
Tolerant of really damp soil, they are usually grown for their elegant plumes of tiny flowers in shades of pink, red and white, but their ferny foliage is equally attractive. Good forms of the tall-growing *Astilbe × arendsii* include the red 'Fanal' and the rose-pink *A. × a.* 'Federsee', while for the front of the border the much smaller varieties, *A. chinensis* 'Pumila', which has mauve-pink flowers, and *A. simplicifolia* 'Bronze Elegance', which has creamy salmon-pink flowers and lovely bronze-tinged foliage, would be excellent choices.

Flowers June to August. Approximate height and spread 120 × 50 centimetres (4 × 1½ feet); dwarf varieties 30 × 50 centimetres (1 × 1½ feet).

Masterwort (Astrantia major)
It makes you wonder how such a beautiful plant got such an ugly common name! Its pink, cream and green flowers with their pincushion centres really are exquisite, like miniature

Victorian posies. There is a form of *Astrantia major* – 'Sunningdale Variegated' – whose foliage is marked with a lighter green fading to cream, to give interest in the border after the flowers have faded.

Flowers June to September. Approximate height and spread 60 × 40 centimetres (2 feet × 16 inches).

Elephant's ears (Bergenia)

They have very attractive, large, rounded, evergreen leaves, some of which take on a bronze or red tint in winter. They also have spikes of white, pink or red flowers in spring and summer. Good varieties to look out for include *Bergenia cordifolia* 'Purpurea' which has large, wavy, round leaves that turn a purplish-red in winter and magenta flowers on and off throughout the summer; *B.* 'Abendglut' with neat, crinkle-edged leaves, good autumn colour and vivid rose-red flowers; and *B.* 'Ballawley', the largest of all, with good autumn colour and rose-red flowers in spring, and occasionally a few in autumn.

Flowers March onwards according to variety. Approximate height and spread 30–60 centimetres × 30–60 centimetres (15 inches–2 feet × 15 inches–2 feet).

Marsh marigold (Caltha palustris)

As the name suggests, this plant likes it really damp and will even grow in shallow water. It has shiny, round leaves and bright, buttercup-yellow flowers in spring. The double-flowered variety, *Caltha palustris* 'Plena', is even more attractive, while the white-flowered variety *C. p.* 'Alba' has

Columbines (*Aquilegia*), in a range of delicate colours, thrive in part-shade.

simple white flowers with bright gold stamens and sometimes produces a second crop in autumn (this one won't grow in water).

Flowers March to May. Approximate height and spread 20 × 35 centimetres (8 × 13 inches).

Above: Christmas rose (*Helleborus niger*).

Left: Bleeding heart (*Dicentra spectabilis*).

Bugbane (Cimicifuga)
Another plant a thousand times more attractive than its name. It has lovely ferny foliage and in autumn produces clusters of 'bottle brush' flowers on tall stems, which turn into attractive lime-green seedheads – a good plant for the back of the border. Look for *Cimicifuga simplex* 'White Pearl'.

Flowers August to October. Approximate height and spread 130 × 70 centimetres (4½ feet × 28 inches).

Bleeding heart (Dicentra spectabilis)
A beautiful, late spring–early summer flowering plant, with graceful arching stems of small flowers like deep pink hearts

175

with a white teardrop underneath. It also has attractive ferny foliage which dies down in mid-summer, so don't panic and think you've somehow managed to kill it off! There is also a very beautiful white version, *Dicentra spectabilis* 'Alba'.

Flowers May to June. Approximate height and spread 60 × 50 centimetres (2 × 1½ feet).

Christmas rose (Helleborus niger) and Lenten rose (Helleborus orientalis)

These are members of a family no shady garden should be without. The Christmas rose (more usually in flower in January than at Christmas, incidentally) has leathery, evergreen leaves, and large, waxy, white flowers with gold stamens that last for weeks. The Lenten rose, which flowers in late winter, has similar-shaped flowers but in a whole range of colours from white and green through mauve-pinks to purple. It's a slightly larger plant than the Christmas rose and both of them are happy in limy soil.

Flowers: January to March – Christmas rose; February to April – Lenten rose. Approximate height and spread: 30 × 40 centimetres (12 × 16 inches) – Christmas rose; 50 × 50 centimetres (1½ × 1½ feet) – Lenten rose.

Coral flower (Heuchera sanguinea)

Makes good weed-suppressing clumps of scalloped evergreen leaves in dappled shade and rich soil and produces tall, thin stems of tiny red or pink flowers. An interesting variety with mounds of bronzy, wine-coloured foliage and sprays of tiny, white flowers is *Heuchera sanguinea* 'Palace Purple' – a good contrast with a silvery-leaved ground-cover plant like dead nettle (*Lamium* species).

Flowers April to June. Approximate height and spread 60 × 50 centimetres (2 × 1½ feet).

Plantain lily (Hosta)

An outstanding foliage plant and a reason all on its own for having a shady area in your garden. There are many different ones to choose from, some with very small leaves, like *Hosta minor*, and some with huge leaves like *H. sieboldiana* 'Elegans' which has blue-green, deeply ribbed leaves almost 30 centimetres (1 foot) wide. There are gold-leaved varieties, like *H. fortunei* 'Aurea', and others in many shades of green and blue as well as the variegated forms like *H.* 'Thomas Hogg', whose elegant, pointed leaves have creamy margins. Hostas also flower, producing spikes of either mauve or white flowers, and have good autumn colour before the leaves finally rot away. The only snag with hostas is that slugs and snails love them almost as much as discerning gardeners, and can reduce a large leaf to something resembling a colander overnight. Some form of anti-slug precaution is essential.

Flowers July to August. Approximate height and spread (of foliage) 30–60 centimetres × 30 centimetres–1 metre (1–2 feet × 1–3 feet).

Dead nettle (Lamium maculatum)

A marvellous ground-cover plant for shade, spreading quickly and covering a large area with attractive, variegated foliage, creating areas of light among the shade. *Lamium maculatum* 'Beacon Silver', *L. m.* 'White Nancy' and *L. m.* 'Shell-Pink' all have silver-variegated leaves and produce clear pink, ivory white and shell-pink flowers respectively. After the flowers have faded, it's worth trimming the plant with shears to remove the dead flower heads and any upward-growing leafy shoots to keep it close to the ground.

Flowers May to July. Approximate height and spread 20 × 50 centimetres (8 × 18 inches).

Omphalodes cappadocica

A very useful ground-cover plant for growing under acid-loving shrubs since it does best in peaty soil and part-shade, but it will still give a good show in neutral soil. Although its oval, slightly crinkled leaves are not spectacular, it produces sprays of the most vivid gentian-blue flowers, not unlike those of forget-me-nots but larger, for weeks on end.

Flowers April to May. Approximate height and spread 20 × 40 centimetres (8 × 16 inches).

Knotweed (Persicaria)

Another large family, some of whose members are true garden thugs, smothering everything in sight and to be avoided, while others are better-behaved and make good, weed-suppressing clumps. They carry masses of pink or red flowers, rather like fluffy pokers, in summer and autumn. A good variety to look out for is the low-growing *Persicaria affinis* 'Dimity', whose pink flowers darken to a rusty red with age and whose fresh green foliage turns russet brown in winter and stays on the plant until new growth appears in spring. If it does get over-ambitious, simply chop it back with a spade. The much taller

Above: Subtle winter colour beneath a tree from the pale green *Helleborus corsicus*, snowdrops and the variegated leaves of *Arum italicum* 'Pictum'.

Above right: Primula pulverulenta thrives in damp shade.

P. bistorta 'Superba' is also a good variety with much larger, dock-like, light green leaves and large, clear pink flowers in early summer and sometimes again in early autumn.

Flowers: July to September – *P. affinis*; May and September – *P. bistorta*. Approximate height and spread 23 × 50 centimetres (9 × 18 inches) – *P. affinis*; 90 × 70 centimetres (3 feet × 2 feet 3 inches) – *P. bistorta*.

Solomon's seal (Polygonatum × hybridum)
One of those woodland plants with a quiet beauty. It has elegant arching stems with long, fresh green leaves all the way up, from which dangle small, white flowers rather like miniature white pears with a green base. There is a variegated form, *P. multiflorum* 'Variegatum', with leaves boldly striped in creamy white. As with hostas, slugs find the foliage irresistible.

Flowers May to June. Approximate height and spread 80 × 40 centimetres (2½ feet × 16 inches).

Primulas
Another large family with members for almost every garden situation. The lovely candelabra primulas (so called because

their flowers are arranged in whorls up their stems), *Primula japonica* and *P. beesiana*, and the drumstick primula (*P. denticulata*) all need a moist neutral or acid soil to do well. The auricula primulas with their lovely, bi-coloured flowers – rich reds, blues with gold markings – are also supposed to dislike lime, but they grow very well in chalky soil. The common primrose (*P. vulgaris*) will grow almost anywhere as long as the soil is rich and moist.

Flowers March to July. Approximate height and spread 30–60 × 30 centimetres (1–2 × 1 foot).

Lungwort (Pulmonaria)
An excellent ground-cover plant for moist shade. It bears sprays of small pink, white or blue flowers in spring, followed by clumps of weed-smothering, attractive leaves – spotted or silver-frosted. Good varieties to look out for include *Pulmonaria officinalis* 'Cambridge Blue', which has heart-shaped, spotted leaves and masses of blue flowers opening from pink buds, giving it a bi-colour effect; *P. saccharata* 'Sissinghurst White',

Busy Lizzie (*Impatiens*), in a wide range of colours, is the ideal annual for a shady border.

179

which has much larger leaves marbled with silver and large, white flowers; and *P. s.* 'Highdown', which has rich blue flowers.

Flowers March to May. Approximate height and spread 30 × 30 centimetres (1 × 1 foot).

Wake robin (Trillium grandiflorum)
A superb woodland plant, not as widely known as it deserves to be. In a moist acid soil (any lime will kill it), it produces clusters of three shiny mid-green leaves, above which appear its pure white, three petalled flowers.

Flowers March to May. Approximate height and spread 40 × 30 centimetres (16 × 12 inches).

Viola labradorica
An excellent ground-cover plant that seeds itself so freely when it's established that it could almost be a nuisance if it weren't so attractive! It has small, round, green leaves flushed with purple, while its flowers, produced in spring, are small mauve violets, whose colour is exactly the right tone for the leaves.

Flowers March to May. Approximate height and spread 10–15 × 30 centimetres (4–6 × 12 inches).

ANNUALS
While the vast majority of annuals really need a sunny position, there are a few which will do well in shade and they are such excellent plants that their quality almost compensates for the very limited choice.

Fibrous-rooted begonia (Begonia semperflorens)
These have flowers in white, red and pink and foliage that's green or wine red and will do very well in shade.

Flowers June to October. Approximate height and spread 15–25 × 25 centimetres (6–10 × 10 inches).

Busy Lizzie (Impatiens)
A superb choice for a shady border because it will go on flowering prolifically from June until the first frosts. It comes in a whole range of colours, from pure white through many shades of pink and salmon to orange, red and even violet, though in a shady spot paler colours – white, very pale pink or mauve – really do seem to gleam while brighter ones rather lose their impact. Again, it's a matter of personal taste, but a

clump, all the same colour, looks more effective than mixed colours. Unfortunately, many garden centres or even street markets sell annuals like busy Lizzie in mixed colours, so it's worth hunting out those which offer trays of a single colour.

Flowers June to November. Approximate height and spread 20–30 × 20 centimetres (8–12 × 8 inches).

Lobelia

An excellent space filler at the front of a border. Look for 'Crystal Palace', which has intense blue flowers set off to perfection by its bronzy foliage; 'Mrs Clibran', deep blue with a white eye; and 'White Lady', which sometimes produces a few pale blue flowers along with the white. For hanging baskets and containers, try a trailing variety like 'Blue Cascade' or 'Sapphire' whose intense blue flowers have a white eye.

Flowers June to September. Approximate height and spread 15 × 15 centimetres (6 × 6 inches).

Monkey flower (Mimulus)

Produces masses of small, trumpet-shaped flowers in a range of brilliant colours – red, orange, yellow, burgundy, pink and white – and many of them are spotted or blotched with a contrasting colour. Once the first flush of flowers is over, trim the plants back to encourage more flowers.

Flowers June to September. Approximate height and spread 20 × 20 centimetres (8 × 8 inches).

Baby blue eyes (Nemophila insignis)

A very pretty, front-of-the-border plant with sky-blue, cup-shaped flowers with white centres carried above slightly trailing, ferny foliage. It's a hardy annual, so it can be sown straight into the ground where you want it to flower.

Flowers June to September. Approximate height and spread 15 × 15 centimetres (6 × 6 inches).

Heartsease (Viola tricolor)

Our native pansy has really delightful small flowers in yellow, violet and mauve – usually all three together. It's happy in dappled shade and in most soil types including sand. It's actually a short-lived perennial but best treated as an annual. Once established, it will seed itself and flower from May.

Flowers May to October. Approximate height and spread 10–20 × 10 centimetres (4–8 × 4 inches).

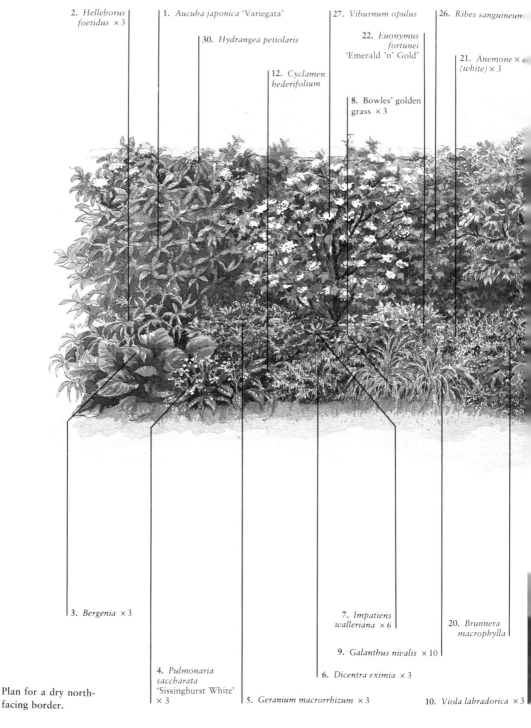

2. *Helleborus foetidus* ×3

1. *Aucuba japonica* 'Variegata'

30. *Hydrangea petiolaris*

27. *Viburnum opulus*

26. *Ribes sanguineum*

22. *Euonymus fortunei* 'Emerald 'n' Gold'

21. *Anemone* × (white) ×3

12. *Cyclamen hederifolium*

8. Bowles' golden grass ×3

3. *Bergenia* ×3

7. *Impatiens walleriana* ×6

20. *Brunnera macrophylla*

9. *Galanthus nivalis* ×10

4. *Pulmonaria saccharata* 'Sissinghurst White' ×3

6. *Dicentra eximia* ×3

Plan for a dry north-facing border.

5. *Geranium macrorrhizum* ×3

10. *Viola labradorica* ×3

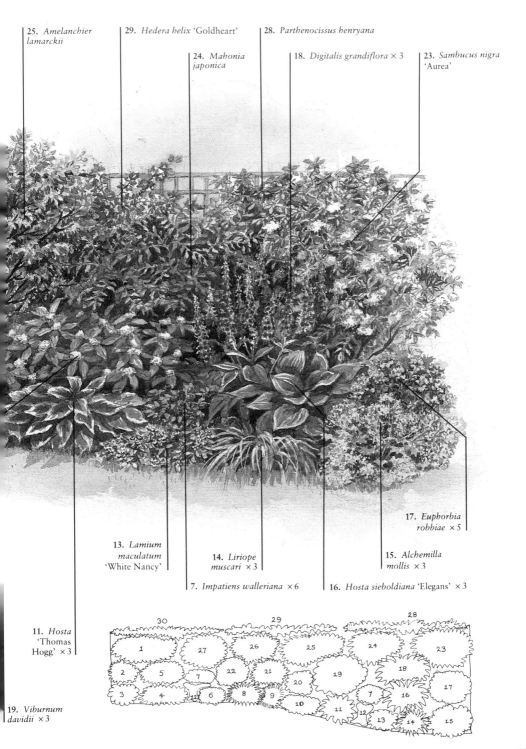

25. *Amelanchier lamarckii*

29. *Hedera helix* 'Goldheart'

28. *Parthenocissus henryana*

24. *Mahonia japonica*

18. *Digitalis grandiflora* × 3

23. *Sambucus nigra* 'Aurea'

17. *Euphorbia robbiae* × 5

13. *Lamium maculatum* 'White Nancy'

14. *Liriope muscari* × 3

15. *Alchemilla mollis* × 3

7. *Impatiens walleriana* × 6

16. *Hosta sieboldiana* 'Elegans' × 3

11. *Hosta* 'Thomas Hogg' × 3

19. *Viburnum davidii* × 3

BULBS

Many flowering bulbs thrive in woodland conditions during spring and autumn when the trees under which they grow are bare of leaves and so allow a reasonable amount of light and moisture through.

Arum italicum 'Pictum'

An exotic-looking plant which produces heads of poisonous, bright orange berries like drumsticks in late summer followed by the leaves, which are spear-shaped, glossy dark green, strikingly marked with grey and cream, and which keep appearing until the spring.

Flowers (insignificant) April to May. Approximate height and spread 30–45 × 30 centimetres (12–18 × 12 inches). Plant 30 centimetres (12 inches) apart.

Glory of the snow (Chionodoxa luciliae)

It has very pretty blue-lilac flowers with a white eye. If left undisturbed, they will seed themselves.

Flowers March to April. Approximate height 5 centimetres (2 inches). Plant 8–10 centimetres (3–4 inches) apart.

Cyclamen hederifolium

Produces masses of deep pink or white flowers which are thumbnail-sized versions of the pot plants we buy. The beautiful, ivy-shaped leaves, which are marbled with silver, follow the flowers. Cyclamen will tolerate some degree of alkalinity, but a soil just either side of neutral suits them best.

Flowers August to November. Approximate height 3 centimetres (1 inch). Plant 8–10 centimetres (3–4 inches) apart.

Winter aconite (Eranthis hyemalis)

With its bright yellow, buttercup-like flowers set on a ruff of dark green leaves, it is one of the first bulbs to appear after Christmas. It's happy in moist soils – acid or alkaline – and in shade. The tubers are usually sold dry, and can become very hard, so soak them overnight in water before planting or, if possible, put them in a seed tray of moist compost for a couple of weeks.

Flowers January to March. Approximate height 3–5 centimetres (1–2 inches). Plant 5–8 centimetres (2–3 inches) apart.

Dog's-tooth violet (Erythronium dens-canis)

Has beautiful, delicate, nodding flowers in shades of white, pink, lilac and carmine, and attractive mottled leaves. Good varieties to look for include *Erythronium dens-canis* 'White Splendour', 'Rose Beauty' and 'Lilac Wonder'. Again, the tubers dislike drying out, so buy them from a reputable supplier who lifts and despatches them the same day, and plant them as soon as you receive them.

Flowers March to April. Approximate height 10–15 centimetres (4–6 inches). Plant 15–20 centimetres (6–8 inches) apart.

Snowdrops (Galanthus nivalis)
These are among the earliest of the spring-flowering bulbs and their pure white flowers show up very well in shade. They tolerate most types of soil, though in a sandy soil you need to dig in plenty of moisture-retaining organic matter before planting. There are lots of different varieties – some with double flowers, like *Galanthus nivalis* 'Flore Pleno', and some with beautiful green markings on the petals, like *G. n.* 'Viridapicis' – and they are best planted 'in the green', just after they have flowered. Although you can also buy them as dried bulbs in autumn, they may take a couple of years to settle down and start growing well.

Flowers January to March. Approximate height 5 centimetres (2 inches). Plant 5–8 centimetres (2–3 inches) apart.

Spring snowflakes (Leucojum vernum)
Related to snowdrops, they have longer stems and more rounded, white, scented flowers.

Flowers March to May. Approximate height 8 centimetres (3 inches). Plant 15–20 centimetres (6–8 inches) apart.

Grape hyacinths (Muscari armeniacum)
With their dense spikes of vivid blue flowers, they are widely grown, though this particular variety, which will tolerate shade, is taller and has paler blue flowers than the most commonly grown variety, *Muscari botryoides*

Flowers April to May. Approximate height 10–15 centimetres (4–6 inches). Plant 10–15 centimetres (4–6 inches) apart.

Daffodils (Narcissus cyclamineus)
Daffodils will cope with shady conditions, provided they are the types of smaller species, not the large garden hybrids. Look for *Narcissus cyclamineus* 'February Gold'; the smaller 'Tête

Winter-flowering *Mahonia*
× *media* 'Charity'.

à Tête', with two or three flowers on each stem which often start opening as soon as the stem has emerged from the ground; or the lovely white 'Jenny'. Like all the members of this family they need well-drained but moisture-retentive soil, and if you feed them after they've flowered with a rose or tomato fertilizer, they'll go on flowering for many years.

Flowers February to April. Approximate height 15–30 centimetres (6–12 inches). Plant 20–30 centimetres (8–12 inches) apart.

DRY SHADE

As already explained, dry shade is one of the most difficult garden situations to fill with suitable plants, but by no means impossible. You can help a lot by improving the soil as much as you are able with moisture-retentive organic matter before you plant, and by mulching the border with a good thick layer of more of the same in the autumn and again in spring. If part of the problem is caused by a dense canopy of overhanging branches, removing a few selectively will improve matters. But

do make sure, before you get busy with the saw, that the tree isn't covered by any kind of preservation order. If it is, you'll have to get permission before you do any work on it.

Snowy mespilus (*Amelanchier lamarckii*) in spring.

CLIMBERS
Ivy (*Hedera helix* or *H. colchica*), the climbing hydrangea (*Hydrangea petiolaris*) and Virginia creeper (*Parthenocissus* species) will all tolerate dry shade. (See pages 160–1.)

SHRUBS
Snowy mespilus (Amelanchier lamarckii)
A shrub (or small tree) with a long season of interest – from its clouds of small, white flowers along with new bronzy foliage in spring to its superb yellow or red autumn colour. It's supposed to grow really successfully only on acid soils, but seems to cope well enough with neutral and even chalky soils (if they are moist) to make it well worthwhile.

Approximate height and spread after five years 4 × 3 metres (13 × 10 feet); after ten years 7.5 × 6 metres (25 × 20 feet).

Barberry (Berberis)

A family of tough, accommodating shrubs, some of which will put on a reasonable show in dry shade. They include the evergreens *Berberis darwinii*, which has small, jagged, evergreen leaves and clusters of bright orange flowers in spring, and *B. stenophylla*, which has long, thin leaves, olive on top, silver underneath, and double, yellow flowers hanging along its curving branches in spring. Among the deciduous barberries, the green- and gold-leaved varieties of *B. thunbergii* will tolerate shade, though the many purple-, red- and pink-leaved ones need sun to maintain their colour.

Approximate height and spread after five years 1.5 × 1.5 metres (5 × 5 feet); after ten years 2.2 × 2 metres (7 × 6 feet).

Spindle (Euonymus fortunei)

A very versatile evergreen shrub that will either climb up a shady wall, if pointed in the right direction, or spread along the ground. There are several good variegated forms: among the green-and-golds look for *Euonymus fortunei* 'Emerald 'n' Gold' and 'Gold Tip'; and among the quieter cream-and-greens *E. f.* 'Emerald Gaiety' and, for climbing, *E. f.* 'Variegatus', both of whose leaves are flushed pink in very cold weather.

Approximate height and spread after five years 60 centimetres × 1 metres (2 × 3 feet); after ten years 60 centimetres × 2 metres (2 × 6 feet); climbing – after ten years 4 × 4 metres (13 × 13 feet).

Holly (Ilex aquifolium)

Like its traditional partner ivy, it will put up with dry shade and the variegated forms will brighten a dark corner. Both *Ilex* 'Silver Queen', with white markings, and *I.* 'Golden King', with gold variegations, are good varieties. To confuse matters, 'Silver Queen' is a male form (no berries) while 'Golden King' is female (bearing berries provided there is a male somewhere in the area). Of the plain green hollies *I.* 'J.C. van Tol' has a lot to offer – almost spineless, it bears glossy green leaves and regular crops of red berries without an extra pollinator.

Approximate height and spread after five years 2 × 1.5 metres (6 × 5 feet); after ten years 4 × 2.5 metres (13 × 8 feet).

Winter-flowering jasmine (Jasminum nudiflorum)

Marvellous value in a small garden and really lights up a north wall. In some years it will start producing its starry yellow flowers on bare green stems as early as November and carry on till March. It's a wall shrub rather than a climber and so will need some support, but it's at its best trailing downwards, so tie it back near the top of the wall or fence and allow it to spill over.

Approximate height and spread after five years 1.5 × 1.5 metres (5 × 5 feet); after ten years 2 × 2 metres (6 × 6 feet).

Oregon grape (Mahonia aquifolium)
A superb shrub for dry shade. It has long, jagged, evergreen leaves, sprays of scented, yellow flowers in early spring, and in autumn the leaves turn a purplish-red. It can get a little straggly, particularly in deep shade, but if you cut back the old, woody growth to ground level every three or four years, it will produce new growth very quickly. *Mahonia japonica* has foliage that is deep green on acid soil and is tinged with red on a limy soil. It also has very fragrant yellow flowers which sometimes appear before Christmas. Look out for the hybrid *M. × media* 'Charity', which is one of the best.

Approximate height and spread of *M. aquifolium* after five years 80 centimetres × 1 metre (2½ × 3 feet); after ten years 1 × 2 metres (3 × 6 feet); of *M. japonica* after five years 1.5 × 1.8 metres (5 × 5½ feet); after ten years 2.5 × 2.8 metres (8 × 9 feet).

Cherry laurel (Prunus laurocerasus 'Otto Luyken')
A useful evergreen that will tolerate anything except extremely dry and/or extremely limy soil. It has glossy foliage and, in spring, candles of small, creamy white flowers.

Approximate height and spread after five years 1 × 1 metre (3 × 3 feet); after ten years 1.5 × 2 metres (5 × 6 feet).

Stag's horn sumach (Rhus typhina)
This seems a very exotic shrub to be growing in such difficult conditions. It has beautiful, fern-like foliage which turns scarlet in autumn, and in winter the bare tree, with the branching form that gives it its common name, is covered in reddish-brown, furry bark. It also has large, velvety, brown cones in autumn. It's suckers and seedlings may cause problems.

Approximate height and spread after five years 2 × 2 metres (6 × 6 feet); after ten years 4 × 4 metres (13 × 13 feet).

Flowering currant (Ribes sanguineum 'Pulborough Scarlet')
With its rose-red flowers in April or early May, it does

Foxgloves (*Digitalis*) thrive in shade and tolerate most soil types.

remarkably well in dry shade, as it does also in heavy clay. It reaches its final height very fast and is a useful shrub for achieving a quick effect.

Approximate height and spread after five years 1.5 × 1 metre (5 × 3 feet); after ten years 2 × 2 metres (6 × 6 feet).

Golden elder (Sambucus nigra 'Aurea')
It will also tolerate dry shade, though it will lose some of its golden colour, becoming more golden-green. (See page 168.)

Skimmia
It will tolerate dry, but not extremely dry, conditions. (See page 169.)

Guelder rose (Viburnum opulus)
It will tolerate dry shade. (See page 172.)

Lesser periwinkle (Vinca minor)
This trailing, ground-covering, evergreen shrub will tolerate deep shade and dry soil. It's more attractive and better suited to small gardens than the ordinary periwinkle (*Vinca major*).

It flowers from April to June and among the best varieties are
Vinca minor 'Bowles' Variety', which has large, light blue
flowers, and 'Gertrude Jekyll', which has small, white ones.

Approximate height and spread after five years 15 × 40
centimetres (6 × 16 inches); after ten years 15 × 60 centimetres
(6 inches × 2 feet).

HERBACEOUS PLANTS
Bugle (Ajuga reptans)
It has short spikes of intense blue flowers in early summer and
is a good carpeter. There are some lovely variegated kinds,
though the green and pale buff 'Variegata' does better in deep
shade than the dark metallic purple 'Atropurpurea' and the
mottled wine-red 'Burgundy Glow'. They don't form such a
dense carpet as they would in a moist soil, but they do well
enough.

Flowers May to July. Approximate height and spread
15 centimetres × 1 metre (6 inches × 3 feet).

Lady's mantle (Alchemilla mollis)
It will also do well enough in dry shade. (See pages 172–3.)

Elephant's ears (Bergenia)
It won't flower as prolifically in dry shade as it will in moister
conditions, but its large, thick, leathery leaves are well worth
having. (See page 174.)

Siberian bugloss (Brunnera macrophylla)
A perennial relation of the forget-me-not, it has sprays of
similar bright blue flowers in spring. It also bears large, heart-
shaped leaves, though these won't be as big or as numerous
as they would be in a moister soil.

Flowers April to May. Approximate height and spread
45 × 45 centimetres (18 × 18 inches).

Eastern bleeding heart (Dicentra eximia)
This is a much bushier plant with more feathery foliage than
its native cousin, though its pink flowers, borne intermittently
throughout the summer after the first main flush in late spring,
are more tubular than heart-shaped. Bleeding heart (*Dicentra
spectabilis*) will tolerate dry shade to a degree, but *D. eximia*
does better.

Flowers May to October. Approximate height and spread
30 × 50 centimetres (12 × 18 inches).

Foxglove (Digitalis)

This plant will do well in most soils, given some shade. Our native foxglove, *Digitalis purpurea*, is, strictly speaking, a biennial (growing one year, flowering the next, then dying), but it may survive a year or two longer. It usually seeds itself pretty well, so continuity is not a problem.

Flowers June to August. Approximate height and spread 90 × 30 centimetres (3 × 1 feet).

Barrenwort (Epimedium)

Does best of all where there is some moisture in the soil, but even in dry shade it gives a good account of itself. They have attractively marked heart-shaped leaves and delicate spring flowers in yellow, crimson, orange, pink and cream depending on variety.

Flowers April to June. Approximate height and spread 30 × 30 centimetres (1 × 1 foot).

Spurge (Euphorbia)

Another large family with members for all situations. For dry shade the best is *Euphorbia robbiae*, which has tall rosettes of leathery, dark green leaves topped all summer long with yellow-green flowers which take on bronze tints in autumn.

Flowers April to June. Approximate height and spread 60 × 60 centimetres+ (2 × 2 feet+).

Cranesbill (Geranium)

These plants do sterling work in dry shade, particularly the *Geranium macrorrhizum* varieties. These have lovely, aromatic, semi-evergreen leaves, which sometimes turn red in autumn, and sprays of flowers in white or pink. Look for G. *m.* 'Album', whose flowers are blush-white rather than pure white; G. *m.* 'Ingwersen's Variety', with soft, mauve-pink flowers; and G. *m.* 'Bevan's Variety', with taller stems of vivid magenta-pink flowers.

Flowers April to July. Approximate height and spread 40 × 40 centimetres (16 × 16 inches).

Stinking hellebore (Helleborus foetidus)

This sounds like a particularly unpleasant insult, but in fact it's an excellent plant for dry shade. It makes neat clumps of deep green, sharply divided, fan-shaped leaves and bears clusters of small, pale green, bell-shaped flowers in winter.

Flowers January to April. Approximate height and spread 60 × 40 centimetres (2 feet × 16 inches).

Dead nettle (Lamium maculatum)
Useful ground cover in dry shade, which is probably the one place in the garden where you could plant its invasive relative, *L. galeobdolon*, which has larger, variegated leaves. Dry shade prevents it from being too vigorous and swamping everything else in sight. (See page 177.)

Flowers May to June. Approximate height and spread 30 centimetres × 1 metre+ (1 × 3 feet+).

Lily-turf (Liriope muscari)
It has narrow, straplike, evergreen leaves and, in autumn, spikes of violet-blue flowers that look like the grape hyacinth.

Flowers August to October. Approximate height and spread 40 × 40 centimetres (16 × 16 inches).

Bowles' golden grass (Milium effusum 'Aureum')
This plant provides a real pool of sunshine in a shady spot, with its very fine golden leaves and sprays of tiny, gold, bead-like flowers in early summer. It looks especially good with the purple-leaved *Viola labradorica* and snowdrops.

Flowers April to May. Approximate height and spread 40 × 30 centimetres (16 × 12 inches).

Lungwort (Pulmonaria)
Does well in dry shade. (See pages 179–80.)

Piggy-back plant (Tolmiea menziesii 'Variegata')
So called because it produces small plantlets on top of its leaves, which will root if carefully removed and pressed into the ground. It has very attractive, round, yellow-speckled leaves, and though it's often sold as a houseplant it's perfectly hardy. The flowers are insignificant.

Approximate height and spread 30 × 30 centimetres (1 × 1 foot).

Viola labradorica
Does well in dry shade, though it's not as invasive as it is in moister soil – no bad thing! (See page 180.)

Waldsteinia ternata
A lovely evergreen carpeter with glossy, dark green, three-lobed leaves, which sometimes take on a bronze tint in winter, and sprays of golden-yellow flowers, rather like strawberry flowers, in spring.

Spurge (*Euphorbia robbiae*) is another good plant for difficult, dry, shady sites.

Flowers April to May. Approximate height and spread 8–10 centimetres × 1 metre (3–5 inches × 3 feet).

ANNUALS

No annuals will really thrive in dry shade, though if you have a few busy Lizzies (*Impatiens*) to spare it would be worth planting them out and taking a chance.

BULBS

Arum italicum 'Pictum'

It will grow well enough in dry shade beneath a wall provided there is some moisture below the surface and the bulbs are planted quite deep. (See page 184.)

Glory of the snow (Chionodoxa luciliae)

Will grow under deciduous trees or hedges. (See page 184.)

Meadow saffron (Colchicum speciosum)

They have pink, mauve or white flowers in September, and leaves that don't appear till spring. The flowers look rather

strange sprouting from naked earth, so you could try planting them among ground-cover plants.

Flowers September. Approximate height 15–18 centimetres (6–7 inches). Plant 10 centimetres (4 inches) apart.

Cyclamen hederifolium
Worth trying if you work plenty of organic matter into the top layer of soil before planting. (See page 184.)

Snowdrops (Galanthus nivalis)
Worth trying since they appear when there is most likely to be some moisture about. (See page 185.)

Bluebells (Hyacinthoides non-scripta)
These are also pretty tough and naturalize well under trees. They produce the classic blue flowers in spring and, if they are happy, will self-seed freely.

Flowers April to May. Approximate height 20 centimetres (8 inches). Plant 8 centimetres (3 inches) apart.

The stinking hellebore (*Helleborus foetidus*) will grow well in dry shade.

195

Ornithogalum nutans
A cousin of the star of Bethlehem, this plant has very attractive, pale grey-green and white star-shaped flowers with petals that curve back.

Flowers April to May. Approximate height 15–40 centimetres (6–16 inches). Plant 15 centimetres (6 inches) apart.

DENSE SHADE
Those plants marked 'C' will also tolerate really heavy clay.

CLIMBERS
Ivy (Hedera helix and H. colchica)
C. (See page 160.)

SHRUBS
Spotted laurel (Aucuba japonica and A. j. 'Variegata')
C. (See page 163.)

False castor-oil plant (Fatsia japonica)
(See page 164.)

Wintergreen (Gaultheria procumbens)
(See page 156.)

Japanese privet (Ligustrum japonicum)
It has very glossy, dark green leaves and is not as attractive as other privets, but it will grow where they won't!

Average height and spread after five years 60 × 40 centimetres (2 feet × 16 inches); after ten years 1.8 × 1 metre (5½ × 3 feet).

Pachysandra terminalis and P. t. 'Variegata'
(See page 165.)

Cherry laurel (Prunus laurocerasus 'Otto Luyken')
C. (See page 189.)

Christmas box (Sarcococca humilis)
(See pages 168–9.)

Snowberry (Symphoricarpos × doorenbosii)
C. (see page 169.)

Greater and lesser periwinkle (Vinca major and V. minor)
C. (See pages 190–1.)

HERBACEOUS PLANTS
Brunnera macrophylla
(See page 191.)

Lily-of-the-valley (Convallaria majalis)
With its superbly scented white flowers, it can become almost
a weed when it's established, though dense shade is likely to
keep it under reasonable control.
   Flowers April to May. Approximate height and spread
20 × 50 centimetres+ (8 × 18 inches+).

Spurge (Euphorbia robbiae)
(See page 192.)

Plantain lily
The variety *Hosta fortunei* only, with large, deeply ribbed,
plain green leaves and mauve flowers, will thrive in dense
shade provided the soil is always moist.
   Flowers June to August. Approximate height and spread
75 × 60 centimetres (2½ × 2 feet) C.

Dead nettle (Lamium maculatum/Lamium galeobdolon)
C. (See pages 177 and 193.)

PLANTING PLAN FOR DRY SHADE
See illustration on pages 182–3.

CLIMBERS
Allow 3 metres (10 feet) for each plant.

Hydrangea petiolaris. Fresh spring leaf colour/early summer
flowers. (See pages 160–1.)

Ivy (*Hedera helix* 'Goldheart'). Evergreen/bright variegation
for winter colour. (See page 160.)

Virginia creeper (*Parthenocissus henryana*). Lovely foliage all
summer/brilliant autumn colour. (See page 161.)

SHRUBS
Spotted laurel (*Aucuba japonica* 'Variegata'). Evergreen/
bright variegation for winter colour. (See page 163.)

Guelder rose (*Viburnum opulus*, e.g. 'Notcutt's Variety').
Lovely white lace-cap flowers/translucent red berries in
autumn. (See page 172.)

Flowering currant (*Ribes sanguineum*). Fast-growing with
attractive rose-red flowers in early summer. If the snowy
mespilus and guelder rose outgrow their space after five years
or so, the currant can be removed. (See pages 189–90.)

Snowy mespilus (*Amelanchier lamarckii*). Clouds of white
flowers in spring and lovely autumn colour. This and the
currant are both deciduous, so the variegated ivy behind takes
over in winter months. (See page 187.)

Mahonia japonica. Evergreen, with bright yellow flowers in
winter before the Virginia creeper is in leaf. Its red tints in
autumn tone with the Virginia creeper's. (See page 189.)

Golden elder (*Sambucus nigra* 'Aurea'). A splash of gold in the
corner. (See page 168.)

PERENNIALS AND SMALL SHRUBS
3 × stinking hellebore (*Helleborus foetidus*). The dark evergreen foliage will show up beautifully against the golden
variegated laurel. (See page 192.)

3 × *Geranium macrorrhizum* 'Ingwersen's Variety'. Attractive
pink flowers in early summer with aromatic, more or less
evergreen foliage. (See page 192.)

Euonymus fortunei 'Emerald 'n' Gold'. A bright evergreen
between two deciduous shrubs (guelder rose and flowering
currant) will give winter colour, and the green and gold
variegation will echo the ivy behind it to the right. (See page
188.)

3 × Japanese anemone (*Anemone × hybrida* 'Alba' or 'Honorine
Jobert'). The white flowers will show up beautifully against
the autumn colour of the snowy mespilus. (See page 173.)

Viburnum davidii. This will form quite a large clump in ten years, but can be cut back. (See pages 169–72.)

3 × foxglove (*Digitalis grandiflora*). The bronze-tinged yellow flowers in summer will show up against the dark green of the mahonia. (See page 192.)

5 × spurge (*Euphorbia robbiae*). The dark green leaves will stand out well against the golden elder and the green-yellow flowers will tone with it. (See page 192.)

GROUND-COVER PLANTS AND BULBS
3 × elephant's ears (*Bergenia* 'Ballawley'). The large, round leaves form an ideal 'stop' to the border. (See page 174.)

Lungwort (*Pulmonaria saccharata* 'Sissinghurst White') has variegated leaves and pure white flowers. (See pages 179–80.)

3 × eastern bleeding heart (*Dicentra eximia*). Its delicate, ferny foliage will contrast well with the elephant's ears and its flowers will take over once the latter's have finished. (See page 191.)

3 × Bowles' golden grass (*Milium effusum* 'Aureum'). A splash of brightness. (See page 193.)

3 × *Viola labradorica*. The purplish foliage contrasts beautifully with its golden neighbour (and with its other ferny, light green neighbour!) Plant snowdrops between Cc and Dd, and between the individual plants in each group. (See page 180.)

3 × *Hosta* 'Thomas Hogg'. Lovely cream-edged leaves. (See page 176.)

3 × *Lamium maculatum* 'White Nancy'. The silvery variegated foliage will look marvellous next to the *Viola labradorica* and in front of the dark green spurge. (See page 177.)

Hosta sieboldiana 'Elegans'. Its huge, rounded, ribbed, blue-green leaves are an excellent contrast with its neighbours. (See page 176.)

Lily-turf (*Liriope muscari*). (See page 193.)

3 × lady's mantle (*Alchemilla mollis*). Another good 'stop' plant; though its leaves aren't as big as the elephant's ears, they're much bigger than the dead nettle's or the viola's. The yellow-green flowers will tone with the spurge and the foliage of the golden elder. (See pages 172–3.)

Busy Lizzie (*Impatiens*) in its pale pink form is well worth trying here. (See pages 180–1.)

Plant *Cyclamen hederifolium* between the *Hosta* 'Thomas Hogg's and *Lamiums* – its flowers will show up well against the silvery dead nettle foliage, and the dark green leaves, marbled silver, which follow will contrast with it – and between the lungwort and eastern bleeding heart. Plant snowdrops between the Bowles' golden grass and violas.

EAST-FACING BORDERS

In a border that faces east, and gets sun for the first part of the day, you can grow many plants that are happy in partial shade, as you can in a west-facing border. The main difference between the two is that a border facing east is cooler – for one thing, the early morning sun doesn't have as much heat in it as the afternoon sun; and for another, winds from the east can be bitingly cold. That rules out plants that are slightly tender like trumpet vine (*Campsis radicans*) and many hebes.

East-facing borders are also not ideal for plants like camellias (even if you have an acid soil) or winter-flowering jasmine. In cold weather the buds freeze, and if they are allowed to thaw out slowly as they would on a north-facing wall, they survive undamaged, but if they are exposed to early-morning sun, as they would be in an east-facing border, and thaw too fast, they are damaged, turn brown and fall off.

However, as always in gardening, there are compensations. Many of the superb, large, pale pink, mauve or striped clematises, like the very popular, pale pink-mauve and carmine, 'Nelly Moser', the lavender-mauve 'Barbara Jackman', or the raspberry-pink 'Carnaby', keep their colour much better on an east-facing wall than they do in full sun, which tends to bleach it out.

Another group of plants that do very well in east-facing borders are those with golden foliage. It's quite hard to strike a balance between too much sun, which can scorch some golden foliage quite badly, and too little, in which case the brilliant gold colour fades to a golden-green. But an east-facing border, which gets full sun in the morning, and loses it at around the middle of the day before it's too fierce for too long, is ideal.

Golden foliage is very attractive in that setting, too, lit up by the early-morning sun. East light can be a little cold so a shrub like the golden-leaved mock orange (*Philadelphus coronarius* 'Aureus') or the small, box-leaved honeysuckle (*Lonicera nitida* 'Baggesen's Gold'), which creates its own warmth and brightness, is ideal.

In order to show off golden foliage to its best advantage you need a fair proportion of plain greens – light as well as dark – and a few variegated plants too. When it comes to flower colour white, and yellow, with just a touch of blue looks very effective indeed. As well as many excellent deciduous trees and shrubs with golden foliage, there are some evergreens – or perhaps 'evergolds' would be a more accurate description – as well. Apart from *Lonicera nitida* 'Baggesen's Gold', there's the new golden form of Mexican orange blossom (*Choisya ternata* 'Sundance') and the low-growing Japanese holly (*Ilex crenata* 'Golden Gem') – ideal for this situation since it needs sun to achieve its brightest colour, but is very prone to damage from scorching.

The majority of golden evergreens, however, are conifers, which come in a wide range of shapes and sizes – bun shapes, mop-heads, pillars, pyramids, cones. But make doubly sure that the little specimen you're buying is in fact a dwarf or very slow-growing conifer and not simply a very young giant! Some change colour as the seasons pass – *Thuja occidentalis* 'Rheingold', for example, turns from gold to coppery-gold in the winter, while the smaller *T. orientalis* 'Golden Ball' is bright yellow in spring and summer, turning green and sometimes bronze in autumn and winter. Most conifers prefer a slightly acid or neutral soil, though junipers and yew will tolerate lime.

As already explained, though, an east border, especially in an exposed garden, can be very cold, and some conifers, particularly when first planted, can be badly scorched by biting winds. They lose so much moisture as a result of the wind drying out their foliage that in effect they are suffering from drought and so the leaves turn brown. It's vital, therefore, that you give them some winter protection, either by planting them in the lee of other, larger, tougher shrubs

Ivy (*Hedera helix* 'Goldheart').

which will act as a windbreak or by making a temporary windbreak from perforated plastic material made specially for the purpose. Don't try to make a solid windbreak which is liable to blow down, but worse still, the wind tends to hit it, whip over the top and swirl and eddy on the other side, doing just the kind of damage to the plants that you set out to prevent.

MOIST SOIL

TREES
Golden birch (Betula pendula 'Golden Cloud')
A golden 'silver' birch which develops the lovely white bark associated with the species within a few years. It can be grown as a small tree or as a shrub if you prune it back in winter. Left alone, it is expected to reach 5 × 4 metres (16 × 13 feet) in 20 years.

Golden honey locust (Gleditsia triacanthos 'Sunburst')
(See page 151.)

Golden Indian bean tree (Catalpa bignonioides 'Aurea'*)*
(See page 151.)

Golden false acacia (Robinia pseudoacacia 'Frisia'*)*
Its branches are brittle and vulnerable to wind damage, so it
needs a sheltered position. (See page 149.)

CLIMBERS
Golden ivy (Hedera helix 'Buttercup'*)*
Has small, bright golden-yellow leaves, while *H. h.* 'Goldheart'
has large, central gold splashes on its leaves, as does the much
larger-leaved Persian ivy (*H. colchica* 'Paddy's Pride'). (See
page 160.)

Golden hop (Humulus lupulus 'Aureus'*)*
A vigorous climber, grown primarily for its foliage which
colours best in full sun. Prune it back hard each spring to
ensure the brightest foliage colour and to keep it in bounds.
    Approximate height (in one season) 4–5 metres (13–16 feet).

Japanese honeysuckle (Lonicera japonica 'Aureo-reticulata'*)*
In fact, it has variegated gold and green leaves, but from a
distance they look gold. It also has yellow flowers. (See page
161.)

CONTRASTS
Irish ivy (Hedera hibernica)
With its large, dark green leaves, it also makes a superb
backdrop for a golden-leaved shrub.

Climbing hydrangea (Hydrangea petiolaris)
Again! With its bright green foliage and flat heads of white
flowers. (See pages 160–1.)

American honeysuckle (Lonicera × *americana)*
It has white and yellow flowers all summer. (See page 161.)
The Chinese woodbine (*L. tragophylla*) has dark green leaves
and bright golden-yellow flowers in June and July. It will cope
with dense shade, and grows up to 6 metres (20 feet).

SHRUBS
Barberry (Berberis thunbergii 'Aurea'*)*
Forms a medium-sized spreading shrub, has bright gold
foliage in spring fading to pale green by the end of the summer

and then turning orange-gold in autumn. It needs protection both from frosts and icy winds and from hot sun. (See page 188.)

Mexican orange blossom (Choisya ternata 'Sundance')
A new golden-leaved form. Unlike its parent it won't do well in full shade, but like its parent needs shelter from cold winds. It has the same white flowers, though some people find them not as strongly scented. (See also page 256.)

Dogwood (Cornus alba)
The golden form, *C.a.* 'Aurea', has soft butter-coloured leaves. Alternatively, you could choose the gold-and-green-variegated 'Spaethii', which looks gold from a distance, and which has brighter red stems in winter. (See page 164.)

Winter-flowering heathers (Erica carnea)
These are tolerant of lime and include a number of varieties with bright gold foliage in winter. Look for *E.c.* 'Aurea', 'Foxhollow', 'January Sun' and 'Westwood Yellow'.

Golden fuchsia (Fuchsia magellanica 'Aurea')
It has the brightest golden foliage in full sun, but in partial shade it's still very attractive. It has small red flowers in midsummer. If the frost doesn't cut it back, prune it hard in spring for brighter foliage.
    Flowers June to August. Approximate height and spread in one season 1 × 1 metre (3 × 3 feet).

Japanese holly (Ilex crenata 'Golden Gem')
A low, spreading, evergreen shrub with small golden leaves which turn green in their second year, though the new growth is always golden. (A standard-sized variegated holly, like 'Golden King', which is as much gold as green, would qualify here too – see page 188.)
    Approximate height and spread after five years 40 × 80 centimetres (16 × 1½ feet); after ten years 60 centimetres × 1 metre (2 × 3 feet).

Box-leaved honeysuckle (Lonicera nitida 'Baggesen's Gold')
This makes a small, 'evergold', rather untidy shrub which works well in mixed, informal planting. It seems to become brighter gold in winter.
    Approximate height and spread after five years 60 centi-

metres × 1.2 metres (2 × 4 feet); after ten years 1.2 × 2 metres (4 × 6 feet).

Mock orange (Philadelphus coronarius 'Aureus')
It has bright yellow foliage in spring turning to yellow-green as the summer progresses. It has fragrant, white flowers in mid-summer. (See pages 261–2.)

Flowering currant (Ribes sanguineum)
The golden form, 'Brocklebankii', has pale pink flowers. (See pages 189–90.)

Golden elder (Sambucus nigra 'Aurea')
And golden cut-leaved elder (*Sambucus racemosa* 'Plumosa Aurea'), or the even hardier new form *S.r.* 'Sutherland') are excellent shrubs for this border. (See page 168.)

Spiraea
There are two excellent golden forms: *S.×bumalda* 'Goldflame' and the newer *S. japonica* 'Golden Princess'. (See page 265.)

Guelder rose (Viburnum opulus)
There is a golden form, *V.o.* 'Aureum'. (See page 172.)

GOLDEN CONIFERS
Chamaecyparis lawsoniana 'Minima Aurea'
Makes a rounded pyramid of golden foliage all year.
   Approximate height and spread (at the base) after ten years 60 × 50 centimetres (2 × 1½ feet).
   C. *obtusa* 'Nana Lutea' is a slow-growing, spreading bush that keeps its golden colour all year.
   Approximate height and spread after ten years 50 × 30 centimetres (1½ × 1 foot).
   C. *pisifera* 'Sungold' makes a golden-yellow mop-head as broad as it's high.
   Approximate height and spread after ten years 60 × 60 centimetres (2 × 2 feet).

Junipers
Junipers are among the hardiest conifers and will tolerate chalky soil. Some of the golden forms, like *Juniperus communis* 'Depressa Aurea', need full sun to give of their best, but others are happy in partial shade. *J.* × *media* 'Gold Coast', which

45. *Cimicifuga simplex*

59. *Hedera helix hibernica*

8. Clematis 'Comtesse de Bouchard'

44. *Campanula lactiflora*

22. *Rosa rubrifolia*

42. *Ajuga* 'Burgundy Glow'

The east-facing border shown in the plan on page 155 five years after planting.

21. *Viburnum davidii*

23. Fuchsia 'Tom Thumb'

43. *Bergenia* 'Ballawley'

39. *Choisya ternata*
'Sundance'

9. *Actinidia
kolomikta*

13. *Sorbus cashmiriana*

25. *Philadelphus
coronarius*
'Aureus'

40. *Dianthus
deltoides*

38. *Allium
schoenoprasum*
'Forescate'

41. *Saponaria
ocymoides*

24. *Skimmia japonica*
'Rubella'

retains its colour through the winter, makes a spreading bush, wider than it is high.

Approximate height and spread after ten years 75 centimetres × 1.2 metres (2½ × 4 feet).

J. × media 'Gold Sovereign', a new introduction, is the smallest of the semi-prostrate golden junipers.

Approximate height and spread after ten years 50 × 75 centimetres (18 inches × 2½ feet).

Mountain pine (Pinus mugo)
A superb small conifer with long, fine pine 'needles'. *P.m.* 'Wintergold' is a deep golden-yellow throughout the winter, turning a light green in summer.

Approximate height and spread after ten years 40 × 90 centimetres (16 inches × 3 feet).

Yew (Taxus baccata)
There are two excellent golden forms: the lovely, old gold, narrow, upright *T.b.* 'Standishii', 1 metre × 30 centimetres (3 × 1 foot), and the low, spreading 'Summergold' (which as its name suggests has its brightest gold colouring in summer), 50 centimetres × 1.4 metres (18 inches × 4½ feet).

Thujas
These conifers are tolerant of most soil types, including a degree of lime, as long as they are not too wet.

Thuja occidentalis 'Rheingold' has a rounded, conical shape and foliage that is gold in summer and coppery-gold in winter.

Approximate height and spread after ten years 1 metre × 80 centimetres (3 × 2½ feet).

T. occidentalis 'Sunkist' eventually makes a pyramid of foliage that stays bright gold all year round.

Approximate height and spread after ten years 1.2 metres × 60 centimetres (4 × 2 feet).

T. orientalis 'Aurea Nana' makes a superb, small, oval bush, golden-yellow in early summer and yellow or even bronze-green in winter.

Approximate height and spread after ten years 60 × 30 centimetres (2 × 1 foot).

T. orientalis 'Collen's Gold' is a pillar of golden foliage all year.

Approximate height and spread after ten years 1.2 metres × 50 centimetres (4 × 1½ feet).

T. orientalis 'Golden Ball' makes a dome-shaped bush,

bright gold in late spring and summer, green and sometimes bronze in autumn and winter.

Approximate height and spread after ten years 40 × 40 centimetres (16 × 16 inches).

T. orientalis 'Pyramidalis Aurea', as its name suggests, makes a narrow pyramid of golden-yellow foliage.

Approximate height after ten years 2 metres (6 feet).

SHRUBS FOR CONTRAST
Spotted laurel (Aucuba japonica)
Either in its plain form or one of the less brightly variegated forms like *A.j.* 'Variegata'. (See page 163.)

Dogwood (Cornus)
Choose non-golden forms. (See page 164.)

Cotoneaster
Look for ground-hugging forms, like *Cotoneaster dammeri* which has deep green, evergreen foliage and so provides good contrast to golden foliage. (See page 256.)

Elaeagnus × ebbingei and E. pungens 'Maculata'
(See page 227.)

Spindle (Euonymus fortunei)
Especially the gold-and-green-variegated forms like 'Emerald 'n' Gold' and the dwarf 'Sunspot'. (See page 188.)

Chinese witch hazel (Hamamelis mollis)
It has sweetly scented, yellow flowers in winter – attractive with 'evergold' foliage. (See page 165.)

Mahonia japonica
(See page 189.)

Osmanthus burkwoodii (formerly Osmarea burkwoodii)
It is similar to *Osmanthus delavayi* only larger and tougher.

Flowers April to May. Approximate height and spread 2–3 metres × 2–3 metres (6–10 feet × 6–10 feet).

Photinia × fraseri 'Red Robin'
Approximate height and spread after five years 1.5 × 2 metres (5 × 6 feet).

Winter-flowering heather (*Erica carnea* 'Westwood Yellow').

Potentilla fruticosa
(See pages 262–4.)

Cherry laurel (Prunus laurocerasus 'Otto Luyken')
With its glossy, dark, evergreen leaves, it is an excellent contrast to golden foliage. It can be pruned to keep it small. (See page 189.)

Firethorn (Pyracantha)
A good, evergreen wall shrub for east-facing borders. (See pages 165–8.)

Christmas box (Sarcococca humilis)
(See pages 168–9.)

Skimmia
Another valuable evergreen, and, if plants of both sexes are grown, red berries in winter result. (See page 169.)

Viburnums
This family includes some very hardy specimens: the winter-flowering *Viburnum tinus*; the spring-flowering *V.*×*burkwoodii*

and *V. plicatum tomentosum* 'Mariesii'; and the evergreens, grown largely for their foliage, *V. rhytidophyllum* (if you have plenty of room) and the much smaller *V. davidii*. (See pages 169–72.)

HERBACEOUS PLANTS
Hosta fortunei 'Aurea'
This plant has lovely, soft, butter-yellow leaves in spring, slowly fading through the summer to light green. *H.f.* 'Albopicta' is a variegated form whose leaves are marbled with yellow, gold and just a little green. Both must have partial shade, and both have lilac flowers from mid-summer onwards. (See pages 176–7.)

Dead nettle (Lamium maculatum 'Aureum'*)*
A very valuable ground-cover plant for moist soils, and will tolerate quite dense shade. (See page 177.)

Creeping Jenny (Lysimachia nummularia 'Aurea'*)*
Another good ground-cover plant for damp soil, with long trailing stems of round, golden leaves and yellow flowers in summer.

Above: Golden creeping Jenny (*Lysimachia nummularia* 'Aurea').

Golden cut-leaved elder (*Sambucus racemosa* 'Plumosa Aurea').

Flowers June to July. Approximate height and spread 5 × 60 centimetres (2 inches × 2 feet).

Lemon balm (Melissa officinalis 'Aurea'*)*
Has rich yellow leaves. (See page 232.)

Bowles' golden grass (Milium effusum 'Aureum'*)*
Has foliage, stems and flowers which are all golden yellow. (See page 193.)

Golden feverfew (Tanacetum parthenium 'Aureum'*)*
Forms small mounds of finely cut, yellow leaves covered with small white daisies throughout the summer. It does best in full sun but grows well enough in an east-facing border, provided the soil isn't too wet or heavy.

Flowering June to September. Approximate height and spread 30 × 20 centimetres (1 foot × 8 inches).

Plants for contrast
Monkshood (*Aconitum*). (See page 172.)
Lady's mantle (*Alchemilla mollis*). (See pages 172–3.)
Japanese anemone (*Anemone × hybrida*). (See page 173.)
Columbine (*Aquilegia*). (See page 173.)
Astilbe. (See page 173.)
Masterwort (*Astrantia major*). (See pages 173–4.)
Elephant's ears (*Bergenia*). (See page 174.)
Bugbane (*Cimicifuga*). (See page 175.)
Hellebores (*Helleborus niger* and *H. orientalis*). (See page 176.)
Day lilies (*Hemerocallis*). (See pages 272–3.)
Hostas. (See pages 176–7.)
Houttuynia cordata. (See page 273.)
Knotweed (*Persicaria affinis* and *P. bistorta*). (See pages 177–8.)
Primulas. (See pages 178–9.)
Lungwort (*Pulmonaria*). (See pages 179–80.)

Rodgersias (R. pinnata and R. podophylla)
Superb, large, bold, foliage plants for a semi-shaded, moist border. Plumes of small pink or cream flowers rise above the mound of foliage. They need a spot sheltered from strong winds.

Flowers July. Approximate height and spread 1 metre × 80 centimetres (3 × 2½ feet).

ANNUALS
Almost all the traditional annuals will do well in this situation, except the few like Livingstone daisy (*Mesembryanthemum*) which really like it hot and dry. Since there are none which have foliage that is truly golden, you can simply choose on the basis of flower colours that fit your scheme.

BULBS
All the usual spring-flowering bulbs will do well here too, though it won't be hot enough for exotics like the belladonna lily (*Amaryllis belladonna*). Again, there are no bulbs with golden foliage, so let flower colour dictate your choice.

DRY SOIL
Again the list is much shorter than that for moist soil, but even so there are enough golden-leaved plants to give you the effect you want.

TREES
Silver birch (*Betula* 'Golden Cloud'). (See page 202.)

Golden honey locust (*Gleditsia triacanthos* 'Sunburst'). (See page 151.)

CLIMBERS
Ivy (Hedera helix and H. colchica)
(See page 160.)

Japanese honeysuckle (Lonicera japonica 'Aureo-reticulata')
It prefers a moister soil, but if you add organic matter when you plant, and mulch it well afterwards, it should do well. (See page 161.)

SHRUBS
Golden privet (Ligustrum ovalifolium 'Aureum')
An evergreen, it will grow well in conditions where many others won't.
    Flowers July. Approximate height and spread 4–5 metres × 4–5 metres (12–15 feet × 12–15 feet).

Box-leaved honeysuckle (Lonicera nitida 'Baggesen's Gold')
(See pages 204–5.)

Right: Japanese
honeysuckle (*Lonicera
japonica* 'Aureo-
reticulata').

Far right: Mountain pine
(*Pinus mugo*
'Wintergold').

*Below: Prunus
laurocerasus* 'Otto
Luyken'.

Left: Golden balm (*Melissa officinalis* 'Aurea').

Below: The nasturtium (*Tropaeolum majus*) is one of the few annuals that thrives in poor, dry soil and part-shade.

Mock orange (Philadelphus coronarius 'Aureus')
It will tolerate dry soil if you add plenty of organic matter when you plant it and mulch it well afterwards. (See pages 261–2.)

Flowering currant (Ribes sanguineum 'Brocklebankii')
(See pages 189–90.)

Golden elder (Sambucus nigra 'Aurea') *and golden cut-leaved elder (S. racemosa* 'Plumosa Aurea')
(See page 168.)

CONIFERS
The golden varieties of *Chamaecyparis lawsoniana* listed on page 205 (provided you add plenty of organic matter when you plant), or *Juniperus × media, Taxus baccata* and *Thuja occidentalis* and *T. orientalis* should all do well.

Plants for contrast
Barberry (Berberis)
In some of its evergreen forms it will cope well enough. (See page 188.)

Spindle (Euonymus fortunei)
These, especially the gold-and-green-variegated forms, will do well, but you must be prepared to mulch and even water in the first season. (See page 188.)

Holly (Ilex × altaclerensis)
I. aquifolium in one of its plain green forms, like 'J.C. van Tol', or golden and green variegated forms, like 'Golden King', is also a valuable evergreen. (See page 188.)

Mahonia japonica or M. aquifolium
(See page 189.)

Skimmia
(See page 169.)

HERBACEOUS PLANTS
Spurge (Euphorbia robbiae)
It has large heads of yellow-green flowers and, from a distance, the effect is yellow. (See page 192.) *E. polychroma* has green foliage but such large heads of sulphur-yellow

flowers in spring that the overall effect is also of a golden plant.

Flowers April to May. Approximate height and spread 40 × 30 centimetres (16 inches × 1 foot).

Dead nettle (Lamium maculatum 'Aureum'*)*
(See page 177.)

Lemon balm (Melissa officinalis 'Aurea'*)*
(See page 232.)

Bowles' golden grass (Milium effusum 'Aureum'*)*
Provided you add plenty of organic matter when planting. (See page 193.)

Piggy-back plant (Tolmiea menziesii 'Variegata'*)*
Looks more yellow than green. (See page 193.)

Plants for contrast
Lady's mantle (*Alchemilla mollis*). (See pages 172–3.)
Elephant's ears (*Bergenia*). (See page 174.)
Foxglove (*Digitalis*). (See page 192.)
Barrenwort (*Epimedium*). (See page 192.)
Cranesbill, especially *Geranium macrorrhizum*. (See page 192.)
Stinking hellebore (*Helleborus foetidus*). (See page 192.)
Lily-turf (*Liriope muscari*). (See page 193.)
Viola labradorica. (See page 193.)
Waldsteinia ternata. (See pages 193–4.)

ANNUALS
Thank goodness for nasturtiums! Most of the other annuals that will thrive in poor, dry soils like gazanias and Livingstone daisies (*Mesembryanthemum*) are sun-lovers that open their flowers only in full sun.

BULBS
Few bulbs really like these conditions, but if you add organic matter to the soil before planting, the following are well worth trying.

Anemone blanda. (See page 283.)
Glory of the snow (*Chionodoxa luciliae*). (See page 184.)
Autumn crocus (*Crocus autumnale*). Flowers September to

1. *Ilex aquifolium* 'Golden King'

26. *Lonicera tragophylla*

23. *Hydrangea quercifolia*

22. *Philadelphus coronarius* 'Aureus'

6. *Polemonium caeruleum*

5. *Ajuga reptans* 'Variegata' × 5

3. *Helleborus foetidus* × 3

8. *Liriope muscari*

9. *Waldsteinia ternata* × 3

2. *Lunaria* – white

7. *Lonicera nitida* 'Baggesen's Gold'

Plan for a dry east-facing border.

4. *Bergenia* 'Silberlicht'

18. *Euonymus, fortunei* 'Sunspot'

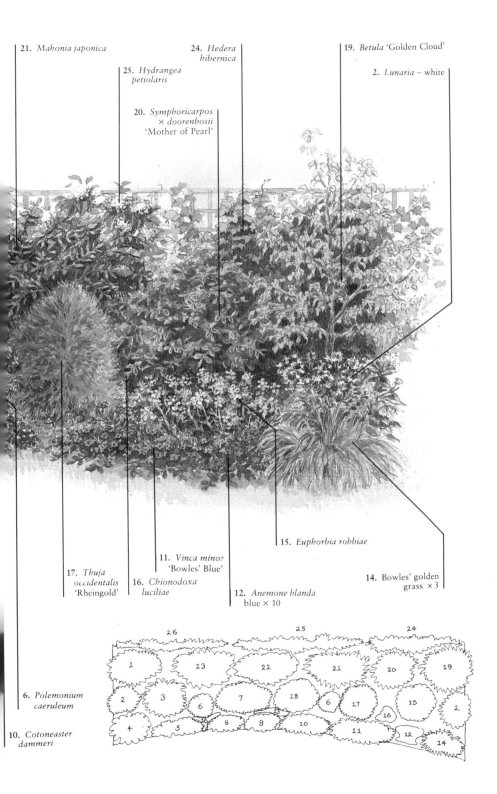

21. *Mahonia japonica*

25. *Hydrangea petiolaris*

20. *Symphoricarpos × doorenbosii* 'Mother of Pearl'

24. *Hedera hibernica*

19. *Betula* 'Golden Cloud'

2. *Lunaria* – white

17. *Thuja occidentalis* 'Rheingold'

16. *Chionodoxa luciliae*

11. *Vinca minor* 'Bowles' Blue'

12. *Anemone blanda* blue × 10

15. *Euphorbia robbiae*

14. Bowles' golden grass × 3

6. *Polemonium caeruleum*

10. *Cotoneaster dammeri*

October. Approximate height 5–12 centimetres (2–5 inches). Plant 8 centimetres (3 inches) apart.
Crocus. (See page 283.)
Grape hyacinth (*Muscari*). (See page 185.)
Ornithogalum nutans. (See page 196.)

PLANTING PLAN FOR A DRY, EAST-FACING BORDER
(See illustration on pages 218–19.)

CLIMBERS
Allow 3 metres (10 feet) for each plant.

Chinese woodbine (*Lonicera tragophylla*). Glowing gold flowers in June–July, followed by red berries for autumn colour. (See page 203.)

Hydrangea petiolaris. (See pages 160–1.)

Irish ivy (*Hedera hibernica*). Glossy, evergreen leaves. (See page 203.)

SHRUBS
Holly (*Ilex aquifolium* 'Golden King'). (See page 188.)

Oak-leaved hydrangea (*Hydrangea quercifolia*). White flowers and good autumn colour. (See page 165.)

Mock orange (*Philadelphus coronarius* 'Aureus'). (See pages 261–2.)

Mahonia japonica. (See page 189.)

Snowberry (*Symphoricarpos × doorenbosii* 'Mother of Pearl'). Pink berries in autumn show up well against the ivy. (See page 169.)

Golden birch (*Betula* 'Golden Cloud') grown as a shrub about 2 metres (6 feet) high. (See page 202.)

PERENNIALS AND SMALL SHRUBS
3 × stinking hellebore (*Helleborus foetidus*). (See page 192.)

Box-leaved honeysuckle (*Lonicera nitida* 'Baggesen's Gold'). Bright against the hydrangea. (See pages 204–5.)

Spindle (*Euonymus fortunei* 'Sunspot'). (See page 188.)

Thuja occidentalis 'Rheingold'. A lovely contrast with the evergreen ivy in winter. (See pages 208–9.)

3 × spurge (*Euphorbia robbiae*). Dark green leaves and yellow-green bracts tone well. (See page 192.)

3 × elephant's ears (*Bergenia* 'Silberlicht'). Pure white flowers in spring, turning faintly pink with age. (See page 174.)

5 × bugle (*Ajuga reptans* 'Variegata'). Beige and green leaves and intense blue flowers in spring. (See page 191.)

3 × lily-turf (*Liriope muscari*). Grass-like foliage and spikes of mauve-blue flowers in late summer. (See page 193.)

Waldsteinia ternata. Attractive, evergreen, mat-forming foliage and buttercup-yellow flowers in spring. (See pages 193–4.)

Cotoneaster dammeri. Ground-hugging with white flowers in spring and red berries in autumn. (See page 256.)

3 × lesser periwinkle (*Vinca minor* 'Bowles' Blue'). Evergreen trailer with small leaves and blue flowers in spring. (See pages 190–1.)

3 × Bowles' golden grass (*Milium effusum* 'Aureum'). Add plenty of organic matter before planting. (See page 193.)

Jacob's ladder (*Polemonium caeruleum*). (See page 276.)

White variegated honesty (*Lunaria annua* 'Alba Variegata'). Flowers April to June. Approximate height and spread 60 × 30 centimetres (2 × 1 foot).

BULBS
Anemone blanda – white and blue. (See page 283.)

Glory of the snow (*Chionodoxa luciliae*). (See page 184.)

WEST-FACING BORDERS

When it comes to choosing the plants for a west-facing border – one which gets the sun from the middle of the day until late evening – bear in mind that many of those which will thrive in south-facing borders are suitable here too. The exceptions are the relatively few plants that need full sun. So when you are designing your west-facing border, other factors need to be considered.

Many people who are out at work all day (or, indeed involved in looking after small children at home) can really enjoy their garden only in the evening. Since the west-facing border is the one which gets the sun until latest in the evening, it makes sense to create some kind of sitting-out area near it, even if it's only a bench on the lawn, and concentrate on plants that give of their best then.

Certain colours look better in evening light than others – bright reds, acid yellows and deep purples are lost, whereas white, cream, pale yellow and the palest pinks seem to gleam in the half-light, as does silvery foliage. Then there are those plants whose flowers open in the evening, like the evening primrose (*Oenothera* species) and those whose fragrance is at its best at that time – climbers like honeysuckle, jasmine and the evergreen climbing species rose, *Rosa banksiae*, which smells of sweet violets; and perennials and annuals like sweet rocket (*Hesperis matronalis*), tobacco plants (*Nicotiana*) and night-scented stocks (*Matthiola bicornis*). Interestingly, many of the plants most fragrant in the evening are white, pale pink, mauve or blue – colours that attract moths rather than butterflies, which prefer brighter colours on the whole, and of course moths come out only after the sun has gone down. Don't forget all the plants with aromatic foliage either – not only culinary herbs like rosemary, sage and thyme, but also others like artemisia, lavender, caryopteris and so on. If you spray them with the hose on a warm summer evening, the fragrance just wafts up in waves. For this reason we decided to make the west-facing border our fragrant border, and to stick largely to colours that look their best in the evening light.

Again, when classifying the plants that you might use, the most useful division seems to be between borders with moisture-retentive but reasonably well-drained soil (clay soils where the drainage has been improved, sandy soils whose ability to retain moisture has been improved, as well as

medium loam) and those with poor, dry soil. Once again, the plants that must have an acid soil are listed separately as are those that will cope with really heavy clay.

Jasmine (*Jasminum officinale*).

FRAGRANT PLANTS NEEDING ACID SOIL
Sweetspire (Itea ilicifolia)
(See page 247.)

Pieris floribunda
It has very intensely fragrant flowers between March and May. (See page 157.)

Rhododendrons
Rhododendrons are mostly unscented but with a few notable exceptions. *Rhododendron luteum* has fragrant orange-yellow flowers in early summer, while a number of white-flowered hybrids like 'Angelo', 'Midsummer Snow' and 'Polar Bear' also have very sweetly scented flowers. Deciduous, Ghent hybrid azaleas, like the pink-flowered 'Norma', the soft

yellow 'Narcissiflora' and the even paler 'Daviesii' have fragrant flowers too. (See pages 157–9.)

FRAGRANT PLANTS FOR MOIST SOIL

TREES
Ornamental crabs (Malus floribunda and M. hupehensis)
Have sweetly scented flowers in spring. (See pages 140–1.)

Flowering cherry (Prunus × yedoensis)
Has lovely almond-scented blossom in spring. (See page 144.)

CLIMBERS
Clematis montana
Has almond-scented white flowers, while *C.m.* 'Elizabeth' has soft pink, fragrant blooms. Both are very vigorous and should be let loose only where space allows. (See page 160.)

Jasmine (Jasminum officinale)
Will produce masses of pure white sweetly scented flowers from summer till autumn. *J. × stephanense* produces even more sweetly scented flowers, but for a shorter period. (See pages 249–50.)

Honeysuckle (Lonicera)
There are many strongly scented varieties. Among the best are *Lonicera × americana*, with honey-scented flowers; *L. heckrottii*, with a similar scent but with yellow rather than cream flowers; and the early and late Dutch honeysuckles (*L. periclymenum* 'Belgica' and *L.p.* 'Serotina'), which between them produce fragrant flowers from May to September. Though they are fragrant in the day, the scent is more intense in the evening and at night. Moths love it. (See page 161.)

Roses
Roses are a must for a fragrant border. Many are scented, but among those that combine the very long flowering period that you want in a small garden with good fragrance are the pink 'Aloha', 'Pink Perpétue' and 'Zéphirine Drouhin', the yellow 'Maigold' and the apricot-pink 'Compassion'. Make an exception for the vigorous, violet-scented *Rosa banksiae* – the

yellow-flowered 'Lutea' – the double white 'Alba Plena' which flowers from April to June, or 'Albéric Barbier' with creamy white flowers. (See page 161.)

Wisteria floribunda and W. sinensis
These have vanilla-scented flowers. (See pages 252–3.)

SHRUBS
Artemisias
All have aromatic foliage. (See page 253.)

Buddleia davidii, B. fallowiana and B. 'Lochinch'
They have a musky, honey-like scent which butterflies love. (See pages 254–5.)

Blue spiraea (Caryopteris clandonensis)
It has aromatic foliage. (See pages 288–9.)

Wintersweet (Chimonanthus praecox)
It has small, yellow, very sweetly scented flowers on bare stems in winter. Tolerates alkaline soil.
   Flowers February to March. Approximate height and spread after five years 1.2 × 1 metre (4 × 3 feet); after ten years 2 × 1.5 metres (6 × 5 feet).

Moroccan broom (Cytisus battandieri)
It has bright yellow flowers that smell like ripe pineapple. (See page 249.)

Broom (Cytisis fragrans or C. × praecox)
Also has fragrant flowers. (See pages 256–7.)

Daphne
There are a number of forms which, between them, produce fragrant flowers from November to August. (See page 257.)

Elaeagnus
All its varieties are usually grown for its foliage. However, many forms, when they are mature, have small but sweetly scented flowers in summer/early autumn. Of the deciduous varieties look for *Elaeagnus angustifolia*, with long, silvery,

Repeat-flowering, scented climbing rose 'Maigold'.

willow-like leaves and very fragrant, yellow flowers in June, and *E. commutata*, with small, silver, slightly wavy leaves and very fragrant, silvery flowers in May. Among the evergreens, look for *E.* × *ebbingei*, with silver-green leaves, or the green-and-gold variegated *E. pungens* 'Maculata', which is widely available; both of these flower eventually, in autumn.

Flowers May to November. Approximate height and spread after five years 1.2 × 1.2 metres (4 × 4 feet); after ten years 2 × 2 metres (6 × 6 feet).

Mount Etna broom (Genista aetnensis)
It is smothered in golden flowers smelling of vanilla in mid-summer. (See page 290.)

Chinese witch hazel (Hamamelis mollis)
It carries very strongly scented, yellow, spider-like flowers on bare wood in winter. *H.m.* 'Pallida' has paler flowers and a less cloying scent. (See page 165.)

Lavender (Lavandula)
All have scented flowers. (See page 290.)

Lemon verbena (Lippia citriodora)
Worth growing simply for the pleasure of rubbing a leaf or two between your palms and sniffing! You can also use it for tea. It's not totally hardy, so plant it close to the wall or fence and shelter it from cold winds. If the frost doesn't cut it back for you, cut the stems to ground level in spring to encourage new aromatic foliage.

Flowers August. Approximate height and spread in one season 80 × 80 centimetres (2½ × 2½ feet).

Winter honeysuckle (Lonicera fragrantissima)
It has very fragrant, small, white flowers on almost bare branches during mild spells from autumn to early spring. Though rather spreading when young, it will eventually form a rounded shrub.

Flowers November to March. Approximate height and spread after five years 1.2 × 2 metres (4 × 6 feet); after ten years 2 × 3 metres (6 × 10 feet).

Tobacco plants (*Nicotiana affinis* 'Nicki' and *Lobelia* 'String of Pearls').

Mahonia japonica
Its long trusses of pale yellow flowers smell of lily-of-the-valley in winter. (See page 189.)

Myrtle (Myrtus communis)
A large, evergreen shrub whose leaves and small, white, fluffy flowers, borne all summer, are both strongly scented.

Flowers July to September. Approximate height and spread after five years 1 × 1 metre (3 × 3 feet); after ten years 2 × 2 metres (6 × 6 feet).

Osmanthus delavayi
It has very sweetly scented, small, white flowers in spring. (See page 261.)

Mock orange (Philadelphus)
An essential ingredient of any scented border. (See pages 261–2.)

California tree poppy (Romneya coulteri)
(See page 264.)

Roses
In their shrub and bush forms, roses are also a must for any scented border. Again there is a huge choice, but where space is at a premium look for those with additional qualities, such as a long flowering season and attractive foliage. Among the many outstanding varieties are the blush-white 'Margaret Merril', the pale pink 'City of London' and 'Bonica' and the dusky scarlet 'Fragrant Cloud'. Among the English roses 'Graham Thomas', 'Heritage' and 'Othello' all have good fragrance. (See pages 264–5.)

Rosemary (Rosmarinus officinalis)
This herb has powerfully aromatic foliage. (See page 292.)

Sage (Salvia officinalis)
In its variegated as well as its plain forms, it has strongly aromatic foliage. Ask any pig. (See page 300.)

Golden elder and golden cut-leaved elder (Sambucus nigra 'Aurea' and S. racemosa 'Plumosa Aurea')
Both have flat heads of white musk-scented flowers, used in home wine making for elderflower champagne. (See page 168.)

Cotton lavender (Santolina)
In all its forms, it has very pungent foliage, sweet yet sharp at the same time. (See page 292.)

Christmas box (Sarcococca humilis)
It is grown largely for its vanilla-scented flowers in winter. (See pages 168–9.)

Lilac (Syringa)
In many of its forms, it has superbly sweet-scented flowers. (See pages 265–6.)

Viburnum
This family includes in its large and varied ranks many of the most sweetly scented shrubs of all. For winter scent *Viburnum farreri* and the smaller-growing *V. × bodnantense* (especially *V. × b.* 'Dawn') are superb, as is the evergreen *V. tinus*. For spring fragrance look for the evergreen *V. × burkwoodii*, which can be in flower as early as January in a sheltered spot; *V. carlesii*, with pink-budded, white flowers smelling like pinks; and *V. juddii*, with exquisitely scented, pale pink flowers in April to May. (See pages 266–7.)

HERBACEOUS PLANTS
Elephant's ears (Bergenia cordifolia, B. crassifolia and B. schmidtii)
All have scented flowers in winter and early spring. (See page 174.)

Wallflowers (Cheiranthus cheiri)
Wallflowers are usually grown as biennials (grown from seed one year, flowering the next, then dying). There are many varieties available, but the most compact, double-flowered Siberian wallflowers (*C. × allionii*) have the best perfume. The perennial wallflowers (*Erysimum*) like *E. cheiri* 'Harpur Crewe' are believed to date from the reign of Elizabeth I. It has small, double, yellow, sweetly scented flowers.

Flowers March to May. Approximate height and spread 40 × 30 centimetres (16 × 12 inches).

Lily-of-the-valley (Convallaria majalis)
Does best in part shade, so plant it beneath shrubs. Sweet, lasting fragrance. (See page 197.)

7. Rose 'Albéric Barbier'
and *Clematis viticella*
'Etoile Violette'

27. *Chamaecyparis
lawsoniana* 'Pottenii'

62. *Lilium regale*

4. *Lonicera
periclymenum*
'Serotina'

The west-facing border
shown in the plan on
page 155 five years after
planting.

61. *Viola cornuta*

29. *Juniperus
squamata*
'Blue Star'

60. *Penstemon*
'Garnet'

28. *Chamaecyparis
lawsoniana* 'Minima
Aurea'

30. *Buddle
fallowiar
alba*

31. *Artemisia* 'Powis
    Castle'.

57. *Corylopsis
    pauciflora*

10. Rose 'Pink Perpétue'
    and *Clematis*
    'Jackmanii Superba'

56. *Viburnum juddii*

14. *Malus* 'Profusion'

62. *Lilium regale*

5. *Rosa bonica*

58. *Liriope muscari*

55. *Geranium nodosum*

17. *Mahonia* 'Charity'

231

Pinks (Dianthus)
In many forms, they have sweetly scented flowers. (See pages 295–6.)

Burning bush (Dictamnus albus)
So called because it gives off a volatile inflammable oil when the seedheads are ripening. The dark green leaves smell of balsam when crushed and it also has very attractive white flowers in summer.

Flowers June to August. Approximate height and spread 80 × 40 centimetres (2½ feet × 16 inches).

Sweet rocket (Hesperis matronalis)
A biennial which seeds itself so freely that once you have it you are never without it. During the daytime its pale mauve or white flowers have a faint violet scent, but in the evening it becomes much stronger like cloves.

Flowers April to May. Approximate height and spread 75 × 30 centimetres (2½ × 1 foot).

Lemon balm (Melissa officinalis 'Aurea'*)*
This plant has lemon-scented leaves which are gold with a green central vein. It needs to be cut hard back in late spring to encourage bright new foliage and to prevent flowering, which makes the plant straggly.

Approximate height and spread 60 × 60 centimetres (2 × 2 feet).

Bergamot (Monarda didyma)
It has aromatic leaves and pink, red or white flowers.

Flowers June to September. Approximate height and spread 75 × 35 centimetres (2½ × 1¼ feet).

Evening primrose
In its biennial form, *Oenothera biennis*, it has sweetly scented flowers, opening at dusk, as does the perennial O. *odorata*, though it's much harder to find. (See page 300.)

Russian sage (Perovskia atriplicifolia)
As its name suggests, it has leaves, stems and flowers that all smell of sage. (See page 291.)

Phlox (Phlox paniculata)
Phlox has a strong fragrance. (See pages 275–6.)

Primula
There are a few sweetly scented forms – some of the rarer ones like *Primula chionantha* and the most common form, *P. vulgaris*, the true primrose. (See pages 178–9.)

Thyme (Thymus)
(See page 301.)

Verbena
There are surprisingly few scented forms. Look for *Verbena rigida*, which has violet-purple flowers all summer long, and the smaller *V. corymbosa*, with clusters of violet-blue flowers.

Flowers July to September. Approximate height and spread 40 × 30 centimetres (16 × 12 inches).

ANNUALS
The following are all half-hardy annuals you buy as plants and flower from June to September.

Heliotrope or cherry pie (Heliotropium arborescens)
It has large clusters of deep violet-blue flowers with a heady, rather fruity scent – hence its common name. 'Marine' and 'Mini Marine' are good varieties, the latter a few inches shorter than the former.

Approximate height and spread 45–50 × 30 centimetres (16–18 × 12 inches).

Stocks
A superbly scented family of showy spring- and summer-flowering cottage garden annuals and biennials in shades of white, yellow, pink, mauve, lavender and red. Ten-week stock (*Matthiola incana*) is a half-hardy annual, while Brompton stock (also *Matthiola incana*) is a biennial. Virginia stock (*Malcolmia maritima*) is an easily grown hardy annual with small flowers in white, pink or mauve, while night-scented stock (*Matthiola bicornis*) is a hardy annual with small, insignificant flowers, but its fragrance at night is superb – it is worth growing among the more attractive-looking stocks.

Approximate height and spread 30–50 centimetres (1–1½ feet).

Tobacco plants (Nicotiana)
All are scented, though the many coloured hybrids – with the exception of a mixture called 'Evening Fragrance' – are not as

Top: Pinks (*Dianthus* 'Doris').

Below right: There are many varieties of sweet pea in a wide range of colours, so be sure to choose a strongly scented one.

Below: Fragrant mauve and white sweet rocket (*Hesperis matronalis*) with the scented, pale yellow rose *Rosa cantabrigiensis.*

sweetly scented, particularly in the evenings, as the white *N. affinis*. If you can find it, the short-lived perennial *N. sylvestris*, which can reach almost 2 metres (6 feet) in height, also has superb fragrance in the evening. It's easy to collect your own seed, so you can keep it going from year to year. (See page 279.)

The following hardy annuals can be sown where they are to flower.

Above: Very fragrant regale lilies (*Lilium regale*), growing here with baby's breath (*Gypsophila paniculata*) and alstroemeria, are among the easiest to grow.

Sweet William (Dianthus barbatus)

Has several biennial and annual forms which have a fragrance slightly reminiscent of cloves. Look for the biennial 'auricula-eyed' form, which has bi-coloured red or pink and white flowers, or one of the annual dwarf mixtures like 'Roundabout' or 'Wee Willie'.

Approximate height and spread 15–45 × 15–30 centimetres (6–18 × 6–12 inches).

Left: Mint, golden balm and chives, growing together in a herb border, demonstrates that herbs are highly ornamental as well as useful.

Sweet peas (Lathyrus odoratus)
(See page 282.)

Lobularia maritima
In its white forms, it has a scent some people describe as like new-mown hay. (See page 281.)

Mignonette (Reseda odorata)
(See page 282.)

BULBS
Ornamental onions
Particularly the yellow *Allium moly* and the white *A. neapolitanum.* (See page 282.)

Belladonna lily (Amaryllis belladonna)
(See page 303.)

Crocuses
They have a delicate scent that is best appreciated close to in window boxes or indoors. (See page 283.)

Summer hyacinth (Galtonia candicans)
It has a perfume which seems to develop once the flowers have been cut and taken indoors. (See page 283.)

Hyacinths
They have a sweet, almost cloying perfume indoors, but outside it's largely lost. (See page 283.)

Lilies
Lilies, especially the white *Lilium regale*, have a pervading fragrance on warm days that seems to intensify in the evening. (See page 284.)

Narcissi
These bulbs, represented by the white 'Cheerfulness', are an essential ingredient of the Queen's Maundy Thursday nose-gay, an indication of how strong their fragrance is. Other good varieties for fragrance includes the jonquil narcissi like 'Trevithian', 'Lintie', 'Suzy' and *Narcissus jonquilla* and *N. × odorus* 'Rugulosus', and the old 'Pheasant's Eye' with its white petals and red and gold 'eye'. (See pages 284–5.)

FRAGRANT PLANTS FOR DRY SOIL

The choice is not as large here as for moist soils, but it's possible to create a very attractive scented border provided that you add lots of organic matter before you plant and, having given the border a thorough drenching once you've planted it, mulch with a generous layer of the same.

CLIMBERS
Jasmine (Jasminum officinale)
(See pages 249–50.)

Honeysuckle (Lonicera)
It prefers a cool, moist soil, but some varieties will tolerate dry and chalky soils, like *Lonicera periclymenum* 'Belgica' and *L.p.* 'Serotina' and the goat-leaved honeysuckle, *L. caprifolium*, with creamy-white flowers in mid-summer which are particularly fragrant at night. (See pages 250–1.)

SHRUBS
Barberry (Berberis stenophylla)
This plant makes a large, impenetrable thicket of arching stems covered in deep green, evergreen leaves and, in late spring, scented gold flowers.

Flowers April to May. Approximate height and spread after five years 1.5 × 1.5 metres (5 × 5 feet); after ten years 2 × 2 metres (6 × 6 feet).

Buddleia
(See pages 254–5.)

Blue spiraea (Caryopteris clandonensis 'Arthur Simmonds')
(See pages 288–9.)

Wintersweet (Chimonanthus praecox)
(See page 225.)

Mexican orange blossom (Choisya ternata)
(See page 256.)

Moroccan broom (Cytisus battandieri)
(See page 249.).

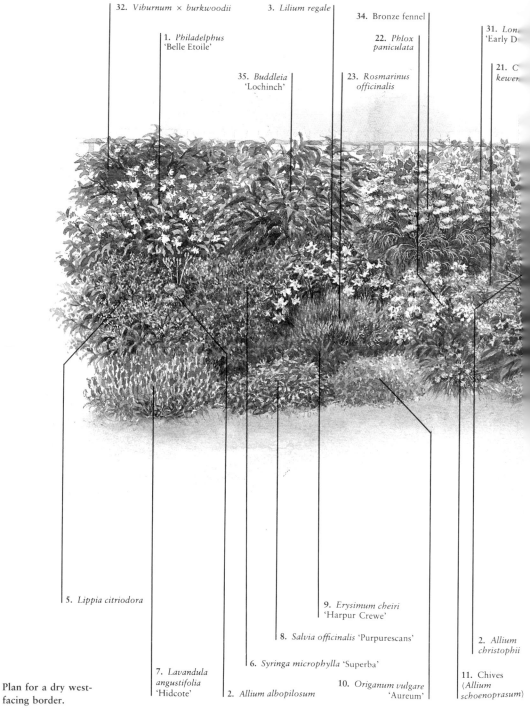

32. *Viburnum × burkwoodii*

3. *Lilium regale*

34. Bronze fennel

31. *Lon.*
'Early D'

1. *Philadelphus*
'Belle Etoile'

22. *Phlox*
paniculata

21. C
kewen.

35. *Buddleia*
'Lochinch'

23. *Rosmarinus*
officinalis

5. *Lippia citriodora*

9. *Erysimum cheiri*
'Harpur Crewe'

8. *Salvia officinalis* 'Purpurescans'

2. *Allium*
christophii

6. *Syringa microphylla* 'Superba'

7. *Lavandula*
angustifolia
'Hidcote'

2. *Allium albopilosum*

10. *Origanum vulgare*
'Aureum'

11. Chives
(*Allium*
schoenoprasum)

Plan for a dry west-facing border.

238

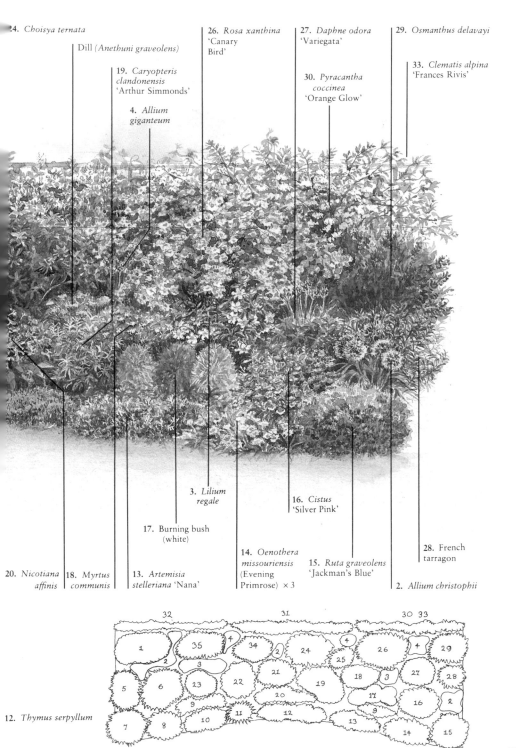

24. *Choisya ternata*

Dill *(Anethuni graveolens)*

19. *Caryopteris clandonensis* 'Arthur Simmonds'

4. *Allium giganteum*

26. *Rosa xanthina* 'Canary Bird'

27. *Daphne odora* 'Variegata'

29. *Osmanthus delavayi*

30. *Pyracantha coccinea* 'Orange Glow'

33. *Clematis alpina* 'Frances Rivis'

3. *Lilium regale*

16. *Cistus* 'Silver Pink'

17. Burning bush (white)

28. French tarragon

14. *Oenothera missouriensis* (Evening Primrose) × 3

15. *Ruta graveolens* 'Jackman's Blue'

20. *Nicotiana affinis*

18. *Myrtus communis*

13. *Artemisia stelleriana* 'Nana'

2. *Allium christophii*

12. *Thymus serpyllum*

Broom (Genista)
(Scc pages 256 7.)

Mahonia japonica
Except in very dry soil. (See page 189.)

Myrtle (Myrtus communis)
(See page 228.)

Osmanthus delavayi
(See page 261.)

Russian sage (Perovskia atriplicifolia)
See page 291.)

Mock orange (Philadelphus)
Provided plenty of organic matter is added when planting. (See pages 261–2.)

Roses
They don't, in general, do well on this type of soil. One very attractive exception is *Rosa xanthina* 'Canary Bird', which makes a tall shrub with arching branches covered in fern-like foliage and, in May, produces masses of single, bright yellow flowers.
  Approximate height and spread 2 × 2 metres (6 × 6 feet).

Rosemary (Rosmarinus officinalis)
(See page 292.)

Sage (Salvia officinalis)
(See page 300.)

Golden elder (Sambucus nigra 'Aurea')
(See page 168.)

Spanish broom (Spartium junceum)
(See page 292.)

Lilac (Syringa)
(See pages 265–6.)

HERBACEOUS PLANTS
Elephant's ears (*Bergenia*). (See page 174.)

Wallflowers (*Cheiranthus cheiri*). (See page 229.)
Lily-of-the-valley (*Convallaria majalis*) in the shade of shrubs. (See page 197.)
Pinks (*Dianthus*). (See pages 295–6.)
Burning bush (*Dictamnus albus*). (See page 232.)
Lemon balm (*Melissa officinalis* 'Aurea'). (See page 232.)
Evening primrose (*Oenothera*). (See page 300.)
Bouncing Bet (*Saponaria ocymoides*). (See page 300.)
Thyme (*Thymus*). (See page 301.)

ANNUALS
Few scented annuals really like dry soil, but the following are worth trying, if you enrich the soil with additional organic matter first.

Heliotrope or cherry pie (*Heliotropium arborescens*). (See page 233.)
Virginia stock (*Malcolmia maritima*). (See page 233.)
Ten-week, Brompton and night-scented stocks (*Matthiola incana* and *M. bicornis*). (See page 233.)
Tobacco plants (*Nicotiana*). (See page 279.)
Mignonette (*Reseda odorata*). (See page 282.)

BULBS
Ornamental onions (*Allium*). (See page 282.)
Belladonna lily (*Amaryllis belladonna*). (See page 303.)
Summer hyacinth (*Galtonia candicans*). (See page 283.)
Lily (*Lilium regale*). (See page 284.)

FRAGRANT PLANTS FOR HEAVY CLAY SOIL
A particularly short list, this one, apart from quite a reasonable selection of shrubs, but you can still make a scented border with a little padding from non-scented herbaceous plants, annuals and bulbs. See pages 304–5 for those that will cope with a sunny site and heavy clay.

TREES
Laburnum (*Laburnum* × *watereri* 'Vossii'). (See page 140.)
Ornamental crab (*Malus floribunda* and *M. hupehensis*). (See pages 140–1.)

SHRUBS
Barberry (*Berberis stenophylla*). (See page 253.)
Mexican orange blossom (*Choisya ternata*). (See page 256.)

Chinese witch hazel (*Hamamelis mollis*). (See page 165.)
Mahonia japonica. (See page 189.)
Osmanthus delavayi. (See page 261.)
Mock orange (*Philadelphus*). (See pages 261–2.)
Roses. (See pages 264–5.)
Golden elder (*Sambucus nigra* 'Aurea'). (See page 168.)
Viburnum × *bodnantense, V.* × *burkwoodii, V. tinus.* (See pages 266–7.)

HERBACEOUS PLANTS, ANNUALS AND BULBS
Apart from day lilies (*Hemerocallis*), some of which are scented, there are few fragrant plants that will grow in heavy clay soil in a sunny position.

PLANTING PLAN FOR A DRY, WEST-FACING BORDER
(See illustration on pages 238–9.)
The months when the flowers are most fragrant are given after the notes on each plant unless it is grown mainly for its foliage.

CLIMBERS
Allow 3 metres (10 feet) for each plant.
Viburnum × *burkwoodii* trained as wall shrub. Evergreen. March–May. (See pages 229, 266–7.)

Early and late Dutch honeysuckle (*Lonicera periclymenum* 'Belgica' and *L.p.* 'Serotina') grown together. May–September. (See pages 250–1.)

Firethorn (*Pyracantha coccinea* 'Orange Glow'). Evergreen. Bright orange berries in winter. Scented flowers June. (See pages 165–8.)

Clematis alpina 'Frances Rivis'. Not scented, but very pretty blue and white flowers in April–May. (See pages 248–9.)

SHRUBS
Mock orange (*Philadelphus* 'Belle Etoile'). June–July. (See pages 261–2.)

Buddleia 'Lochinch'. July–August. (See pages 254–5.)

3 × bronze fennel (*Foeniculum vulgare* 'Purpureum'). Aromatic foliage – good as a flavouring in fish dishes. (See page 297.)

Mexican orange blossom (*Choisya ternata*). Evergreen, pungent foliage. April–June and often again in September. (See page 256.)

Rosa xanthina 'Canary Bird'. May–June. (See page 240.)

Osmanthus delavayi. April. (See page 261.)

PERENNIALS AND SMALL SHRUBS
Lemon verbena (*Lippia citriodora*). (See page 227.)

Littleleaf lilac (*Syringa microphylla* 'Superba'). May–June and again in September. (See pages 265–6.)

Rosmarinus officinalis. (See page 292.)

3 × *Phlox paniculata* 'White Admiral'. (See pages 275–6.)

Broom (*Cytisus kewensis*). Cream, scented flowers. May–June. (See pages 256–7.)

Blue spiraea (*Caryopteris clandonensis* 'Arthur Simmonds'). Aromatic foliage. (See pages 288–9.)

3 × dill (*Anethum graveolens*). Feathery, aromatic, green leaves, 1 metre (3 feet). Good as a flavouring with fish and in pickles.
    Approximate height and spread 1 metre × 30 centimetres (3 feet × 9–12 inches).

Myrtle (*Myrtus communis*). Aromatic, evergreen leaves. July–September. (See page 228.)

Winter daphne (*Daphne odora* 'Variegata'). Variegated evergreen. February–March. (See pages 225, 257.)

3 × French tarragon (*Artemisia dracunculus*). Aromatic foliage.
    Approximate height and spread 45 × 30 centimetres (1½ × 1 foot).

Lavender (*Lavandula angustifolia* 'Hidcote'). (See page 290.)

Sweet rocket (*Hesperis matronalis*). April–June. (See page 232.)

Purple-leaved sage (*Salvia officinalis* 'Purpurascens'). The colour doesn't affect the flavour of the leaves. (See page 300.)

Golden marjoram (*Origanum vulgare* 'Aureum'). Aromatic foliage.
   Approximate height and spread 60 × 30 centimetres (2 × 1 foot).

Chives (*Allium schoenoprasum*). Attractive pink flowers, as well as onion-flavoured foliage. A useful 'vertical' plant among the horizontals.

Thyme (*Thymus serpyllum*). Aromatic foliage. (See page 301.)

Artemisia stelleriana 'Nana'. A dwarf ornamental silver artemisia. Aromatic, non-edible foliage. (See page 268.)

Perennial wallflower (*Erysimum cheiri* 'Harpur Crewe'). March–May. (See page 229.)

Burning bush (*Dictamnus fraxinella* 'Alba'). June–August. (See page 232.)

Evening primrose (*Oenothera missouriensis*). June–September. (See page 300.)

Sun rose (*Cistus* 'Silver Pink'). June–July. (See page 289.)

Rue (*Ruta graveolens* 'Jackman's Blue'). Superb heads of tiny, blue-green bitter-tasting leaves. Cut back hard in spring to ensure the best new foliage.
   Approximate height and spread 60 × 80 centimetres (2 × 2½ feet).

Tobacco plant (*Nicotiana affinis*). June–September. (See page 279.)

BULBS
Ornamental onions (*Allium*). Tall ones like *A. giganteum* and *A. christophii* at the back of the borders. (See page 282.)

Lily (*Lilium regale*). July. (See page 284.)

SOUTH-FACING BORDERS

In many ways a south-facing border which gets sun all day is the easiest of all to plant because there are so many wonderful climbers, shrubs, herbaceous plants, annuals and bulbs which revel in a sunny spot. If there is a problem with south-facing borders it's that the range of suitable plants is so vast that, like a child given *carte blanche* in a sweet shop, you really are spoilt for choice! The temptation to try to cram too much in is very strong, and certainly one way of resisting it is to choose a theme for your border and stick to that. It could be a colour scheme – hot reds, oranges and golds, say – or a particular type of plant – traditional cottage garden plants, for example. Alternatively, you could choose one family of plants as the backbone of your border – small shrub roses, for instance, or the lovely 'English' roses (combining the beauty and perfume of old roses with the compactness, repeat-flowering and vigour of new hybrids) – and then select the other plants to fit in with them. You could choose tall plants to give the border height and form a background for the roses – plants like blue- or white-flowered campanulas, say, regale lilies, the annual white and pink lavateras, verbascums such as the lovely soft yellow 'Gainsborough', the striking, feathery, bronze fennel (*Foeniculum vulgare* 'Purpureum') and silvery artemisia. You could then add some lower-growing, mound-forming subjects like cotton lavender (*Santolina chamaecyparissus*) and, indeed, lavender itself, small hebes like *Hebe pinguifolia* 'Pagei', hardy geraniums like the widely available 'Johnson's Blue', herbs like sage, gold and silver thymes, marjoram . . . it's still easy to get carried away, even when you have imposed some sort of scheme upon yourself!

Again, there are really two main types of sunny border. First there are those with moisture-retentive but reasonably well-drained soil – which includes not only the elusive medium loam, but also soils of a moderate clay content whose drainage has been improved with organic matter and grit, and moderately sandy and even limy soils whose moisture-retaining qualities have been boosted with large amounts of organic matter. Obviously, if you have a limy soil, you still won't be able to grow acid-loving plants, but this time, as well as many of the plants suitable for average soils, you'll also be able to grow some beautiful specimens that do best on lime, like lilac, mock orange, the lovely silver-leaved, blue-flowered *Caryopteris*

SOUTH-FACING BORDERS

A romantic garden in pastel colours – the white sea kale (*Crambe cordifolia*) and mock orange (*Philadelphus*) and the blue delphiniums against a background of pale pink climbing roses.

clandonensis, the long-flowering *Coronilla glauca* with its mass of yellow pea flowers, and the fragrant, winter-flowering wintersweet (*Chimonanthus praecox*).

The other sort of sunny border is the one with a thin, dry soil. Certainly, adding lots of organic matter can help its ability to retain water a little, but it will still be a dry soil. One answer would be to choose plants that need regular watering and to spend a great deal of time in the garden with the hose. But that's the gardening equivalent of washing-up and besides, if we ever get another hot, dry summer, the use of hosepipes will be one of the first things to be banned. And what with privatization and metering, watering the garden can be a very expensive operation. The best solution, again, is to choose plants that actually flourish in the conditions you're offering – in this instance, drought! – but we'll return to these later.

ACID-LOVING PLANTS

SHRUBS
Heather (Calluna vulgaris)
It flowers in the summer, between June and October, is a lime-hater and needs an acid soil to do well. It comes in a range of colours – flowers in white, pink, red and purple and foliage in green, gold, grey, orange and, in the case of *C.v.* 'Winter Chocolate', chocolate brown in winter. A number of plants grouped together quickly make an attractive carpet. Incidentally, you should ignore the advice still given by some garden centres that on a limy soil you can dig a large hole, fill it with peaty soil and plant acid-lovers in that. This is not successful, for no matter how large the hole, it's only a matter of time before limy water from the surrounding soil creeps in and turns your temporarily acid soil alkaline. If you don't have an acid soil and want to grow heathers, build a raised bed filled with acid soil or grow the winter-flowering kind (*Erica carnea*) which comes in as wide a range of flower and foliage colour, but which is happy on neutral and slightly limy soils.

Approximate height and spread after five and ten years 5–50 × 30 centimetres (2–18 × 12 inches).

Winter hazel (Corylopsis pauciflora)
Like its relative, witch hazel, this has sweetly scented, yellow flowers on bare stems, though in this case in spring rather than in winter. Its young foliage is tinged with pink.

Approximate height and spread after five years 1 × 1 metre (3 × 3 feet); after ten years 2 × 2 metres (6 × 6 feet).

Sweetspire (Itea ilicifolia)
A medium-sized, evergreen shrub with holly-like leaves and fragrant, greenish-white flowers, closely packed in tassels rather like catkins, can be grown either free-standing or trained a warm wall.

Approximate height and spread after five years 1 × 1 metre (3 × 3 feet); after ten years 2 × 2 metres (6 × 6 feet).

Calico bush (Kalmia latifolia)
It is rather like members of the rhododendron family in appearance, with large, glossy green, oval leaves which provide an ideal backdrop for the clusters of rose-pink, cup-shaped flowers in early summer. It will tolerate a little shade but does best in full sun.

Approximate height and spread after five years 1.5 × 1.5 metres (5 × 5 feet); after ten years 2 × 2 metres (6 × 6 feet).

Lithodora diffusa

A small, evergreen, carpeting shrub with flowers of the most beautiful vivid gentian blue between May and August. The best variety is *L.d.* 'Grace Ward', which grows more vigorously and has flowers of an even more intense blue, but it's not as widely available as *L.d.* 'Heavenly Blue', which itself is such a wonderful plant that it's no real hardship! A light clipping-over after flowering will make it grow more densely.

Approximate height and spread after five years 15 × 30 centimetres (6 × 12 inches); after ten years 15 × 50 centimetres (6 × 18 inches).

MOIST SOIL

CLIMBERS

Actinidia kolomikta

A superb twining foliage plant for a sunny wall or fence. It has large, heart-shaped leaves that start out green but quickly assume splashes of cream and pink on the lower portion which are so bold that you might think the Queen of Hearts' gardeners had been busy with their paint brushes.

Approximate height and spread after five years 3–4 metres (10–13 feet).

Trumpet vine (Campsis radicans)

Needs a well-protected, sunny wall to do well, but its dramatic, large, orange-red, trumpet flowers, produced from August to October, make it worth taking the chance. It also has attractive, lush green foliage, not unlike that of wisteria.

Approximate height and spread after five years 4–5 metres (13–16 feet).

Clematis

Most like their heads in the sun and their roots in moist, shady, preferably limy soil. They include so many different varieties that it's possible to have one in flower practically the whole year round. In winter there's the evergreen fern-leaved clematis (*Clematis cirrhosa balearica*) whose very delicate-looking foliage is tinged with bronze when the creamy-white, bell-shaped flowers appear. It's rather tender, so I'm afraid it's only for a south-facing wall in the warmest gardens. To follow on in spring there is C. *alpina*, with blue and white or pink nodding flowers, and in late spring/early summer C. *macropetala*, similar to C. *alpina* though its pink, blue or white flowers are semi-double and larger. (C. *montana* flowers at this time, but it is so vigorous that you really ought to think twice about planting it in a very small garden.) Throughout the summer there are any number of large-flowered hybrids, though the pale pink and mauve varieties, like 'Nelly Moser' and 'Barbara Jackman', are better out of full sun since it causes their flowers to fade. In late summer there is C. *viticella*, with small single or double white, wine-red or rich purple flowers, or C. *orientalis*, the 'orange peel' clematis, which has grey-green foliage and nodding, yellow, cup-shaped flowers in September/October, followed by fluffy silvery seedheads that last into the winter.

Approximate height and spread in one season – large-flowered hybrids 2–5 metres (6–16 feet); small-flowered species 3–7 metres (10–23 feet).

Moroccan broom (Cytisus battandieri)
A fast-growing wall shrub which has attractive, large, silvery leaves and plumes of bright yellow flowers that smell of sweet, ripe pineapple. It dislikes both very acid and very alkaline soils, but will grow happily in ordinary and even poor, dry soils.

Approximate height and spread after five years 4.5 × 2 metres (14 × 6 feet); after ten years 6.5 × 4 metres (22 × 13 feet).

Chilean glory flower (Eccremocarpus scaber)
It produces masses of orange-red, tubular flowers from August to October, is only completely hardy in the mildest areas of the country. Everywhere else it will get cut down to the ground by the first hard frost, but don't despair; pile some strawy manure or even peat over the roots to protect them through the cold season and after all but the hardest winters it will shoot again in spring. Alternatively, if you collect seed in the autumn, it's very easy to raise new plants that way in the spring.

Approximate height and spread in one season 3 metres+ (10 feet+).

Jasmine (Jasminum officinale)
It produces small, white flowers with one of the strongest, sweetest fragrances of all, particularly in the evening, which

The extraordinary coloration of *Actinidia kolomikta* is at its best in full sun.

makes it an especially good choice for a west-facing wall (see page 224). It's a twining plant, and a very untidy grower, so you'll need to treat it with a firm hand if it is on a wall or fence. Better still, grow it over an arch, arbour or even a shed, where its untidiness won't matter. There is a pink-flowered variety, *J. × stephanense*, and two lovely ones with variegated leaves, *J.o.* 'Aureum' with pale yellow variegated leaves and *J.o.* 'Argenteovariegatum' with cream variegated leaves, though you'd probably find the latter only in a specialist nursery.

Approximate height and spread after ten years 9 metres (30 feet).

Honeysuckle (Lonicera)

Like clematis, it's happiest with its head in the sun and its roots in the shade, so either plant shrubs in front of the honeysuckle to provide shade, or mulch the roots well with a deep layer of organic matter. For a long flowering period, plant both. *L. periclymenum* 'Belgica', the early Dutch honeysuckle, which in early summer and often again in early autumn has sweetly scented, pale rose-purple, tubular flowers that are yellow

within, and *L.p.* 'Serotina', the late Dutch honeysuckle, whose flowers, darker red outside and paler yellow inside are produced from mid-summer to mid-autumn. For brighter flowers, though without any scent, try *L.* × *brownii* 'Fuchsioides', which has brilliant orange-scarlet flowers in late spring and again in late summer.

Approximate height and spread 4.5–6 metres (15–20 feet).

Clematis macropetala.

Passionflower (Passiflora caerulea)

Provided with a warm, sheltered wall or fence, it will produce a succession of its large, intriguing flowers with white petals with a central ring of fine purple growths in which are the three styles and five anthers, said to symbolize the three nails and five wounds of the Crucifixion that give the plant its common name. The individual flowers are not long-lived, but so many of them are produced between June and September that it doesn't matter. In mild areas it is almost evergreen, but a really hard frost will cut the growth to the ground. If you protect the roots with compost it should produce new growth in spring.

Approximate height and spread (in mild areas) 4 × 3 metres (13 × 10 feet).

Roses
In their climbing and rambling forms, this is another family that leaves you spoilt for choice, both in colour and shape of flower – from the simple, almost flat, creamy-yellow flowers of 'Mermaid' to the elaborate, many-petalled, deep cerise-pink flowers of the thornless 'Zéphirine Drouhin'. Go for a repeat-flowering variety that will flower more or less non-stop from June to October, or even later in a mild autumn, rather than one which flowers for only a few weeks in June. First-class varieties include the pinky-apricot 'Compassion', the deep rose-pink 'Aloha', the deep yellow 'Golden Showers', the white 'Climbing Iceberg', the pearly, blush-pink 'New Dawn', 'Paul's Scarlet Climber' and 'Pink Perpétue', with clusters of double, carmine-pink flowers.

Approximate final height depending on variety 2.5–4 metres (8–13 feet).

Chilean potato tree (Solanum crispum 'Glasnevin')*
A very mundane name for an extremely pretty climber, though, to be fair, it is related to the common-or-garden potato. Given a warm, sheltered wall or fence, and a well-drained soil, it will produce rounded clusters of small, mauve flowers with prominent, bright yellow stamens in abundance from June to October. It's a wall shrub, not a climber, so will need supporting, either on horizontal wires or, better still, on chicken wire (see pages 129–30). Its long stems are sometimes killed by frosts in cold areas, but it takes a really severe winter to kill the plant altogether. Usually it starts into growth again the following spring. It has a beautiful relative, *S. jasminoides* 'Album', which produces clusters of pure white flowers with the same prominent gold stamens.

Approximate height after five years (if not cut back by frosts) 5–6 metres (16–20 feet).

Wisteria
One of the most beautiful climbing plants, with its huge trusses of violet-blue flowers hanging down in late spring and early summer. It does require quite careful pruning of its twining growths in late summer and again in winter if it's to produce flowers, and even so it can take five years or more for it to bloom for the first time. There is also a white variety,

Wisteria sinensis 'Alba', while the much less vigorous *W. floribunda* 'Macrobotrys' has trusses of lilac-blue flowers almost 1 metre (3 feet) long!

Approximate height and spread after ten years 20 metres+ (66 feet+); *W.f.* 'Macrobotrys' 9 metres (30 feet).

SHRUBS

Southernwood (Artemisia abrotanum)
This shrub has sweetly aromatic, very finely divided, grey-green leaves and small, bobbly flowers in early summer. It has a more beautiful relative, *A. arborescens*, with a mass of filigree silver leaves, but sadly this isn't as hardy and a really cold winter will kill it off. Unless you're a gambler, one of the tall perennial artemisias (see page 268) is a safer bet.

Approximate height and spread after five years 80 × 80 centimetres (2½ × 2½ feet); after ten years 80 centimetres × 1.2 metres (2½ × 4 feet).

Barberry (Berberis thunbergii)
In its purple-, red- and pink-leaved forms, it needs full sun to give of its best. Apart from striking foliage, they also have flowers in spring, berries in autumn and, in most cases, lovely autumn colour. There are several different shapes. One of the best stiff, upright varieties is *B.t.* 'Helmond Pillar', with deep purple leaves, while for something tall but with gracefully arching branches look for the brilliant wine-red *B.t.* 'Red Chief'. For a low, semi-spreading shrub, *B.t.* 'Dart's Red Lady', which has deep purple leaves which turn a vivid fiery red in autumn, is hard to beat. The little, bun-shaped *B.t.* 'Bagatelle', which reaches no more than 30 centimetres (1 foot) in height, is ideal in a group for the front of a border.

Approximate height and spread after five years 1 metre × 60 centimetres (3 × 2 feet); after ten years 1.8 × 1.5 metres (5½ × 5 feet).

Brachyglottis (formerly Senecio) greyi
Grown largely for its soft, felty, silvery-green leaves, though it does produce bright acid-yellow, daisy-like flowers in mid-summer. If you are growing it for its foliage and the flowers don't suit your colour scheme, simply cut off the buds when they appear.

Approximate height and spread after five years 60 × 90 centimetres (2 × 3 feet); after ten years 90 centimetres × 1.2 metres (3 × 4 feet).

The repeat-flowering, fragrant climbing rose 'Pink Perpétue'.

Butterfly bush (Buddleia davidii)
It acts like a magnet for butterflies in any garden and is also an attractive summer-flowering shrub in its own right. There are many excellent named varieties from which to choose, with flowers in a range of colours from white to almost black (*B.d.* 'Black Night'), but where space is limited smaller-growing varieties, like *B.d.* 'Nanho Alba' and 'Nanho Purple', are a good choice. Two lovely relatives well worth considering are *B. fallowiana* 'Alba', which has sweetly scented, pure white flowers with an orange eye and foliage that's silver-white when young fading to a very pale grey, and *B.* 'Lochinch', with lavender-blue flowers, again with an orange eye, and similar silvery-grey foliage. All buddleias benefit from cutting back hard every year or two, otherwise they become straggly and produce smaller flowers.

Approximate height and spread after five years 1.2–2.5 ×

1.5–2.5 metres (5–8 × 5–8 feet); after ten years (if unpruned) 2–3.5 × 2–3.5 metres (6–12 × 6–12 feet).

Carpenteria californica
An evergreen, summer-flowering shrub for a sunny wall in a sheltered garden. It has large, saucer-shaped, white flowers and long, glossy, bright green leaves. A really cold winter will cut it back to the ground, and though it will usually produce new growth in the spring, it will take a couple of years before it flowers again.

Flowers June to July. Approximate height and spread after five years 1 × 1 metre (3 × 3 feet); after ten years 1.5 × 1.5 metres (5 × 5 feet).

Californian lilac (Ceanothus)
When it's smothered with bright blue thimbles of flowers in early summer, it is a startling sight. There are both evergreen and deciduous kinds, and some can eventually make very large shrubs indeed, though the evergreen varieties are not totally hardy in colder areas. Among the best deciduous varieties are C. 'Gloire de Versailles', with powder-blue flowers in mid-summer, and the much deeper blue C. 'Topaz'. Among the hardiest and/or smallest-growing evergreen varieties are C. *impressus*, with distinctive, small, glossy green leaves, often curled at the edges, and masses of small, deep blue flowers in late spring, which doesn't grow to much more than 1.3–1.5 metres (4–5 feet) in height and spread; and C. *thyrsiflorus repens* 'Creeping Blue Blossom', which very quickly forms a mound of dense, evergreen foliage no more than 1 metre (3 feet) in height and is smothered in mid-blue blossom in May.

Approximate height and spread after five years 1 × 1.2 metres (3 × 4 feet); after ten years 1.3 × 1.5 metres (4 × 5 feet); C. *thyrsiflorus repens* after ten years 1 × 2.5 metres (3 × 8 feet).

Ceratostigma willmottianum
This plant produces masses of deep blue, saucer-shaped flowers from August to the first autumn frosts. If the stems aren't cut back to the ground by hard frost, prune them back in spring to stop the shrub becoming leggy and to encourage flowering. C. *plumbaginoides*, with bright blue flowers, grows to only about a quarter of the size, making it a useful ground-cover plant.

Approximate height and spread after five years (unpruned) 60 × 60 centimetres (2 × 2 feet); after ten years 1 × 1 metre (3 × 3 feet).

Mexican orange blossom (Choisya ternata)
It has glossy, aromatic, evergreen leaves and profusion of small, white, scented flowers in summer and often again in autumn. It will grow in shade as well as full sun, though it flowers more freely in sun. It forms a large, rounded bush, but can be pruned to keep it within the allotted space.

Approximate height and spread after five years 1 × 1.2 metres (3 × 4 feet); after ten years 2 × 1.8 metres (6 × 5½ feet).

Smoke bush (Cotinus coggygria)
It gets its common name from the clouds of tiny flowers that cover it all summer, turning a smoky grey in the autumn. The purple-leaved varieties, like *C.c.* 'Royal Purple' or 'Notcutt's Variety', are the most beautiful, with wine-red foliage in spring and summer, and superb autumn colour too, as well as the clouds of 'smoky' flowers. You can cut it hard back each spring to produce bigger, brighter leaves, but if you do, you lose the flowers, which are produced on the previous season's wood.

Approximate height and spread after five years 1.5 × 1.5 metres (5 × 5 feet); after ten years 3 × 3 metres (10 × 10 feet).

Cotoneaster
Another large family with members of all shapes and sizes, deciduous and evergreen, some of which will thrive in practically every garden situation. In a small garden, some of the ground-covering, small-leaved evergreens, which can cope with full sun and shade, are ideal. Look for *Cotoneaster dammeri* ('Coral Beauty' is a particularly good form), with white flowers in summer followed by sealing-wax-red berries. The slow-growing *C. microphyllus*, good for covering a bank or for growing over a wall, has masses of tiny, grey-green leaves and dark red fruits in autumn and forms a low mound, rather than growing flat like *C. dammeri*.

Approximate height and spread after five years 30–50 centimetres × 1.2 metres (12–18 inches × 4 feet); after ten years 30–60 centimetres × 2 metres (1–2 × 6 feet).

Broom (Cytisus)
These also come in many different shapes and sizes, and though most people think of them as having yellow flowers, in fact they come in a range of colours from cream through pink and mauve to rich red and maroon. Among the excellent

low-growing varieties, look for *Cytisus kewensis*, with a mass of cream flowers in May; *C. × beanii*, with rich yellow flowers at the same time; and *C. purpureus*, with lovely soft mauve-pink flowers. Among the taller brooms notable varieties are *C. scoparius* 'Lena', which has superb ruby red and pale yellow flowers, and the much taller *C. × praecox* 'Allgold', which is a blaze of golden yellow flowers in spring.

Approximate height and spread after five years – low-growing species 50 × 80 centimetres (1½ × 2½ feet); taller-growing species 60 × 80 centimetres (2 × 2½ feet); after ten years 50 centimetres × 1.2 metres (1½ × 4 feet) and 1.2 × 2 metres (4 × 6 feet) respectively.

Daphne

Another large family, and it includes two of the best winter-flowering shrubs: *Daphne mezereum*, which produces clusters of sweetly scented, purple-red or white flowers on bare wood in February and March, while the small pink and white flowers of *D. odora* are even more fragrant. They do best in deep, rich, moist soil, but will tolerate some lime. The evergreen native daphne, *D. laureola*, which has yellow flowers in early spring, dislikes full sun and does best in medium shade.

Approximate height and spread after five years 60 × 60 centimetres (2 × 2 feet); after ten years 80 × 80 centimetres (2½ × 2½ feet).

Winter-flowering heather (Erica carnea)

Unlike its summer flowering relative, it doesn't need an acid soil. (See page 204.)

Escallonia

A valuable, summer-flowering, evergreen shrub, though in a really cold winter it may lose its leaves and start into growth again in spring. It has masses of small flowers in a range of colours from white through many shades of pink to rich red. Good varieties include *Escallonia* 'Donard Seedling', with very pale pink flowers; *E.* 'Donard Star', with deep green foliage and rose-pink flowers; the taller-than-average *E.*'Iveyi', with very glossy, very dark green leaves and large, pure white flowers; and *E.* 'Peach Blossom', with soft peachy-pink flowers.

Approximate height and spread after five years 1.5 × 1.5 metres (4 × 4 feet); after ten years 2 × 1.8 metres (6 × 5½ feet).

13. *Sorbus cashmiriana*

25. *Philadelphus coronarius* 'Aureus'

6. *Solanum crispum* 'Glasnevin'

The south-facing border shown in the plan on page 155 five years after planting.

38. *Allium schoenoprasum* 'Forescate'

36. Lupin 'Russell Hybrids'

37. *Alstromeria* 'Princess'

32. Delphinium hybrids

26. *Cotinus coggygria*
    'Atropurpurea'

11. Rose 'Mermaid'

31. *Artemisia* 'Powis
    Castle'.

34. *Stachys olympicum*
    'Primrose Heron'

33. *Anthemis
    cupaniana*

35. *Coreopsis
    verticillata*
    'Moonbeam'

Spindle (Euonymous fortunei)
Will grow in full sun as well as in shade. (See page 188.)

Fremontodendron californicum
This makes a large wall shrub in a sunny, sheltered spot, with big, lobed, green-grey leaves covered in down, and large, buttercup-yellow flowers throughout the summer. It is susceptible to frost in the first few years, but once established is pretty hardy. It will also tolerate high alkalinity.

Approximate height and spread after five years 3×3 metres (10×10 feet); after ten years 5×5 metres (16×16 feet).

Chinese witch hazel (Hamamelis mollis)
This plant will also grow in full sun as well as in shade. (See page 165.)

Shrubby veronicas (Hebe)
Mostly from New Zealand, these include many very useful flowering evergreen shrubs. Some of the smaller ones are worth growing for their foliage alone – the ground-covering, blue-grey *Hebe pinguifolia* 'Pagei', for example, and the mound-forming *H. albicans*, with small, densely packed, elliptical grey-green leaves. They won't reach much more than 50 centimetres $\times$ 1 metre ($1\frac{1}{2} \times 3$ feet) in ten years, they are both hardy and have stubby spikes of white flowers from early summer onwards. Of the larger hebes, *H.* 'Midsummer Beauty', *H. × franciscana* 'Blue Gem' and *H.* 'Autumn Glory', which all have mauve or lavender-blue flowers at various times throughout the summer, and the pink-flowered *H.* 'Great Orme' are all good. There are lovely variegated varieties too, like *H. × andersonii* 'Variegata', but they are even less hardy than their plainer relatives and won't survive a very cold winter.

Approximate height and spread after five years 1×1 metre (3×3 feet); after ten years 1.5×1.5 metres (5×5 feet).

Rose of Sharon (Hypericum calycinum)
Best avoided unless you have acres to fill, since it becomes very clear after a season or two that world domination is its ultimate goal! A far better bet is *H. patulum* 'Hidcote', which has shallow, saucer-shaped, golden-yellow flowers all summer long and is semi-evergreen.

Approximate height and spread after five years 60 × 60
centimetres (2 × 2 feet); after ten years 1 × 1 metre (3 × 3 feet).

Beauty bush (Kolkwitzia amabilis)
It has lovely, soft pink, bell-shaped flowers from late spring
to mid-summer on wood at least three years old. It does best
in full sun, but it can be grown against a north-facing wall.
There's a variety called 'Pink Cloud' which has larger flowers
and starts producing them earlier in life than its parent.

Approximate height and spread after five years 1.5 × 1.5
metres (5 × 5 feet); after ten years 2.5 × 2.5 metres (8 × 8 feet).

Tree mallow (Lavatera olbia 'Rosea')
A quick-growing, upright, long-flowering shrub, with large,
silvery-pink flowers. It's good for the back of the border. Hard
pruning in spring encourages better flowering. There is an
attractive newer variety, *L.* 'Barnsley', which has blush-white
flowers with a red centre.

Approximate height and spread after five years 2.5 × 2
metres (8 × 6 feet); after ten years 3 × 3 metres (10 × 10 feet).

Magnolias
Magnolias are among the most beautiful flowering shrubs and
trees, but most are much too large for a small garden. An
exception is *Magnolia stellata*, which is covered in white, star-
shaped flowers with long, slender petals in April and May,
before the leaves appear. *M.s.* 'Royal Star' has larger flowers
which appear a little later.

Approximate height and spread after five years 80 centimetres × 1 metre (2½ × 3 feet); after ten years 1.5 × 2 metres
(5 × 6 feet).

Osmanthus delavayi
A useful evergreen shrub with small leaves and superbly
scented, small, white flowers in spring – ideal for cutting and
taking indoors. It's happy in most soils, including chalk.

Approximate height and spread after five years 2 × 2 metres
(6 × 6 feet); after ten years 3 × 3 metres (10 × 10 feet).

Mock orange (Philadelphus)
Gets its common name from its sweet-scented white flowers,
borne in profusion in June and July. Again there are a number
of good varieties, though those that grow to 3 metres+ (10
feet+) are not ideal for small gardens. Among the best small

varieties are 'Aureus', 'Belle Etoile', which forms an arching shrub covered in superbly scented, large, single, white flowers, and the smallest of all, 'Manteau d'Hermine', whose twiggy branches are smothered in creamy-white, double flowers.

Approximate height and spread after five years 80 centimetres–1 metre × 80 centimetres–1 metre (2½–3 feet × 2½–3 feet); after ten years 1–1.5 × 1–1.5 metres (3–5 × 3–5 feet).

Potentillas (Potentilla fruticosa)

These make small- to medium-sized, rounded bushes which carry their small, pretty, open-faced flowers for months on end. There are many good varieties from which to choose, some well-established like the yellow-flowered 'Katherine Dykes', 'Elizabeth' and 'Goldfinger'; the pure white-flowered 'Abbotswood', with soft grey foliage; the smallest-growing,

The low-growing, long-flowering dwarf rose 'The Fairy' is ideal for a mixed border in a small garden.

Above: A classic cottage garden border, with campanulas, oriental poppies, delphiniums and hardy geraniums.

Left: Daisies (*Bellis perennis*) will also flower in light shade.

cream-flowered 'Tilford Cream'; and some relatively new like the orange-red 'Red Ace' and the pale pink 'Princess', whose flowers fade in prolonged, hot, dry weather to near-white.

Approximate height and spread after five years 80 × 80 centimetres (2½ × 2½ feet); after ten years 1 × 1 metre (3 × 3 feet).

Stag's horn sumach (Rhus typhina)
It will also grow in sun as well as shade. (See page 189.)

Flowering currant (Ribes sanguineum)
Will grow in sun as well as shade. (See pages 189–90.)

California tree poppy (Romneya coulteri)
A deciduous shrub which bears lovely, large, fragrant, white flowers with prominent gold centres, rather like poppies, from mid-summer to mid-autumn. It dies back in winter and any shoots that don't die back should be pruned hard in spring.

Flowers July to September. Approximate height and spread after five years 1 × 1 metre (3 × 3 feet); after ten years 1 × 2 metres (3 × 6 feet).

Roses
Roses are essential for any garden, and they are now available in so many different forms that between them they'll do everything from climbing 20 metres (60 feet) up a tree to growing in a window box! Though hybrid teas are the best-known roses and do produce superb blooms for cutting, their growth habit is rather stiff for mixed borders. Some of the cluster-flowered floribundas are more graceful, and of the many good ones – like the newer, pale pink, superbly scented 'City of London', the blush-white 'Margaret Merril' and the amber-yellow 'Amber Queen' – are all excellent for a mixed border in a small garden. The 'English' roses are also ideal for this purpose, combining the beautiful petal formations, soft colours and fragrance of the old roses, with a compact habit and repeat-flowering. There are many to choose from, but among those widely available are the soft yellow 'Graham Thomas', the white 'Fair Bianca', the peachy-pink 'Heritage', and 'Othello', with crimson flowers turning purple as they age.

Approximate height and spread after five years 80 centimetres–1.2 metres × 80 centimetres–1.2 metres (2½–4 feet × 2½–4 feet).

For something even smaller, look for patio, dwarf or miniature roses – different places sell them under different names, though on the whole the two former are larger than the latter. Again there are many good ones from which to choose, and more are being added all the time as the rose breeders realize there is a growing market for small roses. Among the best patio roses are the orange-red 'Anna Ford', the pale rose-pink 'Gentle Touch', the apricot-pink 'Peek a Boo', the golden-orange-flushed-with-pink 'Sweet Magic' (which sounds awful but looks terrific!), and the old favourite, 'The Fairy', with masses of clear pink rosettes from July to Christmas, given a mild autumn. Of the miniatures 'Baby Masquerade', with yellow flowers flushed pink, the three 'Sunblazes' ('Orange', 'Gold', and 'Pink'), the crimson 'Little Buckeroo' and the white 'Pour Toi' are all good.

Approximate height and spread after five years 50–60 × 40–60 centimetres (18 inches–2 feet × 16 inches–2 feet).

Spiraea

There are varieties which flower in spring, like *Spiraea* × *arguta* (also known as bridal wreath), and those that flower in summer. Some of these also have striking foliage, like *S.* × *bumalda* 'Goldflame', whose new leaves emerge a startling orange-gold and slowly fade to green-gold by the time the dark pink-red flowers are coming through. Another rather curious variety worth thinking about is *S. japonica* 'Shirobana', which carries flowers that are all-white, all-rose-crimson or a mixture of the two at the same time.

Approximate height and spread after five years 40 × 50 centimetres (15 × 18 inches); after ten years 60 × 70 centimetres (2 × 2 feet 3 inches).

Lilacs (Syringa)

These are beautiful, late spring- and early summer-flowering shrubs for a sunny spot on any soil, particularly a chalky one. There are many excellent named varieties, though for small gardens you need to look for the pure white *Syringa* 'Vestale', the dark lilac-red *S.* 'Congo' or the pale yellow *S.* 'Primrose'.

Approximate height and spread after five years 1 metre × 90 centimetres (3 × 2½ feet); after ten years 1.5 × 1.2 metres (5 × 4 feet).

Alternatively, you could try the very slow-growing Korean lilac (*Syringa meyeri* 'Palibin'), which produces numerous sweetly scented, pinky-lilac flowers on a bush which reaches no more than 80 centimetres (2½ feet) in ten years. Slightly larger is *S. microphylla* 'Superba', which has rose-pink flowers in May and June and then again in the autumn. It's now possible to get lilacs which have been micro-propagated and so don't send up suckers from the rootstock.

Approximate height and spread after five years 30 × 25 centimetres (12 × 10 inches); after ten years 80 × 60 centimetres (2½ × 1½ feet).

Viburnum

This really is the most accommodating family of plants. As well as those that thrive in shade, there are many that need full sun. The winter-flowering varieties like *Viburnum* × *bodnantense* and *V. farreri*, which have sweetly scented, pink-white flowers on bare wood from November onwards, certainly need a sunny spot and will tolerate most soils, including limy ones. The winter-flowering evergreen, *V. tinus*, actually prefers a shadier position.

Approximate height and spread after five years 1.5 × 1 metre (5 × 3 feet); after ten years 2.5 × 2 metres (8 × 6 feet).

The summer-flowering *Viburnum plicatum* 'Mariesii' has

Weigela praecox 'Variegata' is attractive in flower but worth growing for its foliage alone.

fresh green, deeply ribbed leaves and, in time, a distinctly layered habit, so the lace-caps of white flowers that appear on the tiered branches make them look as though they are covered in snow. It also has berries in autumn and good autumn colour. *V.p.* 'Watanabe' is a smaller version, reaching only two thirds the height and spread of 'Mariesii'. The guelder rose (*V. opulus*) will also grow in sun. (See pages 169–72.)

Approximate height and spread after five years 2.5 × 2 metres (8 × 6 feet); after ten years 3.5 × 3 metres (12 × 10 feet).

Red hot pokers (*Kniphofia galpinii*) and *Sedum* 'Autumn Joy' provide an arresting contrast in flower colour, foliage shape and form.

Weigela

It has pretty, white, pink or red flowers in May and June. For flowers the ruby-red-flowered *Weigela* 'Bristol Ruby' and the bright scarlet W. 'Evita' are both good; while for the longest possible season of interest look for W. *florida* 'Foliis Purpureis', whose purple leaves tone perfectly with the paler purplish-pink flowers; and, perhaps best value of all, W. *florida* 'Variegata', which has pale pink flowers and very attractive cream and green variegated foliage through till the autumn.

Approximate height and spread after five years 1.2 × 1.2 metres (4 × 4 feet); after ten years 1.8 × 1.8 metres (5½ × 5½ feet).

HERBACEOUS PLANTS

Bugle (Ajuga reptans)
In its red and purple-leafed forms, is an excellent carpeter for a sunny border. Good varieties include A. *metallica*, which has dark purple, crinkly leaves; *A.r.* 'Braunherz', whose purple leaves have a bronze sheen; and *A.r.* 'Burgundy Glow', which has wine-red leaves. They all have spikes of deep blue flowers.
Flowers April to June. Approximate height and spread 10 × 50 centimetres (4 × 18 inches).

Pearly everlasting (Anaphalis triplinervis 'Summer Snow')
It carries pearly-white, everlasting daisies above clumps of grey foliage.
Flowers July to September. Approximate height and spread 40 × 70 centimetres (16 inches × 2 feet 3 inches).

Anthemis cupaniana
It soon makes spreading mounds of fine-cut, silvery foliage, covered in early summer with chalk-white daisies.
Flowers May to July. Approximate height and spread 30 × 40 centimetres (12 × 16 inches).

Artemisia
This, in its many forms, is a superb silver foliage plant for a sunny border with well-drained soil. One of the tallest and hardiest is *Artemisia absinthium* 'Lambrook Silver' with very fine, thread-like foliage and small, bobbly grey flowers, while A. *maritima* 'Powys Castle' is slightly smaller with the same fine silver foliage and no flowers. They keep their leaves all year, but look pretty scruffy by the spring, so prune hard to encourage fresh new growth. A. *ludoviciana* 'Silver Queen' has larger, deeply divided, silvery-white leaves. The smallest of all, A. *schmidtiana*, makes a low mound of silver thread-like foliage – good with a purple bugle or *Viola labradorica*.
Flowers June to July. Approximate height and spread 10–90 centimetres × 30–60 centimetres (4 inches–3 feet × 1–2 feet).

Michaelmas daisies (Aster amellus and A. novi-belgii)
They are a must for autumn colour in a sunny border. They

come in a range of colours – white and pink as well as the usual blue-mauve – and good varieties include *A.a.* 'King George', *A.a.* 'Violet Queen', and the pink *A.a.* 'Pink Zenith'. Other species like *A. novi-belgii* come in a similar range of colours plus red – *A.n.-b.* 'Jenny'. Good varieties include the soft lavender-mauve *A.n.-b.* 'Lady in Blue' and the warm coral pink *A.n.-b.* 'Alice Haslem'.

Flowers September to November. Approximate height and spread 30–70 × 40–50 centimetres (1 foot–2 feet 3 inches × 16–18 inches).

Double daisy (Bellis perennis)
With lots of pretty double flowers in early summer, this is an old favourite, dating back to the sixteenth century and now enjoying a new wave of popularity. Good varieties include *B.p.* 'Dresden China', with shell-pink flowers; 'Alice' with peachy-pink flowers; and the 'hen and chicken' daisy, 'Prolifera', in which a ring of miniature daisies hangs from the central one. Whilst strictly a perennial, this one is grown as a biennial.

Flowers May to July. Approximate height and spread 10 × 15 centimetres (4 × 6 inches).

Bellflowers (Campanula)
Both the tall and the dwarf ones are ideal plants for a sunny border. The very tall specimens like *Campanula lactiflora*, which can reach 1.5 metres (5 feet) or more, have such large heads of powder-blue flowers that they really need staking if they are not to flop, so slightly smaller varieties like the blue or white *C. latifolia* or *C. persicifolia*, which produce stiff stems from neat rosettes of narrow evergreen leaves, are a better bet.

Flowers June to August. Approximate height and spread 90 × 40 centimetres (3 feet × 16 inches).

The dwarf bellflowers, with upturned, cup-shaped or star-shaped flowers, are marvellous value for the front of a border as they go on flowering for months. Good varieties to look for include the blue *Campanula carpatica* 'Chewton Joy', 'Isobel' and 'Blue Moonlight', and 'Bressingham White'. 'Stella', which is smothered in small, star-shaped, blue flowers all summer, is another good variety. One to avoid is *C. porscharskyana*, which is a rampant spreader.

Flowers June to September. Approximate height and spread 20 × 40 centimetres (8 × 16 inches).

Mountain cornflower (Centaurea montana)

A relative of the more widely grown annual, this has lovely, scented, deep blue flowers above mats of green-grey foliage. If you cut it back after flowering, it will bloom again in autumn.

Flowers July to August. Approximate height and spread 50 × 50 centimetres (18 × 18 inches).

Crocosmia

It used to be called montbretia. It adds a blaze of colour from late June onwards, with its fiery orange flowers. Good hybrids include the flame-red Crocosmia 'Lucifer', the deep, burnt orange 'Emberglow' and, for something altogether softer, the pale apricot yellow 'Solfatare'.

Flowers July to September. Approximate height and spread 70 × 40 centimetres (2 feet 3 inches × 16 inches).

Delphiniums

They are without doubt the most spectacular blue-flowered cottage garden plants, and now there are dwarf varieties available they're suitable for the smallest garden. The varieties to look for are Belladona hybrids like D. × belladonna 'Lamartine', 'Peace' and 'Blue Bees', and even smaller dwarf hybrids like D. elatum 'Blue Fountains' and 'Blue Heaven'. The only problems with growing delphiniums is that if the soil is too wet and heavy they will rot, and that the slugs like the young leaves almost as much as hosta leaves, so take precautions. (If you don't want to use pellets, 10-centimetre (4-inch) rings cut from plastic lemonade bottles and pushed into the soil around the young plants work pretty well.)

Flowers June to August. Approximate height and spread 80 centimetres–1.2 metres × 50–80 centimetres (2½–4 feet × 1½–2½ feet).

Cone flower (Echinacea purpurea)

Another good late summer-flowering plant for a sunny border. Its rich mauve-red petals slope away from the large central cone which is a golden brown. Good varieties include 'Robert Bloom' and the white-petalled 'White Swan'.

Flowers July to September. Approximate height and spread 90 × 40 centimetres (3 feet × 16 inches).

Spurges (Euphorbia)

These do well in practically every garden situation, and of

Above: Traditional cottage garden plants like oriental poppies and campanulas are ideal for sunny, south-facing borders.

those that like a sunny spot and moist soil, two forms of *E. griffithii* are outstanding. 'Fireglow' has fiery-red flower heads above attractive light green foliage, while 'Dixter' has deeper orange-red flowers and leaves and stems tinged with a chestnut red.

Flowers June to August. Approximate height and spread 75 × 40 centimetres (2½ feet × 16 inches).

Cranesbill (Geranium)
Another large family with members in all shapes and sizes, the

Left: Ornamental grasses, like the moisture-loving golden sedge (*Carex elata* 'Aurea'), are valuable foliage plants.

flowers ranging from white through blues, pinks and almost fluorescent magenta to a purple so deep it's almost black. Among the most widely available varieties are *G. endressn* 'Wargrave Pink', which produces its salmon-pink flowers from May to November, and 'Johnson's Blue', which has clear blue, cup-shaped flowers for many weeks in mid-summer. Not so widely available but worth seeking out are *G. renardii*, which has lovely, scalloped, sage-green leaves and blush-white flowers veined with purple; *G. sanguineum*, with a profusion of vivid magenta flowers all summer; and the trailing *G. wallichianum* 'Buxton's Variety', which produces trailing stems of blue flowers with a white eye from mid-summer to autumn. It's an ideal plant for growing among small, early summer-flowering plants, because once their flowers have finished, it can trail over them, putting its own flowers in their place.

Flowers May to November. Approximate height and spread 40 × 40 centimetres (16 × 16 inches).

Avens (Geum)

An easy-to-grow plant, forming slowly spreading clumps of rich green leaves and producing brightly coloured flowers in shades of yellow and red. Good varieties include the yellow *Geum coccineum* 'Lady Stratheden' and the brick-red *G.c.* 'Mrs Bradshaw'.

Flowers May to August. Approximate height and spread 50 × 40 centimetres (18 × 16 inches).

Baby's breath (Gypsophila)

It produces sprays of tiny white flowers. Its botanical name means 'chalk lover', so it will obviously thrive on limy soil and dislikes acid conditions. The best white form is *Gypsophila paniculata* 'Bristol White' and there's a very pretty pink one called 'Rosy Veil'. The dwarf varieties, such as *G. repens* 'Dorothy Teacher', like even drier conditions.

Flowers June to September. Approximate height and spread 90 × 70 centimetres (3 feet × 2 feet 3 inches).

Day lilies (Hemerocallis)

These bear flowers that last for only a day, but they are produced in such profusion over many weeks that it doesn't matter. They also form weed-smothering clumps of bright green, strap-like leaves. There are many, many different ones – indeed, there is even a Hemerocallis Society – but a few good varieties that are fairly easily available include the velvety, bright yellow *Hemerocallis* 'Canary Glow', the old, sweetly scented, pale primrose 'Whichford', and the warm peachy-pink 'Pink Damask'.

Flowers June to September. Approximate height and spread 75 × 50 centimetres (2½ × 1½ feet).

Coral flower (Heuchera sanguinea)
It will grow in sun as well as shade. (See page 176.)

Houttuynia cordata 'Chameleon'
This plant has superb, red, cream and green variegated foliage which quickly spreads to form a bright mat. It does have white flowers, but they're insignificant.

Approximate height and spread 20 × 70 centimetres (8 inches × 2 feet 3 inches).

Iris (Iris ensata and I. sibirica)
They will thrive in a sunny spot provided the soil is moist so dig in plenty of organic matter. *I.e.* 'Variegata' has lovely cream and green striped leaves with pale mauve flowers, while the smaller *I.e.* 'Alba' bears beautiful white flowers. Good varieties of *I. sibirica* include 'Alba', 'Flight of Butterflies', with rich blue flowers veined in white, and 'Papillon', with flowers of the softest blue.

Flowers June to August. Approximate height and spread 60–90 × 30 centimetres (2–3 feet × 1 foot).

Red hot pokers (Kniphofia)
As their name suggests, they usually have flowers in glowing orange or red, though there are some forms now available with ivory flowers, green in bud (*Kniphofia* 'Little Maid'), and cream flowers, red in bud ('Strawberries and Cream'). If you plant them in autumn, they should be protected with a heap of bracken or straw for the first winter.

Flowers July to October. Approximate height and spread 60 centimetres–1.2 metres × 70 centimetres (2–4 feet × 2 feet 3 inches).

Shasta daisies (Leucanthemum maximum and Dendranthema)
These are invaluable white flowers for any border, flowering from mid-summer to autumn. Good varieties include the tall 'Wirral Supreme' and the much smaller 'Snowcap', which is

little more than half its size. Other border chrysanthemums (as opposed to their much larger-headed, show-bench relatives) for colour in late summer include the orange *D. rubellum* 'Peterkin', the rich mahogany red *D.r.* 'Duchess of Edinburgh' and the pale apricot-yellow, *D.r.* 'Mary Stoker'.

Flowers July to November. Approximate height and spread 60 centimetres–1 metre × 30–40 centimetres (2–3 feet × 12–16 inches).

Ligularias

They combine handsome foliage with attractive flowers, though different forms have very different flowers. *Ligularia dentata* bears large, yellow or orange, daisy-like flowers, while *L.* 'The Rocket' has tall spikes of small, yellow flowers, not unlike those of bugbane, on black stems. Don't worry if they wilt in hot weather – they'll soon recover, though they should never go short of water.

Flowers July to September. Approximate height and spread 1.5 metres × 70 centimetres (5 feet × 2 feet 3 inches).

Peonies (Paeonia)

These plants undoubtedly have the most beautiful flowers in spring, but in the majority of cases their flowering season is short. There are many superb 'Chinese hybrids' in a whole range of colours, with excellent foliage after their short but flamboyant flowers are over. *Paeonia mlokosewitschii* – known to its many friends, for understandable reasons, as 'mlok' or 'Molly the witch' – is attractive from the time its crimson shoots start pushing their way through the soil in winter. They are followed by buds and leaves, at first tinged pinkish bronze, then becoming a soft grey-green, and the most beautiful large, pale lemon flowers with gold centres. In autumn its unusual seed pods split open to reveal rows of red and blue-black seeds.

Flowers April to May. Approximate height and spread 60 × 60 centimetres (2 × 2 feet).

Oriental poppies (Papaver orientalis)

These are traditional cottage garden plants with their big, blowsy flower heads, not only in the traditional orange-scarlet, but also in different shades of pink, like *P.o.* 'Mrs Perry'; mauve, like 'Blue Moon'; and even black and white! They are inclined to flop, and the foliage may start to die off in mid-summer, so be sure to plant them next to or behind

something that flowers later and to cut them hard back after flowering has finished.

Flowers May to June. Approximate height and spread 80 × 50 centimetres (2½ × 1½ feet).

Phlox (Phlox paniculata)
These plants are also something no self-respecting cottage garden would be without, for their long-lasting, bright flowers range across many shades from white through various pinks and mauves to scarlet and crimson. Good, widely available varieties include *P.p.* 'Balmoral', 'Border Gem', 'Prince of Orange' and 'White Admiral'.

Naturalized winter-flowing bulbs – *Crocus tomasinianus*, snowdrops (*Galanthus nivalis*) and winter aconites (*Eranthis hyemalis*).

Flowers July to September. Approximate height and spread 90 × 50 centimetres (3 × 1½ feet).

The dwarf phlox, *P. douglasii* and *P. subulata*, form low mats of green foliage and produce masses of flowers in the same range of colours as their larger relation, plus blue. Good ones to look for include *P.d.* 'Red Admiral' and 'May Snow', *P.s.* 'Oakington Blue', 'Temiscaming' (a vivid rosy red) and 'White Delight'.

Flowers May to July. Approximate height and spread 15 × 40 centimetres (6 × 16 inches).

Jacob's ladder (Polemonium caeruleum)
Yet another old cottage garden favourite, it gets its name from its ladder-like, bright green foliage, and has clusters of mid-blue flowers throughout the summer. Once it's established, it seeds itself freely, but is easily hoed out if it becomes a nuisance.

Flowers May to August. Approximate height and spread 70 × 50 centimetres (2 feet 3 inches × 18 inches).

Ornamental rhubarb (Rheum)
It is a dramatic foliage plant, though in most of its forms it's too large for a small garden. The exception is *Rheum* 'Ace of Hearts', which has dark green, heart-shaped leaves, veined and backed with crimson, and plumes of dainty, very pale pink flowers.

Flowers May to June. Approximate height and spread 1.2 × 1 metre (4 × 3 feet).

Rudbeckia
It brings a warm glow to the late summer/early autumn border, with golden yellow or orange daisy flowers with their prominent dark central cones. Look for *Rudbeckia fulgida deamii* or 'Goldsturm'.

Flowers July to October. Approximate height and spread 80 × 40 centimetres (2½ feet × 16 inches).

Scabious (Scabiosa caucasica 'Clive Greaves')
It likes limy soil and produces large, violet-blue flowers from mid-summer on. *S.c.* 'Floral Queen' has bigger blue flowers, while there is a creamy-white form, 'Miss Wilmott'.

Flowers June to September. Approximate height and spread 70 × 50 centimetres (2 feet 3 inches × 18 inches).

Kaffir lily (Schizostylis coccinea 'Major'*)*
It produces neat, grass-like foliage and cherry-red flowers in late autumn at a time when there is little else so vivid in flower. In colder gardens it needs some protection in winter: bracken or straw piled over the leaves once flowering is finished.

Flowers October to November. Approximate height and spread 75 × 40 centimetres (2½ feet × 16 inches).

Tradescantia virginiana
Yet another lovely plant discovered by the Tradescants, the seventeenth-century plant hunters, has lovely three-petalled flowers in different shades of blue. The most vivid is *T.v.* 'Isis', with bright gold stamens, and there's a fine white form, 'Innocence'.

Flowers June to September. Approximate height and spread 40 × 40 centimetres (16 × 16 inches).

ORNAMENTAL GRASSES

There are also some ornamental grasses that deserve a place in a sunny mixed border.

Holcus mollis 'Variegatus'
It has variegated green and white leaves, with the white predominating, especially when the new growth appears in spring and again in autumn. It will also grow in partial shade, and though it can be invasive, it's easily pulled out.

Approximate height 15 centimetres (6 inches).

Miscanthus sinensis
A dramatic plant for the back of a border, making clumps up to 2 metres (6 feet) tall. The tallest is *M.s.* 'Silver Feather', with narrow, green leaves and plumes of silvery-pink in autumn. Slightly smaller, *M.s.* 'Variegatus' has strongly variegated green and white leaves arching from rigid stems, while the unusual *M.s.* 'Zebrinus' has dark green leaves marked with distinct, horizontal, yellow bands.

Approximate height 1.5–2 metres (5–6 feet).

Molinia caerulea 'Variegata'
This has short, neat tufts of green and cream leaves, with arching stems of tiny, feathery flowers in late summer, both of which fade to an attractive pale beige in winter.

Approximate height 50 centimetres (18 inches).

ANNUALS

When it comes to choosing annuals for a sunny border with reasonably moisture-retentive soil, the world is your oyster, for they'll flower here better than anywhere else. Annuals fall into two groups – half-hardies, which need to be sown indoors and planted out only after all danger of frost has gone, and hardies, which can be sown straight into the soil. Raise your own from seed sown in gentle heat in March or buy them from the garden centre towards the end of May or even in early June. You'll see half-hardy bedding plants on sale from as early as late March, but don't buy unless you have a greenhouse in which to protect them until the weather warms up.

How you plant your annuals – whether in neat, straight lines, dotted here and there, or in bold drifts – is, as always, a matter of taste. There are no prizes for guessing which we prefer!

The following are good half-hardy annuals to buy as plants, flowering from July to October.

Ageratum

It makes low mounds of fluffy, blue flowers throughout the summer. *Ageratum* 'Blue Mink' is perhaps the most widely available variety, but newer hybrids, like 'Blue Danube' and 'North Sea', form bushier, even more free-flowering plants.

Approximate height 15–30 centimetres (4–10 inches).

Asters

These are good, late summer-flowering plants in many different shades of white, yellow, pink, salmon, carmine, mauve and blue. The taller varieties provide cut flowers too, while the dwarf ones are good for the front of the border.

Approximate height 20–75 centimetres (8 inches–2½ feet).

Begonias (Begonia semperflorens)

The fibrous-rooted kind are not to everyone's taste, but they are unbeatable for providing bright colour – vivid reds, pinks, salmons, white – at the front of a border right through the summer, regardless of how dreadful the weather. (See page 180.)

Approximate height 15–30 centimetres (6–12 inches).

Cosmos (Cosmea)
These produce lovely, open, daisy-like flowers in shades of red, pink and white above very feathery, bright green foliage and are an excellent annual for the middle of the border.
  Approximate height 90 centimetres (3 feet).

Busy Lizzie (Impatiens)
Will flower in sun as well as shade. (See pages 180–1.)

Lobelia
(See page 181.)

Marigolds
The French and African kinds seem to divide the world into those who love them and those who hate them! But they are very easy to grow, will put up with dreadful weather and flower right through the summer. They range from giant drumsticks, like 'Doubloon', which are 90 centimetres (3 feet) tall with flowers 13 centimetres (5 inches) across, to dwarf French marigolds, like the gold-edged 'Red Marietta', only 20 centimetres (8 inches) high. Although *Tagetes* is the botanical name for African and French marigolds, only the very dwarf ones, *T. pumila*, are sold under that name. *T.p.* 'Lemon Gem', 'Tangerine Gem' and 'Golden Gem' are all good.
  Approximate height 20–90 centimetres (8 inches–3 feet).

Nemesias
They come in practically every colour of the rainbow. You can buy them only in mixed colours.
  Approximate height 25 centimetres (10 inches).

Tobacco plants (Nicotiana)
These also come in a wide range of colours – everything from wine red to lime green. The smaller hybrids, like *Nicotiana alata* 'Domino' or 'Roulette', stand up to the rigours of a typical English summer better than the taller varieties and present their flowers upwards rather than drooping down. For the best perfume it's worth tracking down *N. affinis*. It's tall – 75 centimetres (2½ feet) – and its white flowers aren't large, but the scent on a warm summer evening is reason enough to grow it.
  Approximate height 30 centimetres (1 foot).

Petunias

These plants really are a monument to the plant breeders' art, for they now come not only in every colour you can imagine, but also with white edging, with stripes, with stars, double as well as single, frilled as well as plain. The choice is yours, though heavy rain can still make a mess of many of them. Resisto hybrids are bred specially to stand up to the weather.

Approximate height 25–30 centimetres (9–12 inches).

Verbena

It is sometimes available in single colours, but more usually as a mixture. 'Showtime' is particularly good, making an effective weed-suppressing carpet.

Approximate height 25–30 centimetres (10–12 inches).

The following are good hardy annuals for this position.

Pot marigolds, or English marigolds

These are lovely old cottage garden annuals in a range of colours from creamy yellow to burnt orange. Good varieties include *Calendula officinalis* 'Pacific Beauty' and the much smaller *C.o.* 'Fiesta Gitana'.

Approximate height 30–60 centimetres (1–2 feet).

Cornflowers (Centaurea)

They now come in a range of colours, but, to the traditionalists among us, they still look best in deep, rich blue. A good tall variety is 'Blue Diadem', while 'Baby Blue' has similar flowers but grows to less than half the size.

Approximate height 30–75 centimetres (1–2½ feet).

Clarkia

An upright annual that produces double flowers in shades of red, pink and white that could pass for carnations at a distance. *Clarkia elegans* 'Choice Double Mixed' is among the best.

Approximate height 50 centimetres (18 inches).

Godetia

They have lovely, delicate-looking flowers like upturned bells, in shades of pink, salmon red and white, with many bi-colours among them. *Godetia grandiflora* 'Sybil Sherwood', a rich salmon pink edged in white, is one of the most beautiful.

Approximate height 30 centimetres (1 foot).

Sunflowers (Helianthus annuus)
Certainly the giant kind, 'Giant Yellow' or 'Tall Single', are great fun for children – and parrot owners, since the enormous centres produce masses of seeds, which wild birds also like. Not as tall, and with smaller, chrysanthemum-like, double flowers, the variety 'Sungold Double' is good for the back of a border.
   Approximate height 1.2–1.8 metres+ (4–6 feet+).

Candytuft (Iberis)
It has clusters of small flowers in shades of pink, lavender, carmine and white. It's easy to grow and long-flowering. *Iberis umbellata* 'Fairy Mixture' (or 'Mixed') is a good variety.
   Approximate height 25 centimetres (10 inches).

Mallow (Lavatera trimestris)
An easy-to-grow plant for the middle of a border, producing large trumpets of pink or gleaming white flowers for months on end. *L.t.* 'Silver Cup', a rich silver-pink, and *L.t.* 'Mont Blanc', a pure white, are both established favourites, while a newer, paler mauve-pink variety, *L.t.* 'Pink Beauty', seems set to join them.
   Approximate height 60 centimetres (2 feet)

Poached egg flower (Limnanthes douglasii)
This plant is perfectly named, for its small, egg-yolk-yellow flowers are rimmed with white. It's a low-growing annual, ideal for the front of the border, especially with other yellow and white flowering plants.
   Approximate height 15 centimetres (6 inches).

Lobularia
The traditional edging companion for lobelia – they are sold together in street markets as 'blue and white'! It's also good for rock gardens, and in between paving slabs. Often it will seed itself freely. The largest-flowered variety yet is *Lobularia maritima* 'Snow Crystals', though *L.m.* 'Carpet of Snow' is also a good one.
   Approximate height 10 centimetres (4 inches).

Love-in-a-mist (Nigella damascena)
Yet another cottage garden plant, with cornflower-blue blooms surrounded by a mist of fine, green foliage. 'Miss Jekyll' is the best blue, while for the more radical among us

the mixed pinks, blues and whites of 'Persian Jewels' are worth trying.

Approximate height 60 centimetres (2 feet).

Mignonette (Reseda odorata)
It has curious, tiny flowers of yellowish-green and red which give off a superb fragrance, both night and morning. Bees love it.

Approximate height 30 centimetres (1 foot).

Consider planting these climbing annuals.

Sweet peas (Lathyrus odoratus)
These can be treated like other annuals and sown straight into the ground, but the best results come from seed sown under glass in autumn or early spring. Starting them on windowsills isn't very satisfactory as they tend to become very leggy, not bushy as they should be, so if you haven't got a greenhouse or cold frame, you're better off buying them as young plants from the garden centre. There are dozens of different colours to choose from, but try to buy a sweetly scented variety.

Approximate height 2 metres (6 feet).

Canary creeper (Tropaeolum peregrinum)
This is a lovely climber for a sunny fence or for growing through a shrub. It has fresh green leaves and fluffy bright yellow flowers.

Approximate height 3 metres (10 feet).

BULBS
In a sunny spot and a moisture-retentive but not heavy soil you can grow practically any bulbs you like, summer- and autumn-flowering, as well as spring-flowering, so you can afford to be choosy.

Ornamental onions (Allium)
These are dramatic bulbs for sunny borders. They range from the small *A. moly*, which has clusters of butter-yellow flowers in June, to the striking *A. christophii (albopilosum)*, with heads of silvery-lilac flowers the size of grapefruit on stems 60 centimetres (2 feet) high. Also good and easy to find is the small, rosy-pink-flowered *A. ostrowskianum*.

Flowers May to July. Approximate height 6–60 centimetres (10 inches–2 feet). Plant 10–20 centimetres (4–8 inches) apart depending on the size of the bulb.

Anemones

Particularly *Anemone blanda* which is excellent for a sunny border. It has large, daisy-like flowers in white, pink or blue and, given decent soil, will soon multiply into a large patch.

Flowers March to May. Approximate height 10 centimetres (4 inches). Plant 10 centimetres (4 inches) apart.

Glory of the snow (Chionodoxa luciliae)

It likes sun as well as shade. (See page 184.)

Crocuses

These are a must for any sunny border, and there's a huge choice. There are large-flowered Dutch crocuses (*Crocus vernus*) in shades of gold ('Yellow Mammoth'), white ('Jeanne d'Arc'), purple ('Paulus Potter'), purple-and-white ('Pickwick'), and the smaller species crocuses (*C. chrysanthus*), often in softer colours: look out for 'Blue Pearl', a delicate pale blue with a pearly sheen, 'Cream Beauty' and 'Snow Bunting', pure white with a gold centre.

Flowers February to April. Approximate height 5–12 centimetres (2–5 inches). Plant 8 centimetres (3 inches) apart.

Snowdrops (Galanthus nivalis)

They will thrive in sun as well as shade. (See page 185.)

Summer hyacinth (Galtonia candicans)

This is an undervalued summer-flowering bulb with tall spires of sweetly scented, waxy-white flowers. The leaves are long and rather floppy, so these bulbs are best planted among shrubs or herbaceous plants which can disguise them.

Flowers July to August. Approximate height 90 centimetres (3 feet). Plant 15 centimetres (6 inches) apart.

Hyacinths

They do have the most marvellous scent and, with their fat, densely packed heads of flowers, are an ideal way of creating large splashes of colour in sunny border. Good varieties include the deep blue *Hyacinthus orientalis* 'Ostara', the pure white 'L'Innocence', the rich pink 'Jan Bos' and the pale yellow 'City of Haarlem'. Make sure that you don't buy the bulbs prepared for forcing indoors since they aren't suitable for planting outside. Treat as bedding plants.

Flowers April to May. Approximate height 25 centimetres (10 inches). Plant 15 centimetres (6 inches) apart.

Dwarf irises (Iris reticulata)

They are delightful miniatures in many shades of blue, from the pale blue 'Cantab' to the deep reddish purple 'J. S. Dijt', all with delicate 'iris' markings on the lower petals. *I. danfordiae* is a vivid yellow iris of the same size; often, after flowering, it breaks up into smaller, non-flowering bulblets, so for all practical purposes you have lost it. Deeper planting – 12 centimetres (5 inches) instead of 8 centimetres (3 inches) – helps to prevent this happening.

Flowers February to March. Approximate height 15 centimetres (6 inches). Plant 10 centimetres (4 inches) apart.

Lilies

Lilies are so exotic-looking and have such a wonderful fragrance that you might assume they are difficult to grow. Certainly some are, but others are very easy, given a soil that isn't wet enough in winter to rot them and that doesn't dry out in summer. All lilies *must* have excellent drainage. They're tall-growing, but if you plant them among shrubs or perennials, they will support them and they won't need staking. Try *Lilium regale*, which has large, white trumpets, flushed pink on the outside, with such a heady perfume that a potful on a patio can scent a whole house through an open window. They prefer having their roots in shade and their heads in the sun, so planting them among small shrubs is an ideal way of growing them. *L. henryi*, which has large, hanging, orange 'Turk's-cap' flowers in late summer, is also easy, and some of the hybrids, like the orange-red *L.* 'Enchantment' and the white *L.* 'Sterling Star', speckled with brown, are all worth a try. These lilies are lime-tolerant and are all stem-rooting, so should be planted quite deeply – about 20 centimetres (8 inches).

Flowers June to September. Approximate height 1–2 metres (3–6 feet). Plant 20 centimetres (8 inches) apart.

Grape hyacinths (Muscari)

They grow in sun as well as shade. (See page 185.)

Daffodils (Narcissus)

Daffodils really do herald the arrival of spring, and no garden, no matter how small, should be without them. In a small garden some of the more common, large daffodils, like 'King Alfred', take up a lot of space and look rather out of proportion. Dwarf ones are a better bet, and apart from

Narcissus cyclamineus 'February Gold' and *N.c.* 'Tête à Tête' (see pages 185–6) that also tolerate shade, there are many to choose from that thrive in full sun. Look for hybrids like 'Jack Snipe' and the white and pale primrose 'Dove Wings', and the jonquil narcissi like the deep lemon 'Sundial' and the popular yellow and orange 'Suzy'. In a very small space try angel's tears (*N. triandrus alba*) which has two or three small, creamy white flowers on 15-centimetre (6-inch) stems or, from the same family, the slightly taller, free-flowering, robust, butter-yellow 'Hawera' or the exquisite pure-white-flowered 'Thalia'.

Flowers February to April. Approximate height 15–30 centimetres (6–12 inches). Plant 8 centimetres (3 inches) apart.

Nerine (Nerine bowdenii)
A valuable, autumn-flowering bulb for a sunny, sheltered spot (the foot of a south-facing wall is ideal). It bears a head of bright pink flowers with curly petals on a slender stem. The strap-like leaves follow the flowers, but die down in early summer. The bulbs should be planted with the neck level with the surface of the soil.

Flowers September to November. Approximate height 50 centimetres (18 inches). Plant 10–15 centimetres (4–6 inches) apart.

Star of Bethlehem (Ornithogalum umbellatum)
It has heads of starry white flowers, which are green on the outside, in late spring. Unlike its relative, *O. nutans* (see page 196), it needs full sun.

Flowers April to May. Approximate height 23 centimetres (9 inches). Plant 8 centimetres (3 inches) apart.

Tulips
Another must for the late spring garden, though again some of the smaller species tulips are probably less trouble. Look for Kaufmanniana, Greigii or Fosteriana hybrids which flower early and in many cases have attractive variegated leaves as well as lovely flowers. Of the Kaufmannianas, 'Heart's Delight', blush-white with carmine outside, 'Showwinner', a glowing cardinal red, and the creamy white 'Concerto' are all outstanding. Of the Greigiis, look for the deep rose 'Oratorio', the salmon-orange 'Toronto', with two or three flowers on each stem, and the vivid red 'Red Riding Hood'. Among the best Fosterianas, which have slightly longer flowers, are the three 'Emperors' – 'Red', 'Orange' and 'Yellow'. Also lovely

A superb dry garden in spring (above) and again in mid-summer.

are *Tulipa tarda*, whose butter-yellow flowers with a white edging open almost flat; the lovely, rounded, apricot-yellow *T. batalinii* 'Bright Gem'; and a true miniature, *T. linifolia*, with brilliant scarlet flowers on stems 10–12 centimetres (4–5 inches) high.

Flowers March to May. Approximate height 15–25 centimetres (6–10 inches). Plant 10 centimetres (4 inches) apart.

DRY SOIL

If you have a dry, sunny border, the sort of plants you're looking for are those whose native habitat is the thin, dry soil of the Mediterranean area.

Almost all grey- and silver-leaved plants – lavender, artemisias, lamb's ears (*Stachys byzantina*) and sun roses (*Cistus* species) – will thrive in these conditions, for what gives the leaves their silvery colour is a covering of very fine hairs which acts like a sunscreen to prevent the leaf scorching or shrivelling up. Other 'fleshy' plants, like stonecrops (*Sedum* species) or houseleeks (*Sempervivum* species), protect themselves against drought by being able to store water in their leaves, while still others, like the sun-loving spurges (*Euphorbia*) have a waxy coating to protect their surface. Few drought-lovers have large leaves – they have either very small ones, like the cotton lavender (*Santolina chamaecyparis*), or very thin ones, like pinks (*Dianthus* species), or very finely divided ones, like the artemisias, so they don't lose moisture that way. Bergenias are an exception here, but then their leaves are as tough as leather so they're in no danger of shrivelling up.

A number of these Mediterranean plants – rosemary, lemon verbena (*Lippia citriodora*) and lavender – also have aromatic oils in their leaves which helps protect them, and which is released into the air when the leaves are crushed or even just brushed against. That makes them good plants for the front of a border or on the corner of a busy thoroughfare, where that is most likely to happen.

Flower colours are important and here there's an opportunity to use the eye-catching 'hot' shades like the vivid magenta pink of rose campion (*Lychnis coronaria*), the vivid blue of the globe thistle (*Echinops ritro*) and the intense scarlet of *Anemone fulgens*. But as most drought-loving plants produce rather small flowers, they usually appear as small, vivid dots of colour against a largely, though not exclusively, grey background.

Since foliage plays such an important part in maintaining a long season of interest in a dry garden, it's vital to include plenty of contrasts, not just in the colours – golds and deep green like that of the perennial candytuft (*Iberis saxatilis*) as well as blues and greys – but in the shapes of the plants themselves, as well as in the shapes of the leaves. You want round shapes and spiky ones, horizontals and verticals. Mound-forming plants like lavender, cotton lavender, ballota and rue look like 'buns in a baking tray' unless you have some tall, spiky plants or ornamental grasses planted among them. Even at the front of a border, where you will naturally place smaller plants, something upright, like the steely-blue grass *Festuca glauca*, makes all the difference.

CLIMBERS
Climbing hydrangea (Hydrangea petiolaris)
(See pages 160–1.)

Passionflower (Passiflora caerulea)
(See pages 251–2.)

SHRUBS
Barberry (Berberis thunbergii)
In its pink, red and purple forms. (See page 253.)

Brachyglottis (formerly Senecio) greyi
Another attractive grey-leaved foliage shrub which has acid-yellow, daisy flowers in summer. It should be cut back hard in spring to prevent the plant becoming woody and sprawling.
    Flowers June to July. Approximate height and spread after five years 80 × 80 centimetres (2½ × 2½ feet); after ten years 1 × 1 metre (3 × 3 feet).

Buddleia
(See pages 254–5.)

Blue spiraea (Caryopteris clandonensis 'Arthur Simmonds')
A low-growing shrub with green-grey foliage and clusters of pale violet-blue flowers in late summer–early autumn. All its shoots should be cut back to near ground level in mid-spring, and for that reason it never grows larger than 80 × 80 centimetres (2½ × 2½ feet). Good varieties to look out for are 'Heavenly Blue', with bright blue flowers, and 'Kew Blue', with darker blue flowers.

Flowers July to October. Approximate height and spread in one season 80 × 80 centimetres (2½ × 2½ feet).

Wintersweet (Chimonanthus praecox)
(See page 225.)

Sun roses (Cistus)
They produce a succession of single, flat flowers in a range of colours from white, both pure and attractively blotched with crimson or purple, through various shades of pink to crimson. The flowers are short-lived but they are born in succession and such profusion that it doesn't matter. Many sun roses have attractive grey foliage, but only a few varieties are reliably hardy. Look out for the small *Cistus × corbariensis*, with small, white flowers opening from buds tinted crimson; C. 'Silver Pink', with (not surprisingly) silver-pink flowers borne in clusters; the tall *C. × cyprius*, with large, white flowers blotched with crimson; and the equally tall *C. laurifolius*, which has leathery, dark blue-green leaves and white flowers with yellow centres. They like any dry soil, including lime.

Flowers June to July. Approximate height and spread after five years 60 centimetres–1.2 metres × 60 centimetres–1.2 metres (2–4 × 2–4 feet).

Coronilla glauca
A rounded, bushy evergreen with lovely foliage not unlike that of wisteria only blue-green in colour. It produces masses of golden-yellow pea flowers in early summer and then intermittently throughout the summer and autumn. It can be fan-trained against a sunny wall.

Flowers May/June to September. Approximate height and spread after five years 1.5 × 1.5 metres (5 × 5 feet); after ten years 2 × 2 metres (6 × 6 feet).

Smoke bush (Cotinus coggygria)
In its red-leaved forms, like 'Notcutt's Variety', it will tolerate dry conditions. (See page 256.)

Moroccan broom (Cytisus battandieri)
It will do well on a sunny wall. (See page 249.)

Broom (Cytisus)
(See pages 256–7.)

Spindle (Euonymus fortunei)
It will tolerate dry soil once established. Water in times of drought during its first year. (See page 188.)

Fremontodendron californicum
(See page 260.)

Mount Etna broom (Genista aetnensis)
This makes a very large, graceful, arching shrub whose branches are smothered in bright yellow pea flowers, making a golden fountain in summer. It does eventually grow into a very large shrub, and doesn't respond well to pruning once it's mature, so allow plenty of space for it.

Flowers July to August. Approximate height and spread after five years 2.5 × 2.5 metres (8 × 8 feet); after ten years 3.5 × 3.5 metres (12 × 12 feet).

Spanish gorse (Genista hispanica)
Has lighter yellow flowers, makes a much smaller bush (60 centimetres × 1 metre (2 × 3 feet) after ten years), very prickly and rounded, while G. *lydia*, which in the same time reaches only 60 centimetres (2 feet) in height but achieves a spread of 2 metres (6 feet), is ideal for a dry bank or for tumbling over a wall.

Hypericum patulum 'Hidcote'
(See pages 260–1.)

Lavender (Lavandula)
It is an ideal shrub for a dry, sunny situation, with its narrow, silvery foliage and spikes of strongly scented lavender-blue flowers all summer long. It can be planted and clipped to make a low, informal hedge or edging to a border, or allowed to grow into a rounded bush. Good varieties include *Lavandula angustifolia*, the old English lavender with varieties like the dark lavender-blue dwarf 'Munstead'; and the similar sized 'Hidcote', with the most silvery foliage and the most intense blue flowers. You can also plant white- or pink-flowered lavenders like 'Alba' or the dwarf 'Nana Alba' or 'Loddon Pink'.

Flowers July to September. Approximate height and spread after five years 20–50 × 40–60 centimetres (8 18 inches × 16 inches–2 feet); after ten years 30–80 × 30–80 centimetres (1–2½ × 1–2½ feet).

Russian sage (Perovskia atriplicifolia)
This plant loves dry, sunny conditions and, if it gets them, grows into a tall spire of very thin stems so silvery they are almost white. These are covered in spikes of lavender-blue flowers in late summer. The best form is one called 'Blue Spire'. It should be cut back hard each spring to encourage really silvery new stems and to prevent it outgrowing the space allowed for it.

Flowers August to September. Approximate height and spread in one season 90 × 60 centimetres (3 × 2 feet).

Jerusalem sage (Phlomis fruticosa)
This is another grey-leaved shrub from the Mediterranean, with long, slightly wavy leaves that look rather like a giant version of sage leaves and clusters of pale yellow flowers in summer. The young foliage is the most attractive, so it needs to be pruned back in spring.

Flowers June to July. Approximate height and spread after five years 1 × 1 metre (3 × 3 feet); after ten years 1 × 1.2 metres (3 × 4 feet).

New Zealand flax (Phormium)
A dramatic, spiky-foliaged shrub with a number of particularly attractive forms. *Phormium cookianum* 'Cream Delight'

The clove-scented pink (*Dianthus* 'Cantab').

has olive-green leaves with a central cream band; *P. tenax* 'Yellow Wave' has a central yellow band; *P.t.* 'Maori Sunrise' has red-purple leaves with rose-pink and bronze veining; and *P.t.* 'Purpureum' has stiff, broad, bronze-purple leaves. Some varieties do produce flower spikes, but not for several years. In hard winters protect the centre of the plant, from which the new leaves are produced, against frost with bracken or straw. It won't survive in very windy or very cold gardens.

Flowers July to September. Approximate height and spread after five years 80 × 80 centimetres (2½ × 2½ feet); after ten years 1.2 × 1.5 metres (4 × 5 feet).

Rosemary
Like other Mediterranean herbs, it loves these conditions too. With its spiky, dark green leaves, and blue flowers in late spring, it makes a good background shrub for the middle of a dry border. Good varieties include *Rosmarinus officinalis*, the smaller *R.o.* 'Benenden Blue' and the arching *R.o.* 'Severn Sea', which has brilliant blue flowers and reaches about one third the average height and spread.

Flowers May to June. Approximate height and spread after five years 80 centimetres × 1 metre (2½ × 3 feet); after ten years 1.2 × 1.5 metres (4 × 5 feet).

Cotton lavender (Santolina chamaecyparissus)
This plant is grown for its lovely, delicate, silvery foliage, and though it does produce little, yellow flowers in summer, these not only make the foliage duller but also spoil the shrub's attractive bun shape and so hard pruning in spring is advisable. There is also a green variety, *S. virens*, which has bright green, thread-like foliage – very valuable in providing a contrast to the greys in a dry garden.

Flowers June to August. Approximate height and spread after five years 50 × 70 centimetres (1½ feet × 2 feet 3 inches); after ten years 50 centimetres × 1 metre (1½ × 3 feet).

Spanish broom (Spartium junceum)
Like its fellow brooms, it thrives in dry conditions and produces masses of bright yellow, pea-like flowers in mid-summer. It dislikes pruning, so if you need to keep its size in check, prune only the current season's growth.

Flowers June to September. Approximate height and spread after five years 2 × 1 metre (6 × 3 feet); after ten years 3 × 2 metres (10 × 6 feet).

Stranvaesia davidiana

Like *Photinia* × *fraseri* 'Red Robin', it is one of Nature's consolation prizes for those without soils acid enough to grow pieris! A semi-evergreen, it has bright red young leaves in spring and small white flowers in early summer, followed by good autumn colour and bright red berries.

Flowers May to June. Approximate height and spread after five years 1.5 × 1.5 metres (5 × 5 feet); after ten years 2.5 × 2.5 metres (8 × 8 feet).

Yucca

Yuccas come originally from Mexico, though in fact they'll grow happily in British gardens, given full sun and dry soil. They are slow-growing, but eventually produce flowers like huge lilies-of-the-valley on spikes up to 2 metres (6 feet) high. Good varieties include *Yucca filamentosa* and its variegated forms and *Y. gloriosa*, though its leaves are so spiky that it's best not planted where children are likely to run around.

Flowers July to August. Approximate height and spread after five years 1 × 1 metre (3 × 3 feet); after ten years 2 × 2 metres (6 × 6 feet).

HERBACEOUS PLANTS

Bear's breeches (Acanthus mollis)

A tall, striking plant, with spires of curious, purple-hooded, white-rimmed flowers and boldly cut foliage. *A. spinosus* has similar flowers and even more finely cut, positively prickly leaves, while *A. spinosissimus* has leaves so finely cut that they are almost skeletal.

Flowers June to September. Approximate height and spread 1.2 metres × 70 centimetres (4 feet × 2 feet 3 inches).

Yarrow (Achillea)

This is a family with members both small and large which are ideal for dry, sunny conditions. Among the dwarf varieties *Achillea* × 'King Edward', with ferny, green-grey foliage and primrose yellow flowers is good, while among the tall varieties look out for *Achillea* 'Moonbeam' and 'Moonshine', with greyish foliage and flat heads of bright yellow flowers; *A. millefolium* 'Cerise Queen', with flat heads of intense cerise pink; and, quite different, *A. ptarmica* 'The Pearl', which has pure white, double, button flowers.

Flowers June to August. Approximate height and spread 10–75 × 40–50 centimetres (4 inches–2½ feet × 16–18 inches).

African lily (Agapanthus)
It has rounded heads of blue or white on long, bare stems riding above clumps of strap-like leaves. Good varieties include *A. campanulatus* 'Albus'; *A.c.* 'Isis', the darkest blue; and Headbourne Hybrids in various shades of blue. In cold gardens they will need protection in winter.

Flowers July to September. Approximate height and spread 1 metre × 70 centimetres (3 feet × 2 feet 3 inches).

Alyssum saxatile
This is the acid-yellow flowering plant you often see sprawling over a sunny wall next to a bright purple aubretia in late spring/early summer. It has some subtler relatives with grey-green foliage, like *A.s.* 'Citrinum', which has cool lemon flowers, and 'Dudley Neville', with soft apricot-yellow flowers. There's also a variegated form of 'Dudley Neville'.

Flowers April to June. Approximate height and spread 25 × 25 centimetres (9 × 9 inches).

Ox-eye chamomile (Anthemis tinctoria)
Especially the variety 'E. C. Buxton'. Its ferny, green leaves and mass of creamy-yellow daisies carried throughout the summer make it a superb plant for a sunny border. The taller 'Wargrave Variety' with cool lemon-yellow flowers is also good.

Flowers June to September. Approximate height and spread 50 × 30 centimetres (1½ × 1 foot).

Artemisias
Ones like 'Powys Castle', 'Lambrook Silver' and 'Silver Queen' will also grow well in dry, sunny borders. (See page 268.)

Ballota pseudodictamnus
With its long, curving stems of felty, silver-white, round leaves, it revels in dry conditions. It does produce mauve flowers in mid-summer, but these are often thought to spoil the effect of the foliage and so are removed. It will die back naturally in all but the mildest winters, and if it doesn't it should be pruned hard to prevent it becoming straggly.

Flowers June to July. Approximate height and spread 50 × 60 centimetres (1½ × 2 feet).

Convolvulus cneorum
This is a superb plant with fine, silky, silver leaves with a faint sheen and a succession of ivory trumpets that emerge from long, tightly rolled, rose-pink buds. It's not completely hardy so would benefit from winter protection in colder gardens.

Flowers April to July. Approximate height and spread 45 × 45 centimetres (17 × 17 inches).

Coreopsis
It has yellow, daisy-like flowers for a long season in summer. *Coreopsis verticillata* 'Grandiflora' has rich gold daisies, while the new *C.v.* 'Moonbeam' has pale, creamy yellow flowers.

Flowers June to September. Approximate height and spread 40 × 30 centimetres (16 inches × 1 foot).

Crocosmia
This plant will also thrive in dry conditions. (See page 270.)

Pinks (Dianthus)
Pinks in their many forms – Chinese pinks, Cheddar pinks, maiden pinks, border pinks or carnations – all love hot, dry,

Most herbs do best in well-drained soil and full sun.

295

alkaline soils. Of the dwarf varieties look for the mat-forming *Dianthus deltoides* 'Flashing Light' (salmon-red flowers), 'Samos' (carmine) and 'Brighteyes' (red with a white eye), and hybrids like 'Little Jock', 'Nyewood's Cream' and 'Pike's Pink'. Of the taller varieties look for allwoodii pinks like the rose-pink 'Doris' and 'Diane', and among the old favourites the double white 'Mrs Sinkins', and any of dozens of new, longer-flowering hybrids like the Devon pinks – 'Devon Glow', 'Devon Blush' and 'Devon Cream'.

Flowers June to September. Approximate height and spread 10–30 × 25–75 centimetres (4 inches–1 foot × 10 inches–2½ feet).

Globe thistle (Echinops ritro)

This is a striking plant for the back of a border, with prickly, silver-green foliage and steel-blue, round, thistle flowers in late summer.

Flowers June to September. Approximate height and spread 1.1 metres × 70 centimetres (3 feet 6 inches × 2 feet 3 inches).

Sea holly (Eryngium)

This is also a thistle-like plant, only the best of them aren't at all prickly to touch. *E. oliverianum* has deeply cut, green leaves, but its stems and flower heads are all deep blue, while *E. giganteum* 'Miss Willmott's Ghost' – named after the redoubtable Victorian gardener who was said secretly to scatter its seed whenever she visited other people's gardens – has silvery green flowers surrounded by metallic silver, ruffle-like bracts. It's in fact biennial, but seeds itself freely.

Flowers June to August. Approximate height and spread 70 × 40 centimetres (2 feet 3 inches × 16 inches).

Spurge (Euphorbia)

It has forms which will also revel in these conditions. The small, prostrate *E. myrsinites* has stems evenly covered in waxy blue leaves, at the end of which are large heads of yellow-green flowers. The larger *E. polychroma* has heads of sulphur-yellow flowers in early summer, while the most spectacular is *E. wulfenii*, which is a large, dramatic, clump-forming plant with tall stems of blue-grey, evergreen leaves topped by large heads of sulphur-yellow flowers.

Flowers March to May. Approximate height and spread 15 centimetres–1.2 metres × 30–70 centimetres (6 inches–4 feet × 2 feet 3 inches).

Bronze fennel (Foeniculum vulgare 'Purpureum'*)*
It makes a tall pillar of very fine, bronze, thread-like foliage.
It does have yellow flowers in mid-summer, but at the expense
of more foliage being produced, so many gardeners remove the
flower buds. That also prevents the plant from seeding itself
everywhere.

Flowers July to October. Approximate height and spread
1.5 metres × 60 centimetres (5 × 2 feet).

Gypsophila
In its dwarf forms, it does well on dry soil. (See page 272.)

Rock roses (Helianthemum)
These are ground-hugging plants, many with grey foliage,
which have white, pink, red, orange or yellow flowers in great
profusion throughout the summer. Trimming them after
flowering stops them from becoming straggly. Good varieties
include the tawny orange-gold 'Ben Nevis', the double red
'Mrs Earle' (also known as 'Fireball'), the red and white
'Raspberry Ripple' and the three 'Wisleys' – pink, primrose
and white.

Flowers June to August. Approximate height and spread
25 × 60 centimetres (9 inches × 2 feet).

Candytuft (Iberis saxatilis)
This is invaluable in the dry, sunny border not only for its
chalk-white flowers in spring, but also for its spreading mats
of dark green, evergreen foliage.

Flowers April to May. Approximate height and spread 8 ×
60 centimetres (3 inches × 2 feet).

Rose campion (Lychnis coronaria)
This plant has downy grey leaves and branching heads of
small, intense magenta-pink flowers. There's also a white
form, 'Alba'. Both seed themselves freely unless they are
regularly dead-headed.

Flowers June to September. Approximate height and spread
60 × 40 centimetres (2 feet × 16 inches).

Catmint (Nepeta × faassenii)
This plant makes good weed-suppressing clumps of grey-
green foliage, with lavender-blue flowers. It gets its common
name from the fact that cats love rolling in it. The hybrid
'Six Hills Giant' is almost twice the size of its relative, is

1. *Cistus laurifolius*

2. *Achillea* 'Moonbeam' × 3

30. *Hydrangea petiolaris*

4. *Buddleia* 'Lochinch'

29. *Fremontodendr californici*

10. *Yucca gloriosa* 'Variegata'

11. *Caryopteris clandonensis* 'Arthur Simmond'

17. *Chionodoxa luciliae* × 7

6. *Alyssum saxatile* 'Dudley Neville' × 5

3. *Phormium tenax*, 'Maori Sunrise'

9. *Amaryllis belladonna* × 7

8. *Dianthus* 'Pike's Pink' × 5

5. *Echinops ritro* × 3

12. *Lychnis coronaria* 'Alba' × 3

Planting plan for a dry south-facing border.

7. *Santolina virens*

23. *Berberis thunberg* 'Rose Glow'

298

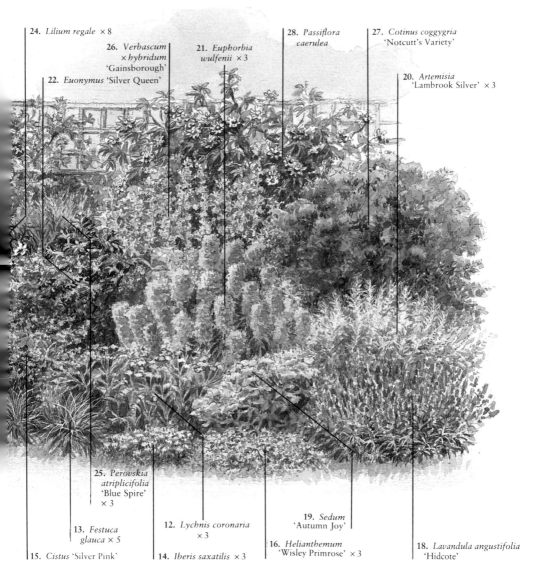

24. *Lilium regale* × 8

26. *Verbascum*
× *hybridum*
'Gainsborough'

22. *Euonymus* 'Silver Queen'

21. *Euphorbia*
wulfenii × 3

28. *Passiflora*
caerulea

27. *Cotinus coggygria*
'Notcutt's Variety'

20. *Artemisia*
'Lambrook Silver' × 3

25. *Perovskia*
atriplicifolia
'Blue Spire'
× 3

13. *Festuca*
glauca × 5

15. *Cistus* 'Silver Pink'

12. *Lychnis coronaria*
× 3

14. *Iberis saxatilis* × 3

19. *Sedum*
'Autumn Joy'

16. *Helianthemum*
'Wisley Primrose' × 3

18. *Lavandula angustifolia*
'Hidcote'

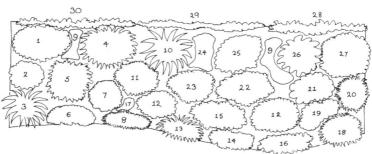

said to be hardier, and will tolerate a bit more moisture in the soil.

Flowers April to September. Approximate height and spread 30–60 × 30–60 centimetres (1–2 × 1–2 feet).

Evening primrose (Oenothera missouriensis)
An excellent choice for the front of a border. It has narrow pointed leaves above which are carried masses of large, trumpet-shaped, lemon flowers from mid-summer onwards.

Flowers June to September. Approximate height and spread 25 × 45 centimetres (9 inches × 1½ feet).

Sage (Salvia officinalis)
This is another herb invaluable for the dry sunny border. Apart from the ordinary culinary form with its sage-green leaves, there's a variegated cream-and-gold-leaved form, *S.o.* 'Icterina', the purple-leaved form, 'Purpurascens' and the smaller 'Tricolor', variegated in white, pink and purple. The latter need winter protection in cold areas. It has purple-blue flowers in mid-summer.

Flowers June to August. Approximate height and spread 40–60 × 40–60 centimetres (16 inches–2 feet × 16 inches–2 feet).

Bouncing Bet (Saponaria ocymoides) This is a vigorous ground coverer, ideal for a sunny bank, covered in bright pink campion flowers in early summer. It's sometimes sold as a rock plant but its vigour means that it soon smothers other plants in the rock garden.

Flowers May to July. Approximate height and spread 15 × 75 centimetres (6 inches × 2½ feet).

Ice plant (Sedum 'Autumn Joy')
It is attractive for most of the year, with its low rosettes of fleshy, pale blue-green leaves in spring, which grow through the summer into a mound of foliage. Then the flower stalks appear, carrying large, flat heads of pale green buds which turn slowly from rose pink to salmon and finally, in late autumn, to bronze. You can leave the flowerheads on through the winter and when you remove them in early spring you'll find the new rosettes of leaves beneath. Butterflies and bees love this plant.

Flowers August to October. Approximate height and spread 60 × 50 centimetres (2 feet × 18 inches).

Lamb's ears (Stachys byzantina)
This is another excellent grey-leafed plant whose flowers, with some exceptions, are rather a disadvantage. The form 'Sheila McQueen' has attractive silvery flower spikes, while 'Silver Carpet' is non-flowering, making an excellent carpeter for the front of a border. 'Primrose Heron' is a fine, yellow-leaved variety.

Flowers June to August. Approximate height and spread 12–30 × 40 centimetres (5–12 × 16 inches).

Thyme (Thymus)
This is a marvellous front-of-the-border plant for a hot, dry spot, with flowers ranging from white through pink to mauve. Among the more upright, bushy ones look out for *Thymus × citriodorus* 'Silver Queen', with variegated green and silver leaves, and *T. vulgaris* 'Golden King'. Among the mat-forming ones the dark green-and-gold-variegated 'Doone Valley', the bright gold 'Golden Carpet' and the grey-leaved, pink-flowered *T. serpyllum* 'Pink Chintz' are widely available and good.

Flowers June to September. Approximate height and spread 5–30 × 30 centimetres (2 inches–1 foot × 1 foot).

Mullein (Verbascum)
This is a stately plant for the back of a border. Apart from the giant *V. olympicum*, which reaches 2 metres (6 feet) and more, and has huge woolly, grey-white leaves and stems and clusters of yellow flowers, there are the smaller hybrids like the primrose yellow 'Gainsborough', the rose-pink 'Pink Domino' and the white 'Mont Blanc'.

Flowers June to August. Approximate height and spread 1.1 metres × 40 centimetres (3½ feet × 16 inches).

ORNAMENTAL GRASSES
Festuca glauca 'Silver Sea'
This is a compact, powder-blue grass that revels in hot, dry conditions. It's an ideal plant to provide a 'vertical' amid horizontal, mat-forming subjects.

Approximate height and spread 25 × 20 centimetres (10 × 8 inches).

Avena (Helictotrichon sempervirens)
It forms arching clumps of vivid, grey-blue foliage up to 45 centimetres (18 inches) high, with plumes of silvery-grey

flowers up to 1.2 metres (4 feet) tall in mid-summer.

Approximate height and spread 1.2 metres × 60 centimetres (4 × 2 feet).

ANNUALS

The following are half-hardy annuals raised in gentle heat from seed or bought as young plants.

Gazanias (Gazania)

These produce large daisy flowers in yellow, orange, pink, and rusty red, some of them single colours, many of them bicolours. The flowers open only in bright sunshine.

Approximate height 30 centimetres (12 inches).

Livingstone daisies (Mesembryanthemum)

These open only in bright sunshine, but they are produced in such numbers that, when they do open, they cover the fleshy, succulent foliage of the plant entirely. They come in glowing shades of pink, carmine, salmon, apricot and gold.

Approximate height 8 centimetres (3 inches).

The following are hardy annuals to be sown where they are to flower.

Star of the veldt (Dimorphotheca)

This is a sun-loving plant whose flowers actually close when it rains. Among the best varieties to try are the Aurantiaca Hybrids, in shades of white, lemon, gold, orange and salmon, or 'Glistening White', whose flowers are described perfectly by their name.

Approximate height 25–30 centimetres (9–12 inches).

California poppy (Eschscholzia)

These will also put on a dazzling display of red, orange and gold flowers on hot, dry soils. Good varieties include 'Monarch Art Shades', with semi-double flowers, and 'Ballerina', with fluted, double and semi-double flowers in the same range of colours.

Approximate height 25 centimetres (10 inches).

Nasturtiums (Tropaeolum)

These are invaluable in a dry, sunny situation and as well as being decorative are also edible. Good varieties for small gardens include T. majus 'Dwarf Jewel Mixed', which has semi-double flowers in several shades of yellow, orange and deep red, and 'Alaska', which has single flowers in red and orange, set off to perfection by marbled green and white foliage.

Approximate height 25–30 centimetres (9–12 inches).

BULBS
Though some of the traditional, spring-flowering bulbs don't enjoy being baked in summer, some of the more spectacular bulbs enjoy hot, dry conditions.

Ornamental onions (Allium)
(See page 282.)

Peruvian lilies (Alstroemeria Ligtu Hybrids)
With their long stems of small, pink, orange and peach flowers, marked with distinct brown dashes, they are increasingly popular as florists' flowers, and are worth trying in a dry, sunny spot, especially if you enrich the soil first with organic matter and mulch them with more of the same once they're planted. They die back after flowering is over, and will need protection in winter.

Flowers June to September. Approximate height 75 centimetres (2½ feet). Plant 30 centimetres (12 inches) apart.

Belladonna lily (Amaryllis belladonna)
This produces scented, pale satiny-pink lily flowers in early autumn on tall, bare stems (the leaves come later). It's an ideal plant for growing behind a medium-sized shrub that has blue flowers at the same time, like *Ceratostigma willmottianum.*

Flowers September to October. Approximate height 75 centimetres (2½ feet). Plant 30 centimetres (12 inches) apart.

Colchicums
(See pages 194–5.)

Regale lilies (Lilium regale)
(See page 284.)

Nerines (Nerine bowdenii)
(See page 285.)

Tulips
In the wild, they grow mainly on sunbaked, rocky hillsides in the Balkans and Central Asia and so do very well in our closest equivalent – limy dry soil in a sunny spot. (See pages 285–7.)

HEAVY CLAY SOIL

CLIMBERS
Ivy (*Hedera*). (See page 160.)
Wisteria sinensis. (See pages 252–3.)

SHRUBS
Barberry (*Berberis thunbergii*) (gold and purple-leaved forms). (See page 253.)
Japonica (*Chaenomeles speciosa*)
    Flowers January to April. Approximate height and spread 1 × 2 metres (3 × 5 feet).
Dogwood (*Cornus alba*). (See page 164.)
Woolly willow (*Salix lanata* and *S. hastata* 'Wehrhahnii'). (See page 168.)
Bridal wreath (*Spiraea × arguta*). (See page 265.)
Viburnum × burkwoodii and *V. plicatum tomentosum* 'Lanarth'. (See *V.p.* 'Mariesii' pages 266–7.)
Weigela florida. (See pages 267–8.)

HERBACEOUS PLANTS
Bear's breeches (*Acanthus mollis*). (See page 293.)
Japanese anemone (*Anemone × hybrida*). (See page 173.)
Michaelmas daisies (*Aster amellus* and *A. novi-belgii*). (See pages 268–9.)
Crocosmia. (See page 270.)
Foxglove (*Digitalis purpurea*). (See page 192.)
Helenium autumnale has large daisy-like flowers in shades of red, orange and gold. It needs regular dividing and staking, which makes it a less useful plant in better soil conditions than others that don't.
    Flowers August to October. Approximate height and spread 90 × 50 centimetres (3 feet × 18 inches)
Ligularia dentata. (See page 274.)
Bergamot (*Monarda didyma*). (See page 232.)
Knotweed (*Persicaria bistorta* 'Superba'). (See pages 177–8.)
Jacob's ladder (*Polemonium caeruleum*). (See page 276.)

ANNUALS
Provided you work plenty of organic matter into the soil, most annuals that thrive in sunny, moisture-retentive soil will do well.

BULBS
The vast majority of bulbs rot in heavy clay soils, but it's worth trying some daffodils, like the large-flowered *Narcissus* 'Golden Trumpet', or the much smaller N. 'W. P. Milner'. Improve the drainage before planting by digging in some coarse grit.

PLANTING PLAN FOR A DRY, SUNNY BORDER
(See illustration on pages 298–9.)

CLIMBERS
(*Allow 3 metres (10 feet) for each plant.*)
Climbing hydrangea (*Hydrangea petiolaris*). (See pages 160–1.)

Fremontodendron californicum. (See page 260.)

Passionflower (*Passiflora caerulea*). (See pages 251–2.)

SHRUBS AND TALL PERENNIALS
Sun rose (*Cistus laurifolius*). One of the tallest and hardiest with white flowers in early summer. (See page 289.)

Buddleia 'Lochinch'. (See page 254.)

Yucca gloriosa 'Variegata' is evergreen and, surrounded by deciduous shrubs and climbers, is good in winter. (See page 293.)

3 × Russian sage (*Perovskia atriplicifolia* 'Blue Spire'), its blue flowers in late summer contrasting with the bright yellow of the *Fremontodendron.* (See page 291.)

3 × mullein (*Verbascum × hybridum* 'Gainsborough'), the soft, yellow flowers attractive against the white and purple passion-flowers. (See page 301.)

Smoke bush (*Cotinus coggygria* 'Notcutt's Variety'). (See page 256.)

SMALLER SHRUBS AND PERENNIALS

3 × yarrow (*Achillea* 'Moonbeam'). Large, flat heads of clear lemon flowers, attractive against the dark green foliage of the cistus behind. (See page 293.)

3 × globe thistle (*Echinops ritro*). Its round, hard blue flowerheads good against the long, slender, silver leaves of the buddleia. (See page 296.)

Cotton lavender (*Santolina virens*). The bright green form provides necessary contrast among the surrounding blue and silver foliage. (See page 292.)

Blue spiraea (*Caryopteris clandonensis* 'Arthur Simmonds'). (See pages 288–9.)

Barberry (*Berberis thunbergii* 'Rose Glow'). Its variegated pink, purple and white leaves blend with the pale grey foliage and blue flowers of the caryopteris on one side and the euphorbia on the other. (See page 253.)

Euphorbia wulfenii. (See page 296.)

3 × *Artemisia* 'Lambrook Silver'. Its delicate silver foliage looks superb in front of the deep red cotinus. (See page 268.)

3 × rose campion (*Lychnis coronaria* 'Alba'). The branching heads of white flowers are attractive against the caryopteris and the berberis. (See page 297.)

Spindle (*Euonymus fortunei* 'Silver Queen'). An attractive evergreen. (See page 188.)

3 × rose campion (*Lychnis coronaria* 'Alba'). A patch of white against the variegated euonymus and the dark green euphorbia. (See page 297.)

3 × ice plant (*Sedum* 'Autumn Joy'). Its pale green, fleshy foliage in summer and its pink flowerheads in autumn are both attractive against the artemisia. (See page 300.)

Sun rose (*Cistus* 'Silver Pink'). (See page 289.)

New Zealand flax (*Phormium tenax* 'Maori Sunrise'). Its deep red, pink and bronze spiky leaves are an interesting contrast in colour and shape to the plants around it. The red also picks up the foliage colour of the berberis and the cotinus in a diagonal line across the border. (See pages 291–2.)

LOW-GROWING SHRUBS AND PERENNIALS
5 × *Alyssum saxatile* 'Dudley Neville'. (See page 294.)

5 × pinks (*Dianthus* 'Pike's Pink'). (See pages 295–6.)

5 × *Festuca glauca*. A vertical plant for contrast among the horizontal ones, and attractive against the silver and pink of the cistus. (See page 301.)

3 × candytuft (*Iberis saxatilis*). Another valuable green plant among the greys. Its white flowers in spring are valuable too. (See page 297.)

3 × rock rose (*Helianthemum* 'Wisley Primrose'). (See page 297.)

Lavender (*Lavandula angustifolia* 'Hidcote'.) This forms a neat, round bush at the corner of the border. (See page 290.)

BULBS
Belladonna lilies (*Amaryllis belladonna*). (See page 303.)

Regale lilies (*Lilium regale*). (See page 284.)

Glory of the snow (*Chionodoxa luciliae*). (See page 184.)

FRUIT AND VEGETABLES

Setting up a vegetable plot
In small modern gardens, a vegetable plot is really a luxury. In our garden in Birmingham, we had to make do with growing vegetables in the borders with the flowers and restricting our fruit mainly to the fences. Mind you, there's nothing wrong with that. In fact, vegetables can be quite attractive, especially those that take up least space, like the salads. And I reckon they'll be the ones you'll most want to grow.

Fruit trees can be almost as handsome as trees bred especially for the blossom. Apples, pears, plums, cherries, peaches, apricots and nectarines can all be grown in the shape of a fan on the fence, all have marvellous blossom in the spring and all have the added beauty of fruit to look at and to eat too. Who could ask for more?

What to grow
First of all, decide what is sensible to grow in the space available. There's absolutely no point in growing maincrop potatoes, for example, if space is limited. The farmer can do them just as cheaply and of equal quality to yours. Peas are probably even better frozen than home-grown (now *there's* a terrible thing for a gardener to admit!), because the processors pick them at just the right time, when they're at their sweetest. They take up a lot of space, so is it worth bothering?

Mind you, most vegetables, and especially the salads, are much, much better picked fresh from the garden. By the time they've been harvested, stood in the wholesale market, then in the shop and finally in your car getting them home, they're limp and tasteless. So, the first rule is to grow what is much better picked absolutely fresh. I would include in that all the salads, beans of every description, marrows and courgettes, spinach and sweetcorn.

Then look to grow what's most expensive or impossible to

buy. I wouldn't be without my annual feast of globe artichokes, for example, but you can't find them in many greengrocers at a price you can afford!

Deep-bed growing

If you're short of space, then a deep-bed is what you want. I've found that with this method you can increase the yield of vegetables by *at least* 100 per cent and with some crops you can triple it! What's more it's easier to weed and cultivate and a productive deep-bed looks very attractive indeed from the kitchen window.

It's really a very simple system, based on the practice of growing everything in 120-centimetre (4-foot) wide beds rather than in conventional rows. All the work is done from the side-paths, just by reaching in as far as the middle, so you never actually tread on the beds.

It's pretty obvious that just by doing away with the access paths in between each row of vegetables, you can save yourself a lot of space. Of course, the vegetables still need room to grow, but they can be put much closer together. Lettuces are a good example. If you grow them in a block of, say, six rows with 20 centimetres (8 inches) between each plant, you'll take up 1.2 × 1.2 metres (4 × 4 feet) of space. If you leave a 30-centimetre (1 foot) path between each row on the conventional method, you'll take up 1.8 × 1.2 metres (6 × 4 feet). Put it another way; by the traditional row method you'd get 28 lettuces out of a 1.2 × 1.2-metre (4 × 4-foot) space, while by using the bed method, you'd get 42.

That would work if you cultivated the soil by single-digging only, but if you double-dig (see pages 44–5) there's a bonus. By extending the depth of the root-zone, you bring more soil area into use. If you improve the lower levels of the soil with organic matter to make it desirable for root growth, you extend the area they have from which to draw nutrients and water. That means they'll spread out less nearer the surface so you can space the vegetables a little closer. So doing it this way, you can get even more out of the restricted space than ever you thought possible.

And there's one other great advantage with double-digging. You'll raise the surface of the bed by about 15 centimetres (6 inches) above the rest of the garden. That means that drainage will be greatly improved so the soil will be drier and warmer and easier to work. And that's certainly the answer if your soil is heavy.

Mind you, there is a price to pay. Naturally, when you're growing as intensively as this, it's necessary to put back into the soil as much, or even a little more, than you take out. But that cost, believe me, is a fraction of the money you'll save by growing your own.

There are one or two crops that are not worth growing by this method. Brussels sprouts, for example, need a lot of room whichever way you grow them. I've experimented with them closer than 60 centimetres (2 feet) apart and, though the plants grow well enough, the sprouts are too small to be worth while. They need that extra light, so there's no point in skimping on space.

Digging the bed

Start by marking out a 1.2-mctre (4-foot) width with a couple of garden lines. Leave yourself at least 30 centimetres (1 foot)

Deep-beds are raised above the surrounding soil. They can be edged with boards to make them neater.

from the fence and between beds or you'll not get your bottom in the space when you bend down! If you find that reaching into the centre of a 1.2-metre (4-foot) wide bed is uncomfortable, there's no reason at all why you shouldn't make it a bit narrower.

If space is very restricted, it's a good idea to edge the beds with boards to keep the soil in. They look a lot neater that way too, though it's not absolutely necessary.

Then, if you have enough energy and enthusiasm to go the whole hog, double-dig the 1.2-metre (4-foot) strip, digging in plenty of manure, spent mushroom compost or peat. As I've suggested in my description of double-digging, it's necessary to work the organic matter through all levels of the soil, not just in the bottom trench, and I like to put a layer on the top too.

Make shallow drills by resting the edge of the planting board on the soil and working it backwards and forwards.

There's no need for extra soil to raise the beds; you'll find that the breaking up of the subsoil and the extra organic matter will do the trick.

You'll be pleased to hear that the hard work of double-digging need only be done once. After the initial effort, you single-dig at the end of each season, but don't neglect the organic matter each year.

You'll read, by the way, that you should never use manure on land that is to be used for growing root crops because it makes them fork. Well I've certainly never found this to be true, provided the manure is well-rotted, so I would use it whatever you're growing. The same goes for spent mushroom compost and garden compost.

Neither is there any need to bother with the complicated rotation plans that many traditional veg growers use. On a small scale like this, it will do nothing to avoid pests and diseases and, though you may deplete the soil of some essential nutrients, you'll be putting plenty back every year anyway. Just sow or plant wherever there's a convenient space.

Sowing and planting

I use a planting board for all sowing and planting. It's simply a length of wood with saw-cuts at 7.5-centimetre (3-inch) intervals along it. This not only gives you a reference for spacing, but it can be used instead of a line to give you a straight line.

If you're sowing small seeds, put the planting board across the bed in the right position, turn it on edge and just work it backwards and forwards so that it makes a shallow dent in the soil. Sow the seed thinly in the drill and then cover it by dragging the back of the rake gently down the middle of the drill. Tap it down gently with the back of the rake, mark each end with a label and Bob's your uncle. If the soil is dry when you come to sow, make the drill and run a little water into it from a can *before* you sow – never afterwards. Cover the drill with dry soil.

Large seeds need a slightly deeper drill, but don't go over the top. More seeds fail because they're sown too deeply than anything else, so never put them deeper than twice the depth of the seed itself, if you see what I mean. So broad beans should go about 2.5 centimetres (1 inch) deep. Make the drill with a stick, first anchoring your planting board into position with a couple of short canes behind it.

This is the way to use the board for planting as well, so you

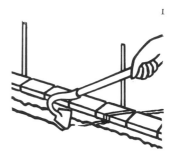

1. Deeper drills are made with a draw hoe, using the edge of the planting board as a guide.

2. By planting or sowing in blocks rather than in rows, you can save a great deal of space.

3. A simple wooden bridge is not difficult to make and will save miles of walking if the bed is long.

have a good indicator for the spacing and the straight line too.

Always plant in blocks rather than rows, staggering the plants to save further on space.

Before you sow or plant anything, sprinkle a bit of general fertilizer over the area and rake it in. Use about three to four handfuls of Growmore or blood, fish and bonemeal over every metre (yard) run of bed.

If your deep-bed is any length at all, you'll find that to avoid treading on the soil you'll walk miles! When sowing or planting, you can only do half a row from one side-path and then you have to walk round to get at the other half. If the bed is short, that's no problem but, if it's long, you'll be cursing my name before very long! So I should advise you to build yourself a wooden bridge. It's not difficult to make out of scrap timber and, if you fix a length of rope to the top, you'll find it quite easy to move about. I use mine all the time and it saves miles of walking.

Deep-bed spacings
Beetroot – 7.5 cm (3 in)
Broad beans – 23 cm (9 in)
Spring cabbage – 15 × 30 cm (6 × 12 in)
Summer cabbage – 30 cm (12 in)
Winter cabbage – 45 cm (18 in)
Chinese cabbage 25 cm (10 in)
Peppers – 45 cm (18 in)
Carrots – 15 cm (6 in)
Summer cauliflower – 45 cm (18 in)
Autumn and winter cauliflower – 60 cm (24 in)
Self-blanching celery – 23 cm (9 in)
Ridge cucumber – 60 cm (24 in)
French beans – 45 cm (18 in)
Leeks – 15 cm (6 in)
Lettuce – 15–23 cm (6–9 in) (depending on variety)
Marrow and courgette – 60 cm (24 in)
Onion – 15 cm (6 in)
Parsnip – 15 cm (6 in)
Early potatoes – 23 cm (9 in)
Shallot – 15 cm (6 in)
Spinach – 15 cm (6 in)
Swede – 30 cm (12 in)
Sweetcorn – 45 cm (18 in)
Bush tomatoes – 45 cm (18 in)
Turnip – 15 cm (6 in)

Radish and salad onions should be sown in a 10-cm (4-in) wide band and scattered thinly. They need no thinning.

Vegetables in the borders

If, like us, you don't even have room for a small deep-bed, you'll have to resort to growing a few veg in the borders. They do, in fact mix in very well. Ideally, think ahead a little when it comes to planning the ornamental plantings and leave the odd space here and there. In this case, it would look quite wrong to sow or plant in long, straight rows. Here you grow in clumps so, if you are raising the vegetables from seed, sow very short rows in patches exactly as advised for hardy annuals.

Climbing vegetables, like beans, peas, marrows and cucumbers, can be grown against the wires or trellis fixed to the fences, where they'll fit in very well and add an unusual touch of interest as well as a useful crop.

Some plants are particularly decorative and better suited to the border than the deep-bed. I grow all my globe artichokes in the borders, for example, where they provide exotic grey foliage with dramatic great thistle-like leaves up to 120 centimetres (4 feet) tall.

On a smaller scale, a clump of beetroot looks very attractive, especially planted in conjunction with grey foliage or white flowers. The bright-red-leaved rhubarb chard looks even better. And, of course, a clump of rhubarb itself makes an excellent foliage effect.

One of the great advantages with growing vegetables mixed in with the flowers in this way is that they are much less likely to suffer from pests or diseases. Often insects home in on their victims by sight and the camouflage provided by surrounding ornamental plants has been shown to help hide the vegetables away. The wide diversity of planting also helps to make characteristic scents which could give insects a clue, and it attracts the insect enemies of the pests, which themselves make for a very effective means of control.

Growing herbs

Of course, herbs can also be grown in the borders to good effect. This is an essential ingredient of a *real* cottage garden, I suppose, and certainly it's the best way to grow the taller varieties like lovage and angelica. But it's nice to have a small area devoted to herbs for use in the kitchen somewhere near the back door where they're readily available. In our Birming-

A small herb garden can make a very attractive feature, but make sure you choose carefully to avoid the really rampant growers. We planted out culinary herbs right outside the kitchen window where they scented the kitchen and were in easy reach of the back door.

ham garden, we included a small patch of mixed herbs right under the kitchen window. You simply can't get them fresher than that!

But it's important to get to know a little about the way the plants grow and to stick to those that aren't going to take over. Where room is limited, I would suggest that it's best to grow only those that are in constant use in the kitchen. Our own list was necessarily limited.

Perhaps the most popular of all herbs is mint, and that's where the problems start. This is a really invasive plant with underground runners that will very quickly take over the whole garden if you're not careful. It's often suggested that to prevent it getting out of hand it should be grown in a bucket sunk into the ground in the herb garden. My own experience is that even that is risky. You only need one shoot to pop over the top of the bucket and root into the soil (which it will do very readily indeed), and it's away. So my suggestion would be to grow it in a container on the patio. There it can never do any harm and it'll make a nice-looking pot too.

Parsley is widely used but difficult to grow from seed. Either germinate it on the windowsill and plant it out later or buy the plants from the garden centre. It makes a very good edging to the bed.

Chives also make an attractive edging and a very useful culinary herb too. But you don't need to buy enough plants to edge the whole bed. Buy one, plant it out as a clump and then split it up the following year. You'll have more than enough and some to give away too!

Garlic is a matter of opinion. I wouldn't be without it, but some more sociable folk would never eat it! If you do grow it, buy a bulb from the greengrocer or the seed merchant and split it up into individual cloves. These are planted in March in the sunniest spot in the garden.

Sage and thyme are best bought as plants. There are several coloured varieties of both, which will brighten up an uninteresting corner. The variegated varieties are just as good in the kitchen as the plain ones.

One other herb that no good cook should be without is bay. You can buy plants from the garden centre but do bear in mind that it's tender and will suffer in a hard winter. So unless you live in a favoured spot, grow it in a tub and bring it inside for the winter.

Growing fruit

Fruit-growing in small gardens used to be difficult. Trees like apples, pears, plums and cherries grew to such enormous dimensions that most modern gardens would certainly only have room for one. That, of course, could also mean problems of pollination, because most fruit needs another variety to ensure that the fruits set. Today, I'm pleased to report, no such problems exist.

First of all, several types of fruit can now be grown on 'dwarfing rootstocks'. This is a technique where the variety is grafted onto a special set of roots which will control the vigour of the tree. So even monsters like the cooking apple 'Bramley's Seedling', which is so vigorous on its own roots it would take up the whole of a small garden, can now be reduced to a tree no bigger than 2.5–3 metres (8–10 feet).

Training methods have also undergone changes, so very simple pruning methods will keep trees down to a manageable size too. What's more, they enable you to grow trees that look really attractive.

Tree fruit

In order to keep trees fruitful and within bounds, they need to be pruned every year. And I know it's that which puts most new gardeners off growing them. The instructions for pruning are generally so complicated they become totally incomprehensible. If it's any consolation, I've never understood them either!

In fact, if you stick to growing small, trained trees, the method is so simple you'll wonder why you ever worried. To

We planted some espalier apples in our small garden where space was too limited to grow them as free-standing trees.

315

Cordon apples are grown at an angle and take up very little space.

grow apples and pears, you need to learn one method which will do for everything, so once you know how to prune a cordon, you've got the whole story. I have to admit that fan-trained peaches, apricots and nectarines do get a bit complicated so I would suggest you stick, in the first instance, to apples, pears, plums and cherries and graduate to the more difficult stuff when you've mastered those.

Cordons are single-stemmed trees, generally grown at an angle of 45 degrees and trained onto wires either free-standing or fixed to the fence. They're planted 75 centimetres (2½ feet) apart. This is a method suitable for apples and pears in the main though I have seen plums grown as cordons too.

Buy one- or two-year-old plants from a fruit specialist. They'll consist of a strong main stem and perhaps, though not necessarily, a few side-branches. Plant them 75 centimetres (2½ feet) apart against a cane tied at a 45 degree angle to the fence or wire structure. Immediately after planting, prune the main stem back, cutting off about a third of its length. When you prune, cut back cleanly, just above a bud. Cut the side-branches back to leave them 5 centimetres (2 inches) long.

That's all the pruning you do in the winter. Next August, the side-shoots you pruned in the winter will have grown out. Cut back all of the new growth to leave little shoots 2.5 centimetres (1 inch) long. If new side-shoots have grown out from the main stem, cut them back to 7.5 centimetres (3 inches). And that's it! Remember, new side-shoots coming from the main stem cut to 7.5 centimetres (3 inches) and any coming from those to 2.5 centimetres (1 inch).

Fans are also grown against a fence in, believe it or not, the shape of a fan. You can buy trees already trained so there's no need to worry about the initial formation of the shape. Before planting, fix 20-centimetre (8-foot) canes to the wires so that the shoots can be tied in to those instead of directly onto the wires, which will chafe.

Plant these 3.5 metres (12 feet) apart. To prune them, look at each branch separately and treat it just as if it was a cordon.

Espaliers are much the same as fans except that the branches are trained out horizontally, one above the other, to form a series of 'tiers'. This shape is used mainly for apples and pears, and again, you can buy them already trained.

Once more, take each branch separately and treat it like a cordon.

Free-standing trees can be kept down to size by a method known as 'festooning', where branches are bent down and tied onto the main stem or the branch below.

Plant one- or two-year-old trees not less than 1.8 metres (6 feet) apart. Then pull the main stem carefully into an arc and tie it to the trunk at the bottom. If there are other strong branches, these can be treated in the same way.

In August, you'll find that side-shoots have grown out all along the curved stem. Then, select about four more branches for tying down in the same way and treat the rest like cordons. Cut new shoots arising from the main stem back to 7.5 centimetres (3 inches) and any coming from them to 2.5 centimetres (1 inch). Repeat that every August and you'll get an interesting shape and a small, very fruitful tree.

Bear in mind that no apple or pear will set a full crop of fruit without being pollinated, so two trees are needed and they should be different varieties that flower at the same time. The fruit-grower you buy the trees from will certainly be able to advise.

Plums are no more difficult. You can grow a small festooned tree, pruning it in just the same way as described for apples, or you can fan train it against the fence.

It's essential to buy a self-pollinating variety, so I would advise you to stick with 'Victoria', which is just about the best dessert plum there is anyway. It's also important to buy a tree that has been grafted onto a dwarfing rootstock, so ask for 'Victoria' on 'Pixy', which will keep the tree quite small.

For fans, it's best to start out with a ready-trained tree. Plant it against a south- or west-facing fence if you can, though they will also do quite well elsewhere. You'll need some horizontal wires fixed to the posts again and you should tie to these a number of 2.5 metre (8-foot) canes in the shape you require. Then tie the shoots of the tree to the canes.

The only pruning that's necessary is to pinch out the growing tips of shoots you *don't* want in the summer as soon as they've made about six leaves. Any shoots that are overcrowded or have just outgrown their space should be treated like this. Then, as soon as the fruit has been picked, cut those shoots you've pinched back again, this time to leave three buds.

Sweet cherries can be treated in the same way. Again, a self-pollinating variety is essential and there's only one – 'Stella' – so that solves that little problem! This time, buy it grafted onto the rootstock 'Colt', but since this is only semi-dwarfing, you'll be well advised to grow the tree as a fan, where you can control the growth. Prune in the same way as a plum.

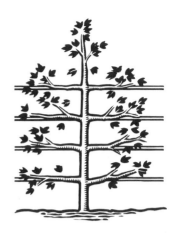

Espaliers can be grown to the top of the fence, with several 'tiers' spaced about 30 centimetres (1 foot) apart. They are very productive and make a bright show of blossom and fruit.

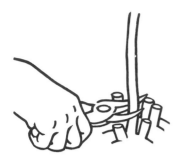

Black currants should be pruned right down to the ground immediately after planting.

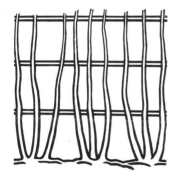

Raspberries must be trained against a post and wire structure or on the fence.

Soft fruit

Soft fruit – strawberries, raspberries, gooseberries, black and red currants – are invaluable, so try to find a space for some.

Black currants take up quite a bit of space but are very rewarding. Choose a modern variety like 'Ben More' or 'Malling Jet', which are very heavy cropping. If you're growing more than one bush, plant them at least 1.5 metres (5 feet) apart. A new variety 'Ben Sarek' is less vigorous and bushes can be planted 1 metre (3 feet) apart. They're very heavy feeders and don't like competition. Plant the bushes a little deeper than they grew at the nursery, and afterwards cut all the shoots right back to 2.5 centimetres (1 inch) above the ground. This will mean that you lose the first year's fruit, but you'll build yourself a strong bush with new growth coming right from the bottom. Every year, the wood that has fruited should be cut out in this way.

Red currants and gooseberries are treated alike, but a bit differently to black currants. They are grown on a 'leg', so plant them with the top of the pot at soil level and prune the shoots back by no more than half. Again, plant 1.5 metres (5 feet) apart. The best gooseberries are either 'Jubilee' or 'Invicta' and the favourite red currant is 'Red Lake'.

Raspberries need a post and wire support, or again, wires on the fence-posts. Choose a variety like 'Glen Clova' or 'Malling Jewel' and plant about 45 centimetres (18 inches) apart. Again, the shoots should be cut right back to leave just a short stem to encourage shoots to come from the base. New canes will arise from the bottom and these should be tied onto the wires, directly this time, not on canes, spacing them about 10 centimetres (4 inches) apart along the wires. They'll provide the crop for the following year and should be cut right out after fruiting, to leave space to tie in the new canes. Autumn-fruiting varieties like 'Autumn Bliss' need no support. Plant them in the same way and cut them right down hard every February. They'll grow up to give you a crop the same year.

Strawberries are the quickest to produce a crop. Ideally, buy new plants in September and you'll get your first picking the following June. If you have room, buy a few varieties to give a longer succession of picking. 'Honeyoye' is a good early, followed by 'Elsanta' and finally the autumn-fruiting 'Aromel'. Plant them in beds with three rows 45 centimetres (18 inches) apart and 60 centimetres (2 feet) between plants. When you plant, make sure that the 'crown' of the plant, where the leaves join the roots, is exactly at soil level.

PLANTS ACCORDING TO THEIR
PRIMARY SEASONS OF INTEREST

WINTER
The following plants are grown for their flowers, bark, catkins, etc. Plants bearing berries, which in some cases last through the winter, are listed under Autumn.

TREES
Acer capillipes (bark). See page 139.
Acer griseum (bark). See pages 138–9.
Betula pendula 'Laciniata' (bark). See pages 148–9.
Betula utilis jacquemontii (bark). See page 149.
Prunus subhirtella 'Autumnalis' (flowers). See pages 144–5.
Salix alba e.g. *vitellina* 'Britzensis' and *S. daphnoïdes* (bark). See page 138.

SHRUBS
Camellia (flowers). Acid soils only. See page 156.
Chimonanthus praecox (fragrant flowers). See page 225.
Cornus alba e.g. 'Westonbirt' and 'Elegantissima' (bark). See page 164.
Daphne odora (fragrant flowers). See page 257.
Erica carnea (flowers). See page 204.
Garrya elliptica (catkins). See page 164.
Hamamelis mollis (fragrant flowers). See page 165.
Jasminum nudiflorum (flowers). See pages 188–9.
Lonicera fragrantissima (fragrant flowers). See page 227.
Mahonia japonica (fragrant flowers). See page 189.
Rhododendron (flowers). Acid soils only. See pages 157–9.
Sarcococca humilis (fragrant flowers). See pages 168–9.
Viburnum × *bodnantense* and *tinus* (fragrant flowers). See page 266.

HERBACEOUS PLANTS
Grown for their flowers.

Helleborus niger, orientalis and *foetidus*. See pages 176, 192.

BULBS
All except *Arum italicum* 'Pictum' grown for their flowers.
Arum italicum 'Pictum' (variegated leaves). See page 184.
Crocus. See page 283.
Galanthus nivalis. See page 185.
Iris e.g. *reticulata*. See page 284.
Narcissus e.g. 'February Gold' and 'W.P. Milner'. See pages
    284–5, 305.

SPRING

TREES
Acer pseudoplatanus 'Brilliantissimum' (foliage). See page
    139.
Amelanchier lamarckii (flowers). See pages 150–1.
Crataegus laevigata (flowers). See page 140.
Malus floribunda (flowers). See pages 140–1.
Prunus (flowers). See pages 143–6.
Pyrus nivalis and *P. salicifolia* 'Pendula' (foliage). See pages
    146–7.

CLIMBERS
Clematis alpina and *macropetala* (flowers). See pages 248–9.

SHRUBS
Berberis darwinii (flowers). See page 188.
Camellia (flowers). See page 156.
Chaenomeles (flowers). See page 304.
Corylopsis pauciflora (flowers). See page 247.
Daphne mezereum (fragrant flowers). See page 257.
Magnolia stellata (flowers). See page 261.
Osmanthus delavayi (fragrant flowers). See page 261.
Pachysandra terminalis (flowers). See page 165.
Pieris (foliage and flowers). Acid soils only. See page 157.
Rhododendrons/azaleas (flowers). Acid soils only. See
    pages 157–9.
Ribes sanguineum (flowers). See pages 189–90.
Salix hastata 'Wehrhahnii' (catkins). See page 168.
Spiraea × *arguta* (flowers). See page 265.
Viburnum × *burkwoodii, carlesii* and *juddii* (fragrant flowers).
    See page 229.
Vinca major and *minor* (flowers). See pages 190–1.

HERBACEOUS PLANTS
All grown for their flowers except where stated.
Alyssum saxatile. See page 294.
Bergenia. See page 174.
Dicentra spectabilis. See pages 175–6.
Epimedium. See page 192.
Euphorbia polychroma. See pages 216–17.
Iberis saxatilis. See page 297.
Lamium. See page 177.
Polygonatum. See page 178.
Primula. See pages 178–9.
Pulmonaria saccharata. See pages 179–80.
Waldsteinia ternata. See pages 193–4.

BULBS
Anemone blanda and *nemorosa*. See page 283.
Chionodoxa luciliae. See page 184.
Crocus. See page 283.
Erythronium dens-canis. See pages 184–5.
Leucojum vernum. See page 185.
Muscari. See page 185.
Narcissus. See pages 284–5.
Ornithogalum. See pages 196, 285.
Tulips. See pages 285–7.

SUMMER

Since there are so many flowering plants in this category, they are subdivided into 'Early' (May–July) and 'Late' (July–September). Those that aren't marked flower all summer.

TREES
Laburnum × *watereri* 'Vossii' (flowers). See page 140.
Malus e.g. 'Liset', 'Red Jade' and *sargentii*. See pages 141–2.
Prunus e.g. 'Kanzan' and *serrula*. See pages 143, 144.
Sorbus e.g. *cashmiriana* and *vilmorinii*. See pages 147–8.

CLIMBERS
Campsis radicans. Late. See page 248.
Clematis – Early include *montana*, 'Nelly Moser', 'Mrs Cholmondeley', 'Marie Boisselot'. Late include 'Jackmanii', *texensis* and *viticella*. See pages 160, 248–9.
Eccremocarpus scaber. Late. See page 249.
Fremontodendron californicum. See page 260.

Hydrangea petiolaris. Early. See pages 160–1.

Lonicera – japonica, 'Halliana'. Early include *periclymenum* 'Belgica' and × *americana*. Late include *periclymenum* 'Serotina', *heckrottii* 'Goldflame', 'Dropmore Scarlet', and × *tellmanniana*. See pages 161, 224.

Passiflora. See pages 251–2.

Roses. Most ramblers flower early. Repeat-flowering climbers flower all summer. See page 252.

Solanum crispum. Late. See page 252.

Wisteria. Early. See pages 252–3.

SHRUBS

Berberis. Early. See page 188.

Buddleia davidii, fallowiana and 'Lochinch'. Late. See pages 254–5.

Carpenteria californica. Early. See page 255.

Caryopteris clandonensis. Late. See pages 288–9.

Ceanothus. Evergreens early, deciduous varieties late. See page 255.

Ceratostigma willmottianum. Late. See page 255.

Cistus. Early. See page 289.

Convolvulus cneorum. Early. See page 295.

Cytisus (including *battandieri*). Early. See pages 249, 256–7.

Escallonia. Early (except 'Iveyi'). See page 257.

Fuchsia. Late. See page 204.

Hebe. Some early – e.g. *elliptica* 'Variegata' and 'Carl Teschner'. Some late – e.g. 'Autumn Glory', 'Great Orme' and 'Midsummer Beauty'. See page 260.

Hydrangea. Early – *paniculata*. Late – lace-caps and mop-heads. See page 165.

Hypericum patulum 'Hidcote'. Late. See pages 260–1.

Itea ilicifolia. Late. See page 247.

Kalmia latifolia. Early. Acid soils only. See pages 247–8.

Kolkwitzia amabilis. Early. See page 261.

Lavender. Late. See page 290.

Myrtus communis. Late. See page 228.

Perovskia. Late. See page 291.

Philadelphus. Early. See pages 261–2.

Pieris. Early. Acid soils only. See page 157.

Potentilla fruticosa. See pages 262–4.

Prunus laurocerasus e.g. 'Otto Luyken'. Early. See page 189.

Pyracantha. Early. See pages 165–8.

Rhododendrons/azaleas. Early. Acid soils only. See pages 157–9.

Romneya. Late. See page 264.

Roses. See pages 264–5.

Skimmia. Early. See page 169.

Spiraea. Late – × *bumalda* and *japonica.* See page 265.

Syringa. Early (*S. microphylla* 'Superba' also Late). See pages 265–6.

Viburnum – e.g. *opulus* and *plicatum.* Early. See pages 266–7.

Weigela florida. Early. See pages 267–8.

HERBACEOUS PLANTS

Since the vast majority of herbaceous plants flower in the summer, and their flowering period has already been given in their descriptions in the different chapters, it seems pointless to list them all again. So unless a herbaceous plant is listed under Winter, Spring, or Autumn, you can safely assume it flowers in summer.

ANNUALS

All annuals flower in summer.

BULBS

Allium. Early–mid-summer. See page 282.

Amaryllis belladonna. Late summer–early autumn. See page 303.

Galtonia candicans. Late summer. See page 283.

Lilies. Mid–late summer. See page 284.

AUTUMN

Plants grown mainly for berries, or autumn foliage colour.

TREES

Acer griseum (autumn foliage colour). See pages 138–9.

Amelanchier lamarckii (autumn foliage colour). See pages 150–1.

Cercidiphyllum japonicum (autumn foliage colour). See page 151.

Malus – e.g. 'John Downie' (the best 'crabs' of all), 'Golden Hornet', 'Red Jade', 'Royalty' (berries). See pages 141, 142–3.

Prunus e.g. *sargentii,* and × *yedoensis* (autumn foliage colour). See pages 144, 145–6.

Sorbus e.g. 'Joseph Rock', 'Embley', *cashmiriana* and *vilmorinii* (autumn foliage colour and berries). See pages 147–8.

PLANTS ACCORDING TO THEIR SEASONS

CLIMBERS

Clematis orientalis (flowers and seedheads). See page 249.

Parthenocissus e.g. *henryana* (autumn foliage colour). See page 161.

SHRUBS

Acer palmatum 'Dissectum' (autumn foliage colour). See pages 161–2.

Aucuba japonica (berries). See page 163.

Berberis. Berries and some, like *B. thunbergii*, autumn foliage colour. See page 188.

Cotinus coggygria (autumn foliage colour). See page 256.

Cotoneaster. Berries and some, like *C. horizontalis*, autumn foliage colour. See page 256.

Gaultheria procumbens. Acid soils only. Berries. See page 156.

Ilex. Berries. See page 188.

Pernettya mucronata. Acid soils only. Berries. See pages 156–7.

Pyracantha (berries). See pages 165–8.

Rhus typhina (autumn foliage colour). See page 189.

Skimmia (berries). See page 169.

Stranvaesia (berries). See page 293.

Viburnum – *davidii* and *opulus* berries. *V. opulus* also autumn foliage colour. See pages 169–72, 266–7.

HERBACEOUS PLANTS

Many late summer-flowering plants will still be flowering.

Anemone × *hybrida*. See page 173.

Aster amellus, novae-angliae and *novi-belgii*. See pages 268–9, 304.

Cimicifuga. See page 175.

Crocosmia. See page 270.

Kniphofia. See page 273.

Rudbeckia. See page 276.

Schizostylis coccinea. See page 277.

Sedum 'Autumn Joy'. See page 300.

BULBS

Autumn crocus. See pages 217–20.

Colchicums. See pages 194–5.

Cyclamen hederifolium. See page 184.

Nerine bowdenii. See page 285.

SPECIALIST NURSERIES

TREES AND SHRUBS
Hilliers, Ampfield House, Ampfield, Romsey, Hants SO51
9PA.
Notcutts Garden Centres, Woodbridge, Suffolk IP12 4AF.

CLEMATIS
Fisk's Clematis Nursery, Westleton, nr Saxmundham,
Suffolk IP17 3AJ.
Treasures of Tenbury, Burford House, Tenbury, Wells
WR15 8HQ.

DWARF CONIFERS
Bressingham Gardens, Diss, Norfolk IP22 2AB.

RHODODENDRONS AND AZALEAS
Hydon Nurseries, Clock Barn Lane, Hydon Heath,
Godalming, Surrey GU8 4AZ.
G. Reuthe, Crown Point Nursery, Sevenoaks Road,
Ightham, nr Sevenoaks, Kent.

ROSES
David Austin Roses, Bowling Green Lane, Albrighton,
Wolverhampton WV7 3HB. New 'old roses'.

HARDY PERENNIALS
Bernwode Plants, Wotton Road, Ludgershall, nr Aylesbury,
Bucks.
Unusual Plants, Beth Chatto Gardens, Elmstead Market, nr
Colchester, Essex CO7 7DB.

GROUND COVER PLANTS
Eileen Moore, Growing Carpets, Christmas Tree House,
High Street, Guilden Morden, nr Royston, Herts SG8 0JP.

SPECIALIST NURSERIES

ALPINES
Hartside Nursery Garden, Low Gill House, Alston,
Cumbria CA9 3BL.
W. E. Th. Ingwersen, Birch Farm Nursery, Gravetye, East
Grinstead, W. Sussex RH19 4LE.

DELPHINIUMS AND BEGONIAS
Blackmore & Langdon, Pensford, Bristol BS18 4JL.

PEONIES AND IRIS
Kelways Ltd, Langport, Somerset TA10 9EZ.

BULBS
Broadleigh Gardens, Barr House, Bishops Hull, Taunton,
Somerset TA4 1AE.

SEEDS
Chiltern Seeds, Bortree Stile, Ulverston, Cumbria LA12
7PB.
Samuel Dobie & Son Ltd, Broomhill Way, Torquay,
Devon TQ2 7QW.
Mr Fothergill's Seeds, Gazeley Road, Kentford,
Newmarket, Suffolk CB8 7QB.
Thompson and Morgan, Poplar Lane, Ipswich, Suffolk IP8
3BU.

INDEX

INDEX

PICTURE CREDITS

BBC Books would like to thank the following for providing the photographs and for permission to reproduce copyright material. While every effort has been made to trace and acknowledge all copyright holders, we would like to apologize for any errors or omissions.

All photographs taken by Stephen Hamilton except:
A–Z Botanical pages 146, 158, 175, 251, 264, 267, 291; Bruce Coleman 106; Jerry Harpur 153, 154, 178 left, 246, 271 top, 286; Andrew Lawson 134, 271 bottom; S & O Mathews 174, 178 right, 190, 234 bottom right, 235 right, 263, 266, 275; Photos Horticultural 58 bottom, 114, 115, 138, 142, 143, 147, 150, 162, 163, 179, 186, 187, 194, 195, 202, 210, 211, 214, 215, 223, 226, 227, 234 top right & bottom left, 235 bottom, 250, 254, 262, 295, 314 left; Harry Smith Collection 39, 58 top, 59 bottom, 103, 314 right; Whiting & Associates 46, 59 top.

Garden plans by Gillian Tomblin.